The South American Expeditions, 1540–1545

❧La relacion y comentarios del gouerna
dor Aluar nuñez cabeça de vaca, de lo acaescido en las
dos jornadas que hizo a las Indias.

Con priuilegio.

¶ Esta tassadapor los señores del consej een ○ ⦿ ⦿

Original imperial coat of arms, 1555 edition of the Comentarios.

Facing page: Original title page, 1555 edition, of the Comentarios.

The South American Expeditions, 1540–1545

COMMENTA RIOS DE ALVAR NVNEZ CABE ca de vaca, adelantado y gouernador dela pro uincia del Rio dela Plata.

Scriptos por Pero hernandez scriuano y secre- tario de la prouincia. Y dirigidos al serenis. muy alto y muy poderoso señor el Infante don Carlos. N.S.

Álvar Núñez Cabeza de Vaca

Translated with notes by Baker H. Morrow

UNIVERSITY OF NEW MEXICO PRESS

Albuquerque

LIBRARY OF CONGRESS CATALOGING-IN-PUBLICATION DATA

Núñez Cabeza de Vaca, Álvar, 16th cent.
[Relación y comentarios. English. Selections]
The South American expeditions, 1540–1545 /
Álvar Núñez Cabeza de Vaca;
translated with notes by Baker H. Morrow.
p. cm.
Includes bibliographical references and index.
ISBN 978-0-8263-5063-3 (cloth : alk. paper)
ISBN 978-0-8263-5065-7 (electronic)

1. Núñez Cabeza de Vaca, Alvar, 16th cent.
2. South America—Discovery and exploration—Spanish.
3. South America—Description and travel—Early works to 1800.
4. Rio de la Plata Region (Argentina and Uruguay)—
   Discovery and exploration—Spanish.
5. Rio de la Plata Region (Argentina and Uruguay)—
   Description and travel—Early works to 1800.
6. Governors—Rio de la Plata Region
   (Argentina and Uruguay)—Biography.
I. Morrow, Baker H., 1946–
II. Title.

E125.N9A3 2011
980'.013—dc23

2011018934

This publication is made possible in part by a generous contribution
from the Program for Cultural Cooperation Between Spain's
Ministry of Culture and United States Universities

For Susan Morrow,

my daughter,

a most remarkable young woman

Alvar Núñez

CABEZA DE VACA

THE SOUTH AMERICAN EXPEDITIONS
1540–1545

The Commentaries of Alvar Núñez Cabeza de Vaca,
Adelantado, Governor
and
Captain-General of the Rio de la Plata Province
Author of the Naufragios

by Pero Hernández
1555

---

translated, with notes, by Baker H. Morrow

The above text indicates the official positions held by
Cabeza de Vaca in South America in the 1500s.

Contents

Translator's Note

I.

IN 1555, CABEZA DE VACA PUBLISHED THE *COMENTARIOS, OR COMMENTARIES*, THE TALE OF HIS SOUTH AMERICAN EXPEDITIONS, IN VALLADOLID. THEY ARE a detailed account of his time from 1540 to 1545 as governor of Spain's new province of the Río de la Plata in South America, an ill-defined area centered in his day in Paraguay but including much of modern Argentina and parts of Brazil and Uruguay.

The *Commentaries* are one of the great first-person accounts of the Spanish conquest of the Americas in the sixteenth century. Ulrich Schmidel (or Schmidt), a German soldier serving under Cabeza de Vaca, and Hans Staden, another German who explored the coast of Brazil in the decade after Cabeza de Vaca, also wrote valuable memoirs of their time in South America. Schmidt's account is exactly contemporary; it is an earnest but often-garbled counterpoint to Cabeza de Vaca's narrative, as the German thought poorly of the governor and was very much a loyal partisan of Cabeza de Vaca's archnemesis, Domingo Martínez de Irala. Staden's time in South America lasted from 1547 to 1554, and his account was published in English in 1874, with notes and comment by Sir Richard Burton.

But Cabeza de Vaca has continued to outshine his contemporaries. R. B. Cunninghame Graham calls him "the one great man in . . . the history of the River Plate . . ." He was already a celebrated explorer by the time he went to La Plata, known for his great trek across North America in the 1520s and '30s and for the *Relación* he wrote recalling it, and the river and forest explorations he describes in the *Commentaries* show that he had lost none of his early curiosity and drive. He tells a more moving and wide-ranging tale of the strange new world of the South American wilderness than do any of his rivals.

Who actually wrote the *Commentaries*? Cabeza de Vaca himself says the writer was his loyal friend and secretary, the notary Pedro (or Pero) Hernández. But this is probably only true in a technical sense. The indispensable background to this book lies in the legal proceedings (four concurrent lawsuits and actions) in which Cabeza de Vaca was embroiled from 1545 to 1555, after he returned to Spain under the grimmest of conditions from the Río de la Plata. In the court records, we find the subject matter of the *Commentaries* in early outline, with good examples of the writing styles of both men. The narrative itself is sometimes inconsistent; it refers to Cabeza de Vaca generally as the "Governor," but he also speaks of himself as "I" or "we" often enough to strike the reader's eye. The *Commentaries*, then, are most likely a collaboration between Cabeza de Vaca and Hernández, intended as an apologia of the great explorer's term as governor and created to catch the ears of King Charles I and his son Philip II but also for popular consumption.

The period of the lawsuits was a particularly thorny time for Cabeza de Vaca. He was an aristocrat and an adelantado (a synonym for "governor" that conveys the sense of a "man out in front"), and his honor had been very much in question for ten years. It is tempting in this context to think of Churchill's methods of composing his books in the last century: the painstaking assembling of notes and the creation of an accurate outline, a great deal of late-night pacing back and forth, and a long dictation to a faithful scribe who fleshes out the bones of the narrative. And who, in Cabeza de Vaca's case, cannot resist adding his own flourishes from time to time.

Before his last return to Spain after nearly two decades of service in both North and South America, Cabeza de Vaca had become the greatest secular champion of the Indians in the sixteenth century. In their service he was matched only by the extraordinary cleric Bartolomé de las Casas, whose denunciations of Spanish misconduct in the Americas were well known in Iberia. In the Río de la Plata, and much to his detriment, Cabeza de Vaca's insistence on paying all the Indians he met for goods and services rendered enraged his fellow Spaniards, to whom plunder and imposition seemed the more natural course of affairs during a conquest.

Cabeza de Vaca was also the only Spaniard to explore, in excruciating detail, the coasts and the interiors of two continents. In North America, he was famous as a roving shaman and a healer among the Indians of Texas and the northern Sierra Madre. Among his own countrymen, the tales of cities of gold lying in the far north attributed to him and his companions

Dorantes, Castillo, and the Moor Estevanico made them very popular figures in the 1530s. In Mexico and Spain, Cabeza de Vaca was renowned as a wanderer, a bearer of marvelous stories, and a tough survivor.

But none of this counted in South America, where his discoveries of such natural wonders as Iguazú Falls never registered. Domingo de Irala, the very proprietary lieutenant governor of the Río de la Plata, and the other royal officials—Cáceres, Garci-Vanegas, Cabrera, and their colleagues—all asked the same question about Cabeza de Vaca: Just who did this interloper think he was?

II.

Álvar Núñez Cabeza de Vaca, one of six children of don Francisco de Vera and his wife, doña Teresa Cabeza de Vaca, was likely born in Jerez de la Frontera, an Andalusian city near Seville, as early as 1485 but perhaps as late as 1492. From his own legal testimony, 1488 seems the likeliest year, but birth dates were loose matters in his time. His family on both sides, the Veras and the Cabeza de Vacas, were caballeros, or midranking nobility. The young Cabeza de Vaca grew up hearing conquistador tales on the knee of his formidable grandfather, don Pedro de Vera, the renowned conqueror of Grand Canary Island in the 1480s. Don Pedro had fought for Ferdinand and Isabella in their Granada campaigns of the Reconquest and in North Africa, and some historians say that he had financed his Canary Island ventures by pawning two of his sons—one of whom, of course, was Cabeza de Vaca's own father, Francisco de Vera—to his Moorish bankers. A ruthless fellow, perhaps, but he was successful as governor in the Canaries, and he eventually built a fine house in Jerez.

By the first decade of the sixteenth century, however, Cabeza de Vaca and his brothers and sisters were orphans. They went to live with his aunt, his mother's sister doña Beatriz Cabeza de Vaca, who was herself the mother of his trusted lieutenant-to-be in the Río de la Plata, his first cousin Pedro Estopiñán Cabeza de Vaca.

The young Álvar Núñez found employment in the Spanish armies bound for Italy, where he began his military service in 1511. His first notable distinction in the Italian wars was his appointment as Alférez, or Lieutenant, of Gaeta, a town near Naples, following the Battle of Ravenna in 1512. Returning to Spain, he served the dukes of Medina Sidonia in Seville in several capacities for a considerable time, most remarkably as one of their stewards. It was indeed a long service, lasting until his departure in 1527 at the age of about thirty-nine for the New World, where he assumed a fateful position as treasurer of the expedition of Pánfilo Narváez to Florida.

Cabeza de Vaca's fortunes were much dependent on those of his sovereign, Charles I of Spain. Charles, a Hapsburg prince raised in Flanders who was the grandson of the Catholic Monarchs Ferdinand and Isabella, began his reign as king of Castile and Aragón in 1517 with no knowledge of the Spanish language. His inexperience in dealing with the aspirations and the traditional rights of the cities of Spain, which in his day exercised considerable democratic power as members of the Cortes of Castile and Aragón, led almost immediately to the Comuneros Revolt of 1520–1521.

The revolt affected Cabeza de Vaca directly. His employers, the dukes of Medina Sidonia, were protectors of the *conversos*, or converted Jews, of southern Spain, against whom much of the wrath of the comuneros was directed. Cabeza de Vaca fought to suppress the insurrection on behalf of Alonso Pérez de Guzmán, the duke in 1520, and King Charles I.

But by 1520 he had also married María Marmolejo, the daughter of an Andalusian converso family directly threatened by the comuneros, and so his loyalist military service takes on perhaps a much more personal meaning.

Cabeza de Vaca rarely mentions María in the course of his writings— neither in the *Relación* nor the *Comentarios*—and we only hear of her indirectly in the voluminous documents of his lawsuits and trial proceedings after 1545. In his pleadings before the Council of the Indies, he says she is much reduced in means from defending his honor and meeting his obligations. María's patience with her husband's long absences must have been considerable, though, as he was gone to the Indies, a bit like Odysseus, for the better part of twenty years. And of the children, if any, of María and Álvar there is likewise not a word.

Cabeza de Vaca's North American journey of nine years is by any measure an epic story of discovery, privation, and endurance. By 1528, he and most of the other soldiers of the Narváez expedition were castaways, their ships gone and the men left utterly without means on the unfriendly coast of Florida. From there they slowly made their way west by raft and on foot along the northern shores of the Gulf of Mexico, where the Indians they met enslaved them. They died in droves: six hundred men by some accounts (Cabeza de Vaca himself mentioned three hundred) eventually dwindled to only four—Dorantes, Castillo, Cabeza de Vaca, and the Moorish bondsman Estevanico, a Moroccan from Azamor. This tiny band crossed Texas, went up the Rio Grande, wandered through the Sierra Madre, and emerged at the Sea of Cortez. From the Pacific seacoast they were taken to Mexico City and hailed as heroes.

Back in Spain by 1537, Cabeza de Vaca reported to the king, wrote his classic memoir of North America, the *Relación* (an update of the *Joint Report* he had prepared earlier with his companions from the long trek, later called *Naufragios*), and bided his time.

Charles I of Spain was also the Holy Roman Emperor Charles V, monarch of much of the rest of Europe, and always more preoccupied with Italy and his other continental holdings than with the distant New World. His income never matched his expenses, and Charles was a skinflint, gaining his enormous New World empire and its revenues through the audacity and toil of his conquistadors (and, in the end, entirely at the expense of the unfortunate Indians) but never paying for it. In fact, he mortgaged the gold and silver of Mexico and Peru against advances given him by his German bankers, the Fuggers.

So, when don Pedro de Mendoza, the first governor of the Río de la Plata, died in mid-ocean and Charles offered a *capitulación* to Cabeza de Vaca to serve as the second governor of the province, it came with strings. Cabeza de Vaca had to promise ships, men, equipment, provisions, and money (about eight thousand ducats, a king's ransom) in his contract, all furnished from his own means. He agreed to relieve the beleaguered Spanish garrisons in La Plata, find and claim new territories for the king, spread Christianity, and make the colony prosper. As an additional condition, the entire arrangement only applied if Juan de Ayolas, the man Mendoza had left in charge when he sailed for Spain, had *died* by the time Cabeza de Vaca arrived in the province.

Álvar Núñez nevertheless eagerly gave his assent. He assembled his ships and his company and set off for South America from the docks of Seville in October of 1540. What happened to him next is the subject of his *Commentaries.*

III.

This book was first translated into English in 1891, some 336 years after it was originally published in Spanish, in a limited edition issued by the Hakluyt Society in London. The *Commentaries* were part of *The Conquest of the River Plate*, with notes and an introduction by Luis L. Domínguez. Accompanying Cabeza de Vaca's account was *The Voyage of Ulrich Schmidt*

[Schmidel] *to the Rivers La Plata and Paraguai,* by Ulrich Schmidel (or Schmidt), the German mercenary adventurer who had served in Cabeza de Vaca's company.

Domínguez was the Argentine minister to Great Britain at the time but notably not the translator of either of the two volumes in his work. He wrote his own explanatory remarks in Spanish and apologized for having to translate them into English. Schmidt's German-English translator is unknown; so, most curiously, is Cabeza de Vaca's translator.

The prose in this early English version of the *Commentaries* is now a little dated, somewhat stiff in a Victorian way. The anonymous translator has the notion of sometimes changing what the Spanish says for something else when he (or she) doesn't agree with the sense of it: changing "cricket" for "cock," for instance, in the second chapter. "Then a cricket began to chirp" is given as "had not a cock began to crow [*sic*]" in the Domínguez edition. In addition, Cabeza de Vaca's endlessly ambivalent language sometimes weighs down Domínguez's translator. In chapter 37, a good example of muddy syntax in the original Spanish that deals with confusing events in Buenos Aires, the translator leaves out entire phrases altogether. On the whole, however, this nineteenth-century work conveys a good sense of the perplexity and isolation the Spaniards must have felt in this new province in the South American interior—the center of Spanish colonization, to be sure, but rather poor, away from the sea, far from the great mineral wealth of Peru and Mexico, and struggling in the midst of a smoldering mass of hostile tribes.

Domínguez's unyielding introductory notes also retain their interest. He believes, for instance, that the only Native American language east of the Andes is simply Guarani, or its variants, instead of Cabeza de Vaca's multiplicity of tongues, and that the rampant cannibalism in the Americas reported by Schmidt, Cabeza de Vaca, Bernal Díaz del Castillo, Father Las Casas (the great ecclesiastical champion of the Indians), and Columbus himself is simply a pack of lies. But his characterization of the *Commentaries* as an essential eyewitness narrative of the conquest of South America is perfectly accurate.

This new translation of the *Commentaries* makes Cabeza de Vaca's adventures in South America available to a wide, English-speaking audience for the first time.

I have used three Spanish versions of the book as my main sources: the *Naufragios y Comentarios* Espasa-Calpe edition of 1942 (reprinted in 1992), which popularized Cabeza de Vaca again in the Spanish-speaking world; the *Cartas de Relación de la Conquista de América, Vol. II*, published by the Editorial Nueva España and annotated by Dr. Julio Le Riverend, c. 1950; and the *Colección de Libros y Documentos Referentes a la Historia de América, Vol. 5*, published in Madrid in 1906 by the Librería General de Victoriano Suárez and edited by Miguel Serrano y Sanz. This last edition preserves the original archaic spelling and format of the book.

Only a few errors of Spanish transcription and typesetting emerged in the course of the translation, and these I have corrected to reflect the original work as it appears in Serrano y Sanz's 1906 edition. The writing conventions of the sixteenth century posed a greater challenge. The *Commentaries*, like the *Relación*, are memoirs but also travel books, forms quite new in Spanish literature in Cabeza de Vaca's day. Originating in the Río de la Plata, Cabeza de Vaca's descriptions of curious animals such as tapirs, river rays, and vampire bats are perhaps the first ever to appear in Europe. His accounts of the sodden jungles and vast swampy wilder-nesses of the Pantanal and the Gran Chaco are equally new and fresh. And his fascination with the bewildering variety of Indian tribes along the Paraguay and Paraná rivers led him to produce, as in North America, land-mark early cultural studies. Remarkably, he often lets the Indians speak for themselves. In chapter 25, for instance, Cabeza de Vaca pursues the Guaycuru Indians deep into the Gran Chaco, where they taunt his Guarani allies. *Come and join us*, they say. *We are the lords of this place, the lords of the deer and all the other animals of the wilderness, lords of the rivers and of the fish that swim in them.*

Yet much of his descriptive work is uncertain, or tentative, because the novelty of the Paraguayan countryside is unsettling to the newly arrived Spaniards. They are not yet quite as sure of themselves as they will become.

The writing in the *Commentaries* is often formal, addressed carefully to Charles I (Carlos I), and the original sentences can easily run on for half a page. At times they can even stretch to an entire page or more. Sentences frequently display double nouns and verbs for a formalized sort of emphasis ("The Christians he had sent to *scout* and *look for* a way to achieve an *entry* into and *exploration* of the province . . ."), and they are loaded with torrents of independent and dependent clauses, often unbroken by punctuation.

Chapters in the original Spanish are largely unparagraphed, with action and comment usually set in the passive voice and hobbled by the vagueness of an old Latin favorite, the subjunctive mood expressed in the imperfect tense. To accompany this thick, archaic prose, there is the backdrop of an unfamiliar, quite strange country never before imagined and certainly incompletely understood by the Europeans who attempt to subdue it and describe it at the same time.

In this new English version, I have made use of shorter sentences, quotation marks, more frequent paragraphs, and a clarifying note or two where needed for greater precision. I have also offered more extensive background explanations for several important figures, events, and locations. Islands, rivers, river ports, mountains, towns, and provinces are located on the maps that accompany the translation. I hope this approach will make Cabeza de Vaca more accessible to the modern reader.

But the *Commentaries* themselves, the South American expeditions, with their endless conquistador intrigues and unfiltered encounters with the native peoples, are heartfelt, and they remain as fresh and compelling as if they had been written yesterday. The essential story of Cabeza de Vaca's attempt to achieve a rescue, create some order, and exercise a bit of decency in the forbidding Río de la Plata is surprisingly poignant, with an enduring appeal, and as you will see the man himself tells it best.

Translator's Acknowledgments

I AM GRATEFUL TO MR. LUTHER WILSON AND MS. BETH HADAS, BOTH FORMER DIRECTORS OF THE UNIVERSITY OF NEW MEXICO PRESS, FOR GIVING me the opportunity and time to translate this second important memoir by Cabeza de Vaca.

I would also like to thank Ms. Amy Duckert Bell and Ms. Rosine McConnell, as well as Mr. Chris Porosky, for their invaluable technical help in preparing the manuscript for the publisher.

My good friends, Mr. V. B. Price and Mr. Jeff Romero, and my nephew, Mr. Matthew Huchmala, offered many helpful comments and other kindnesses over the long course of the translation.

And for their unending patience and unflagging support, I am indebted to my wife, JoAnn Strathman, and my daughter, Susan Morrow.

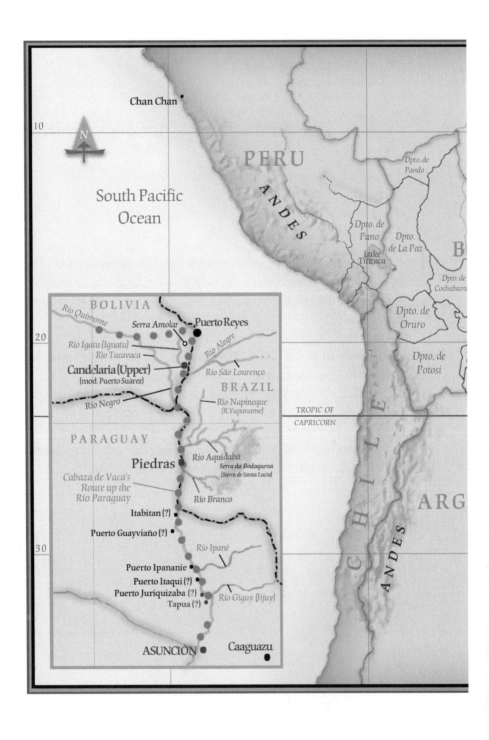

Chan Chan

*South Pacific
Ocean*

PERU

ANDES

Dpto. de
Pando

Dpto. de
Puno   Dpto.
de La Paz

Lake
Titicaca

B

Dpto. de
Cochabam

Dpto. de
Oruro

Dpto. de
Potosí

BOLIVIA

Río Quimome

Serra Amolar   **Puerto Reyes**

Río Igatu (Iguatu)
Río Tucavaca

Candelaria (Upper)
(mod. Puerto Suárez)

Río Alegre

Río São Lourenço

BRAZIL

Río Negro

Río Napineque
(R. Yapaname)

TROPIC OF
CAPRICORN

PARAGUAY

Piedras

Río Aquidabá
Serra da Bodoquena
(Sierra de Santa Lucia)

*Cabaza de Vaca's
Route up the
Río Paraguay*

Río Branco

Itabitan (?)

Puerto Guayviaño (?)

Río Ipané

Puerto Ipananie

Puerto Itaqui (?)

Puerto Juriquizaba (?)

Tapua (?)

Río Giguy (Jijuy)

CHILE

ANDES

ANDES

ARG

ASUNCIÓN   **Caaguazu**

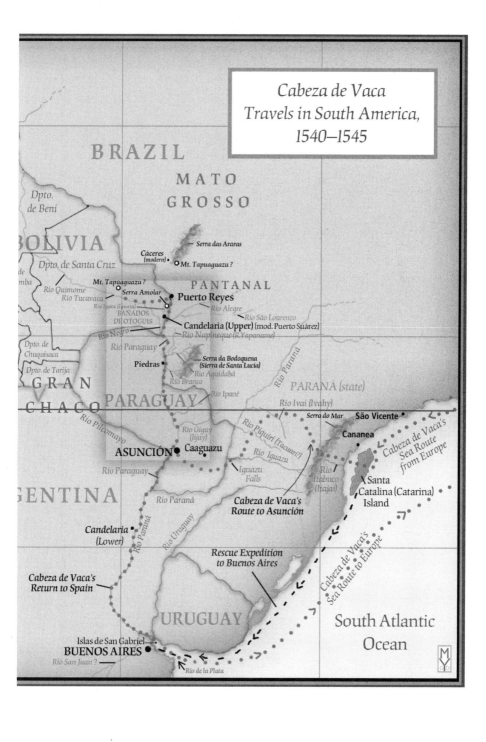

Cabeza de Vaca
Travels in South America,
1540–1545

BRAZIL

MATO
GROSSO

Dpto.
de Beni

BOLIVIA

Dpto. de Santa Cruz

Serra das Araras

Cáceres
(modern)

Mt. Tapuaguazu ?

PANTANAL

Mt. Tapuaguazu ?

Río Quimome
Río Tucavaca
Serra Amolar
Puerto Reyes

de
mba

BAÑADOS
DE OTOGUIS

Río Igatu (Iguazu)

Río Alegre

Río São Lourenço

Candelaria (Upper) (mod. Puerto Suárez)

Río Negro

Río Napineque (R. Yapaname)

Dpto. de
Chuquisaca

Río Paraguay

Dpto. de Tarija

Piedras

Serra da Bodoquena
(Sierra de Santa Lucía)
Río Aquidabá

GRAN

Río Branco

Río Ipané

PARANÁ (state)

CHACO

PARAGUAY

Río Ivai (Ivahy)

Río Pilcomayo

Río Giguy
(Jijuy)

Río Piquiri (Tacuari?)

Serra do Mar

São Vicente

Cananea

ASUNCIÓN

Caaguazu

Río Iguazu

Cabeza de Vaca's
Sea Route
from Europe

Río Paraguay

Iguazu
Falls

Río
Itabuco
(Itajaí)

Santa
Catalina (Catarina)
Island

ARGENTINA

Río Paraná

Cabeza de Vaca's
Route to Asunción

Candelaria
(Lower)

Río Paraná

Río Uruguay

Rescue Expedition
to Buenos Aires

Cabeza de Vaca's
Sea Route to Europe

Cabeza de Vaca's
Return to Spain

URUGUAY

South Atlantic
Ocean

Islas de San Gabriel
BUENOS AIRES

Río San Juan ?

Río de la Plata

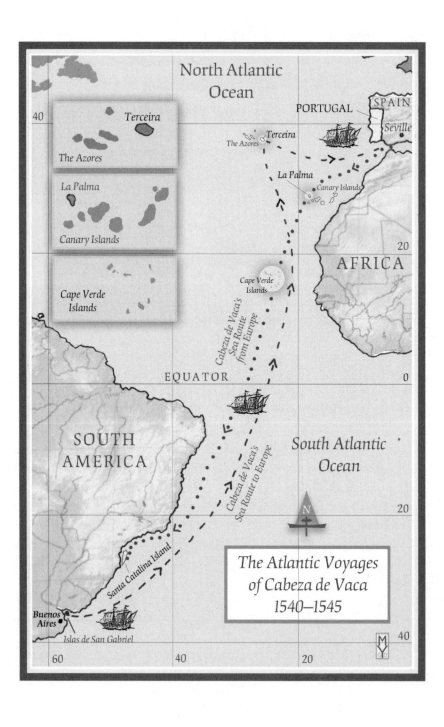

North Atlantic
Ocean

40

Terceira

The Azores

La Palma

Canary Islands

Cape Verde
Islands

PORTUGAL   SPAIN

Seville

Terceira

The Azores

La Palma

Canary Islands

20

AFRICA

Cape Verde
Islands

Cabeza de Vaca's
Sea Route
from Europe

EQUATOR   0

SOUTH
AMERICA

Cabeza de Vaca's
Sea Route to Europe

South Atlantic
Ocean

20

N

The Atlantic Voyages
of Cabeza de Vaca
1540–1545

Santa Catalina Island

Buenos
Aires

Islas de San Gabriel

60   40   20   40

CHAPTER ONE

A Word About the Commentaries
of Álvar Núñez Cabeza de Vaca

AFTER OUR LORD GOD WAS SERVED BY RELEASING ÁLVAR NÚÑEZ CABEZA DE VACA FROM THE CAPTIVITY AND LABORS OF SOME TEN YEARS IN Florida, he came to these kingdoms in the year of Our Lord 1537. He remained in Spain until 1540, in which year there arrived at the court of Your Majesty several persons from the Río de la Plata to give an account of the armada taken there by don Pedro de Mendoza and of the hardships and calamities their party had escaped.[1] Mendoza's party wished to request, should it serve Your Majesty, that you send them provisions and assistance before they all perished, as only a few of the original company were left.

Once all this became apparent to Your Majesty, you ordered that a contract and royal charter be executed with Álvar Núñez Cabeza de Vaca toward the end of helping the colonists. These were drafted and signed, stating that the aforesaid Cabeza de Vaca would go to aid the colony and that he would spend the sum of eight thousand ducats on his journey and on such means of assistance as horses, arms, clothing, and other provisions.[2] In the contract and royal charter, Your Majesty granted to Cabeza de Vaca general administration of that land—the Río de la Plata province—as Captain-General, along with the title of Governor.

Your Majesty also granted to Cabeza de Vaca one-twelfth of everything there might be in the province and of all the commerce of the place, coming and going, with the understanding that he would indeed spend the aforementioned eight thousand ducats on the journey.

And so, Cabeza de Vaca, in complying with the charter Your Majesty had executed, soon left for Seville to set things in motion for the relief effort and provision his fleet. He quickly bought two naos and a caravel, which would sail to meet up with another caravel in the Canary Islands.[3] One of the naos was brand-new, ready to go on its first voyage, and some

350 tons; the other was a 150-ton vessel. Cabeza de Vaca refitted both these ships nicely and loaded them with good supplies, pilots, and sailors. He also outfitted four hundred soldiers very thoroughly—quite a good thing for his relief mission. Everyone who offered to go on the expedition was heavily armed.

To purchase and outfit the ships took Cabeza de Vaca from the month of May till the end of September, and so the company was very eager to set out. He was detained in the city of Cadiz by contrary weather from the end of September until the second of November, when he was finally able to set sail.[4] Nine days later he arrived at the island of La Palma, where he disembarked with the whole company.[5] He stayed there for twenty-five days, awaiting favorable weather to resume his journey.

At last Cabeza de Vaca was able to sail for Cape Verde. While en route, the flagship leaked badly, taking on water some twelve palm-widths deep in the hold. Five hundred quintals of hardtack got soaked and were lost, as was much oil and other supplies.[6] This put the party in a bind. And so it was that we were all at the pumps day and night until we came to the island of Santiago, which is part of the Cape Verde group.[7] We disembarked there and led the horses out onto dry ground so that they might refresh themselves and rest a little from the strain of the sea. We also had to unload the nao to repair the leak. Once we had done so, her master plunged into the water and plugged the holes, as he was the best diver in all Spain.

The fleet had gone from La Palma to Cape Verde in ten days, a distance of three hundred leagues.[8] The port on the isle of Santiago is very poor, because in the place where ships' crews must lift up and cast out their anchors there are many rocks lying below. These gnaw on the anchor cables, and when you go to pull in the lines the anchors stay at the bottom. That's why the sailors say that the port has a lot of "rats," because the rocks gnaw the anchor lines. So it's a dangerous port for a ship if a storm should catch you in it.

It is a vicious sort of island, full of sickness in the summer. In fact, it is so bad that the greater part of those who land there simply die within a few days. Our fleet was there for twenty-five days, during which time no man perished from sickness. This spooked the people of that country, and they reckoned it was a great wonder.

The residents of the island, all told, gave our company a very good reception. It is quite a rich place, with more doubloons than reales, which the slave traders who are off to sell the blacks in the Indies give them.[9] On Santiago, they will give you one doubloon for twenty reales.

CHAPTER TWO

We Leave the Island of Cape Verde

ONCE WE REPAIRED THE LEAKS IN OUR FLAGSHIP, WE LOADED NEW STORES OF MEAT, WATER, AND OTHER NECESSITIES AND LEFT TO CONTINUE OUR journey. We soon crossed the equator.

As we were sailing, the ship's mate needed some of the fresh water the flagship carried. Out of the hundred casks he had put away, he found no more than three.[1] And these would have to supply some four hundred men and thirty horses. Facing these dire straits, the Governor ordered that they find land, and they were three days in search of it.[2] On the fourth day, an amazing thing happened an hour before dawn. And as it is not exactly irrelevant, I have related it here.

As we made toward shore there were rocks hidden beneath the waves, and no one in the entire fleet saw or sensed them at all. Then a cricket began to chirp. He had been brought aboard the nao in Cadiz by a soldier who had longed to hear the music he would make, and we had sailed for two and a half months without hearing him or even knowing he was there. The little cricket's long silence had angered our soldier, but that morning the little fellow sensed land and began to sing. His music woke up the crew, and they saw the rocks, which were only a crossbow shot from the nao. Everyone shouted to throw out the anchors, as we were about to crash into them.

So we dropped anchor, and it was certainly something we were not ever likely to forget. Had the cricket not chirped, all four hundred men and thirty horses would surely have drowned. Everyone thought it was one of God's miracles. From then on, as we traveled down the coast for more than a hundred leagues, the cricket played his music for us every night.

And so, accompanied by his delightful songs, the fleet arrived at a port past Cape Frío called Cananea, which you will find at 24 degrees south latitude.[3] Cananea is a good port. There are some little islands in its mouth.

It is a clean place, and the harbor is eleven fathoms deep. The Governor took possession of the place for Your Majesty and sailed away after having done so. He passed by the river and bay they call San Francisco, some twenty-five leagues from Cananea.[4] From there, the fleet left for the island of Santa Catalina, where the Governor arrived after suffering many hardships and switches in fortune along the way.

They made landfall in Santa Catalina on the twenty-ninth day of the month of March, 1541. Santa Catalina lies just short of 28 degrees south latitude.

The Governor and His Fleet Arrive at Santa Catalina, in Brazil, Where the Company Disembarks

THE GOVERNOR AND HIS FLEET ARRIVED AT THE ISLAND OF SANTA CATALINA, WHERE HE ORDERED HIS COMPANY TO DISEMBARK WITH THE TWENTY-SIX horses that had escaped the wrath of the sea. These were what were left of the forty-six horses he had put aboard the ships in Spain.

The Governor knew that both animals and men would need to restore themselves on land after the hardships of the long voyage. He also wanted to find an interpreter and become acquainted with the native Indians of that country. By chance, he also hoped to find out something of the condition of the Spanish colonists of the Río de la Plata, whom he and his men had come to help.[1]

The Governor intended to let the Indians know that he had come by royal command to bring aid to the colonists of La Plata and take possession of the island of Santa Catalina in the king's name. At the same time, the Governor wished to claim the port of Cananea, which lies on the coast of Brazil at more or less 25 degrees south latitude. This port is some fifty leagues from the island of Santa Catalina.

During the entire time the Governor spent on the island, he treated the Indians there, as well as those of the other parts of the coast of Brazil (who are all vassals of Your Majesty), very well. These Indians told him there were two Franciscan friars fourteen leagues away from the island at a place called Biaza. One was named fray Bernardo de Armenta, a native of Córdoba, and the other fray Alonso Lebrón, a native of Grand Canary Island.

These two friars showed up at Santa Catalina a few days later. They were quite scandalized by the Indians of that country and much afraid of them.

It seems that the Indians wanted to kill them because the friars had earlier burned down certain houses of theirs. As a result of this action, the Indians had already killed two Christians who had been living in that country.

Once the Governor found out about this situation, he began to assuage and soothe the native people. He took the friars along with him, making peace between the parties and charging these clerics with the peaceful conversion of the Indians of Santa Catalina and the nearby areas on the mainland.

CHAPTER FOUR

Nine Christians Come to the Island

THE GOVERNOR CONTINUED WITH HIS AID TO THE SPANIARDS OF THE PROVINCE. DURING THE MONTH OF MAY IN THE YEAR 1541, HE SENT A caravel with Felipe de Cáceres, Your Majesty's auditor, to enter into the river they call La Plata to visit the town founded there by don Pedro de Mendoza.[1] They call the place Buenos Aires. As the season was winter and the weather quite contrary for sailing up this river, he was not able to make any headway, and he returned to the island of Santa Catalina, where the Governor was.

Just then, nine Christians fleeing the town of Buenos Aires arrived in a small vessel. They were escaping the mistreatment of the captains presiding in that province, and the Governor found out firsthand from them the sort of life the Spaniards led there. They told the Governor that Buenos Aires was now resettled and provisioned with people and supplies. But they also said that after don Pedro de Mendoza had reestablished himself there, he sent off Juan de Ayolas to explore the land further and get to know the people of that province.[2] Ayolas had returned from his travels to retrieve certain brigantines he had left in a port called Candelaria along the Río Paraguay, and a tribe of Indians called the Payaguos, who lived along this river, had killed him and all the Christians, as well as a large number of Indians bearing goods who had come out of the interior with Ayolas.[3] These Indians were from a tribe called the Chameses.

Of all these unfortunate Indians and Christians, only one young man, a Chames tribesman, had escaped with his life. This all happened because Ayolas had not been able to find the launches he left behind in the port of Candelaria to be guarded, under his clear orders, by one Domingo de Irala.[4] Ayolas had left behind Irala, a Biscayan, as captain. But Irala withdrew before the aforesaid Juan de Ayolas had returned, abandoning the little port of Candelaria.

So the unfortunate Juan de Ayolas found no refuge: there was no one there. The Indians simply destroyed Ayolas and his men, and it was entirely the fault of that Biscayan Domingo de Irala, the captain of the brigantines.

The nine newly arrived Christians also told the Governor that along the banks of the Río Paraguay, some 120 leagues beyond the port town of Candelaria, there was a town called Asunción.[5] This town lived in friendship and harmony with a tribe called the Carios, and it was here that most of the Spanish people in the province resided.

In the town of Buenos Aires, the nine Christians said, which lies on the Rio Paraná, there were perhaps seventy Christians.[6] From that port to Asunción, which is on the Río Paraguay, it was 350 leagues upriver, all of them very hard sailing. The lieutenant governor of the province was Domingo de Irala, the Biscayan, at whose hands came about the deaths and great loss of Juan de Ayolas and all the Christians he had with him.

The nine Christians told the Governor that Domingo de Irala had left Asunción to go upriver with certain brigantines and men, saying that he was off looking for Juan de Ayolas and that he intended to help him. Irala had subsequently entered a country of troublesome waters and swamps, because of which he was not able to press onward into the interior. Then he had come back, having taken prisoner some six Indians of the Payaguos tribe—the very men who had killed Ayolas and his party.

These prisoners had told Irala of the death of Juan de Ayolas and his Christians, confirming that it had happened. At the same time, there had fallen into Irala's hands a Chane Indian named Gonzalo, who had escaped when the Payaguas Indians killed Ayolas's Christians and all the members of his tribe who had been carrying goods for Ayolas.[7] Gonzalo had been held captive by the Payaguas.

Domingo de Irala had fallen back from his expedition to the interior, losing sixty men to illness and to his own bad treatment of them. Furthermore, Your Majesty's officials residing in the province had committed terrible offenses against the Spanish conquistadors and settlers and against the native Indians of the land, who are vassals of Your Majesty as well. As a result of this, everyone was unhappy and much disturbed.

For these reasons, and because the Spanish captains had also so misused their people, the nine Christians who came to see the Governor had filched a small vessel in the port of Buenos Aires and fled, their intention being to inform Your Majesty of everything that had happened in the province.

These nine souls arrived completely naked. The Governor had them clothed and soon after collected them to return with him to the Río de la Plata. They were useful men and good sailors; besides, among them was a pilot, and he would be of good service as we sailed up the river.

CHAPTER FIVE

The Governor Makes Haste on His Journey

HAVING HEARD THE NEWS FROM THE NINE CHRISTIANS, THE GOVERNOR WISHED TO COME TO THE AID OF THE RESIDENTS OF THE CITY OF ASUNCIÓN and the people of Buenos Aires as quickly as possible. To do so, he would have to look for a route across the mainland from the island. He would need to pass through the places and regions we have already mentioned, where the Christians were. And at the same time his ships could go back to Buenos Aires.

Against the objections and considered opinions of the royal auditor Felipe de Cáceres and the pilot Antonio López, both of whom wanted the Governor to go with the entire party to the port of Buenos Aires, he sent the commissioner, Pedro Dorantes, from the island of Santa Catalina to explore the place and look for a road on the mainland.[1]

"Find out whatever you can about the country," he told Dorantes.

Earlier, during the original exploration of the place, the king of Portugal had lost a lot of men, who were killed by the Indians.

At any rate, this Pedro Dorantes, as ordered by the Governor, left with a certain number of Spanish Christians and Indians, who went along to act as guides and companions during the expedition.

The commissioner, Pedro Dorantes, returned to the island some three and a half months after he had left Santa Catalina to explore the interior. The Governor had been awaiting him eagerly. Among other items in his report, Dorantes said he had crossed great sierras and mountains and very empty lands and had finally come to a place they called the Plain. "The populated lands begin there," he said. The natives of Santa Catalina said it was more of a sure thing—not to mention shorter—to gain entry to these populated regions by going upstream along the Rio Itabucu. This river lies at the tip of Santa Catalina, about eighteen or twenty leagues from the port where we were.

Once he had heard this, the Governor sent someone to explore that river and the land roundabout. This was likely the route the party would have to travel. Once this latest probe had been accomplished, he was determined to make his entry into the country at the Itabucu. He was doing all this, of course, both to be able to explore those unknown lands *and* quickly come to the aid of the Spanish people who were in the province.

And so, the Governor resolved to make his initial incursion there. He told two friars, Fr. Bernaldo de Armenta and his companion, Fr. Alonso Lebrón, to stay on the island of Santa Catalina to continue to teach and indoctrinate the native Indians. In particular, he wanted them to support and refine their recent converts.

But they didn't want to do it. Their excuse was that they wanted to go along with the Governor's party and live in the city of Asunción, where the Spaniards they had actually come to help resided.

CHAPTER SIX

The Governor and His People Begin Their First Ventures into the Interior

T HE GOVERNOR WAS NOW WELL INFORMED ABOUT WHERE HE NEEDED TO SET OUT ON HIS EXPEDITION TO EXPLORE THE COUNTRY AND AID THE SPANIARDS of that province. He was also well equipped with necessary supplies for the journey. On the eighteenth day of October 1541, he gave the men of his company the order to proceed, with the twenty-six horses and mares that had survived the sea voyage. He sent the party across the Río de Itabucu, which he thereupon declared to be in the possession of Your Majesty as newly discovered territory. He left 140 persons on the island of Santa Catalina, all of whom were to go by ship to the Río de la Plata, where they would find the port of Buenos Aires.

The Governor ordered Pedro Estopiñán Cabeza de Vaca, whom he had left on the island as captain of the remaining force, to reoutfit the nao with supplies before leaving Santa Catalina.[1] This would benefit the company that Estopiñán took along with him as well as the Spaniards in the port of Buenos Aires. Before the Governor left the island, he gave the native Indians of Santa Catalina a lot of presents to make them happy.

The Indians of the island freely offered a number of their own people to go along with the Governor and his company. They intended to serve as guides and in a number of other needed capacities, and he took full advantage of their help.

And so, on the second day of November of that year, the Governor ordered everyone in the party to take up whatever he could handle for the journey. This was in addition to all the supplies the Indians would carry for the Spaniards. The Governor began his travels on that day with 250 harquebusiers and crossbowmen, all very handy with their weapons. He also had 26 cavalrymen, the 2 Franciscan friars, and the Indians from Santa Catalina. He sent his own nao back to Santa Catalina to tell Pedro Estopiñán Cabeza de Vaca to set sail and make his way to the port of Buenos Aires.

So the Governor at last marched off into the interior, where the going was arduous both for him and his company. For nineteen days they crossed great mountains, felling a lot of trees and slashing underbrush in the forests and woodlands, opening up paths so that the party and its horses could pass through. The country was empty of human beings.

And at the end of these nineteen days the men finished off the provisions they had set out with. They had nothing left to eat. But it pleased the Lord that without losing a single person of that considerable host they at last came to the first settlements of the place the Indians called the Plain. In these villages, the chief was named Añiriri, and a day's journey away was another place where the chief was called Cipoyay. Yet farther on was another Indian town, in which Tocanguanzu was the chief.

The Indians in all these settlements already knew about the arrival of the Governor and his party, and they came out to greet him along the road, loaded with provisions, very happy and showing great pleasure in his arrival. When the Governor saw all this, he welcomed the Indians with relish and love, as well. And after paying the Indians what their goods were worth, he greeted the village chiefs graciously and showered them with gifts of shirts and other trade goods and trinkets, with which they seemed very pleased.

These people are of a tribe called the Guaranis.[2] They are farmers who plant corn twice a year, and they also plant cassava.[3] They raise chickens in the same way that we do in Spain and ducks as well.[4] They have a lot of parrots and macaws in their houses. And they occupy a very large amount of land indeed, with the same language spoken everywhere.

These people eat human flesh—as often that of their Indian enemies as the flesh of Christians. They even eat each other. They are also a people very fond of war, which they engage in and look forward to on a regular basis. And the Guaranis are a *vengeful* people as well.

Well, the Governor took possession of these settlements in the name of Your Majesty. It was all newly discovered territory, and he graced this novel province with the name of Vera.[5] The record of this appears in the acts of possession recorded in front of Juan de Araoz, Your Majesty's notary.

With all this accomplished, the Governor and his party left the village of Tocanguanzu on the twenty-ninth of November. They traveled for two days, and on the first of December the Governor came to a river that the Indians called Iguazú, which means "big water."[6] Our pilots measured the level of its flow.

What the Governor and His People Went By Along the Road, and What Sort of Country It Is

From that river called Iguazú, the Governor and his people set out to explore the country, and on the third day of December they came to another river that the Indians called Tibagi. This is a stream walled in by tremendous, overlapping slabs of stone, placed in such an orderly manner that they look man-made.[1] Traveling along one stretch of this river was quite hard work, as the men and the horses slipped and couldn't gain any traction. They held on to each other to counteract this. Although the river wasn't particularly deep, the water ran with a strong and furious current.

From as far as two leagues away from this river the Indians came in, much pleased to see us, to bring food for the army. So we lacked nothing in the way of provisions, to such an extent that we sometimes left the surplus along the side of the trails we took. This sort of generosity caused the Governor to give back a great deal to the Indians as well and linger with them for a while—especially with the chiefs. After he paid them for the food, he gave them a number of trade goods and trinkets, as well as various other favors. It was good treatment all around.

The Governor's fame raced through the province as a result of these actions, and all the natives lost their fear of the Spaniards, came to see them, and brought along everything they had. They were paid for their trouble, as we have said.

On that same day, we were near another settlement of Indians whose principal lord was a man named Tapapirazu.[2] An Indian arrived who was a native of the coast of Brazil; his name was Miguel, and he was a new convert. He came to us from the city of Asunción, where the Spaniards we were going to help lived. This Miguel was going back to the Brazilian coast because he had been among the Spaniards for quite a long while. The Governor spent a fair amount of time with him, as he knew a great deal about conditions around Asunción and about the Spaniards and Indians there. These Spaniards were in dire peril because of the deaths of Juan de Ayolas and the other Spanish captains and their men who had been killed by the Indians.

Once Miguel had told his story, he volunteered to go back with the Governor to the city of Asunción, from which he had just come, to serve as a guide and advise the Governor's party on the proper routes to take. The Governor then discharged the Indians who had accompanied him from Santa Catalina Island, sending them back to the coast. So these fellows left, quite happy and pleased with the Governor's good treatment and the many presents he had given them.

The Governor's men lacked experience in the proper treatment of Indians, and he did not want them to harm or even aggravate the natives.[3] Consequently, he ordered the men in general not to barter with the Indians or talk to them. "Furthermore," he said, "the Spaniards of our party are not to go into their houses or settlements, because the temper of the natives is such that any small thing might scandalize them or set them off. And that could result in great damage and discontent all across this country." In addition, the Governor ordered that only people within our company who were familiar with the Indians should trade with them and *purchase* provisions to be shared among all the Spaniards, and all this at the Governor's expense.

The result was that the Governor divided up provisions in person among his men every day, handing everything out graciously and with nothing in it for himself.

It was quite remarkable to see how all the Indians of that country feared our horses. This dread of theirs drew them to our route with a lot of things in hand for the horses to eat, including chickens and honey. "We don't want these creatures to get angry with us," they said, "so we'll make sure they eat well." To pacify the Indians, the Spaniards habitually made camp some distance away from where they lived, hoping to keep them from abandoning their towns. The Governor also did not want any of his men to use force with the Indians or to bother them in any way. And with this order firmly in place, and because the Governor was punishing any-one who angered the Indians in any respect, the native people came in with their wives and children very confidently. It was quite a thing to see. They came from great distances carrying provisions of all kinds, just to look at the Christians and their horses. They wanted to catch a glimpse of people the likes of which no one had ever seen in those lands.

The Governor and his men continued their travels through that country. They came to a town of the Guarani Indians, and the chief of the place and all his people came out to the road to meet them, happy to welcome them. They brought honey, ducks, and chickens, as well as cornmeal and ears of corn. Through his interpreters the Governor spoke with them and allayed their fears. "Thank you for coming to greet us," he said. "Let us pay you for everything you've brought."

They were pleased with this. In addition, the Governor graciously gave some scissors, knives, and other presents to the chief of the town, a man named Pupebaje. The Spaniards then continued their journey, leaving behind these Indians, who were so happy that they danced and sang all across their town.

On the seventh of December they arrived at a river that the Indians call Tacuari.[4] This is a stream that carries a considerable amount of water and has a good current. On its banks they found a town of Indians whose chief was named Abangobi, and he and all the Indians of the place—even the women and children—came out to greet the Spaniards. They showed considerable pleasure at the arrival of the Governor and his people, and they brought a substantial quantity of provisions out to the roadside. We paid them for these, as was our custom.

All these people are of the same tribe and they speak the same language.[5]

From this place we again pushed forward, leaving the natives very happy and pleased. And the news of the good treatment to be had from our party also went forward from one settlement to the next; the Indians showed each other the many things they had gotten from us. The result was that we found all the settlements we were about to enter already pacified, and the people came out to receive us loaded with supplies for our use *before* we got to their towns. And, of course, we paid them for their trouble, as we have said.

Continuing on the trail, by the fourteenth of December the Spaniards had passed through a few more settlements of the Guarani Indians in which they were nicely received and outfitted with whatever provisions the natives had. The company came to a town of Indians whose chief was named Tocangucir. Here they rested for a day because the men were exhausted. The road they followed was to the west-northwest and a quarter to the northeast. The pilots measured our position at 24½ degrees south latitude, about a degree off the Tropic of Capricorn.[6]

All along the road the Governor traveled, from the time he first came into this province, he found the towns to be cheerful places, with their sweeping countrysides, groves of trees, and rivers and fountains. Here there are brooks and narrow rills, and in summary the whole country is a handsome place in which to farm and raise livestock.

Hardships Along the Way for the Governor and His People, and the Kinds of Pines and Pine Cones in That Land

From that place of Tugui, the Governor and his men traveled until the nineteenth of December without finding any people.[1] The route was very arduous, with many rivers and rough country to cross. On one day alone they had to construct eighteen bridges to allow the men and their horses to continue. And the way forward was terrible with the rivers and swamps the party encountered, which were many and awful. The Spaniards went across a number of great mountain ranges and hills that were harsh places indeed, smothered and closed in by vast brakes of thick canes covered with strong barbs. There were many trees, too, and for the party to be able to get through, it took twenty men hacking away constantly to make a path. They were many days traveling in this place, and because of its malevolence they often looked up and could not see the sky.

Finally, on the nineteenth of December, the party came to a settlement of the Guarani tribe, who with their chief and even their women and children came out to receive the Spaniards some two leagues from their town. They brought along a lot of provisions, including chickens, ducks, and honey, as well as sweet potatoes and fruits. They also had corn and a sort of meal made of pine nuts (of which they produced a great quantity), as there are very great pine groves in that country. The pines are immense, so much so that four men touching each other with their arms extended would not be able to circle them. These trees are tall and straight, good for the masts of a nao or a carack because of their size.[2] The cones of these pines are themselves large, the seeds the size of acorns, and their big hulls like chestnuts. They don't taste quite like the pine nuts of Spain. The Indians collect them and grind the seeds into vast quantities of meal for their sustenance.

In that country there are also lots of javelinas and monkeys who feed on the pine nuts in the following way: The monkeys climb up to the top of the trees, where they hang on to the branches with their tails.[3] Then they use their hands and feet to grab the cones and throw them down to the ground. When they have torn off and tossed down a considerable quantity, they scamper down the trees to eat the nuts. Often they find that the javelinas have expropriated the cones and are standing there guarding their hoard. The pigs then charge the monkeys, running them off and eating their pine nuts. The monkeys retreat to the trees, screaming and yelling while the javelinas feed.[4] There are also many fruits here of different shapes and flavors, all of which bear twice during the year.

In this settlement of Tugui, the Governor and his party spent Christmas —as much to celebrate the holiday itself as to rest and restore the men.[5] Everyone was able to eat his fill here, as the Indians were very generous with all their food. So, the Spaniards celebrated, very happy with their holiday and the good care of the Indians.

But it was a dangerous thing to do. With all that food around, the Spaniards didn't exercise their bodies, and they ate anything that came their way and too much of it. It gave them fevers. That had never happened while they were marching along during their previous journeys, when they simply threw off their illnesses and were entirely well.

As they were about to start up their travels again, the company plagued the Governor with requests to rest for a few days. He didn't want to allow this, because he had had enough of everyone falling ill. But the men only thought that he wanted to create more hardship for them. Finally, with their own experience growing a little, they came to understand that he did what he did for their own good. Eating so much just made them ill, and along these lines the Governor had a great deal of experience.

The Explorers Starve, but Save Themselves with Worms, Which They Get from Some Canes

O N THE TWENTY-EIGHTH OF DECEMBER, THE GOVERNOR AND HIS PARTY
TOOK LEAVE OF THE PLACE CALLED TUGUI, WHERE THEY LEFT THE INDIANS
quite happy. They traveled cross-country all day without finding any settlements and finally arrived at a wide and massive river, with tremendous
currents and running very deep. Along its banks were a number of groves
of cypresses and cedars and other trees.[1]

Crossing this river was arduous and took that day and three more. They
traveled cross-country again and passed five settlements of the Guarani
tribe. All these people came out to receive the Governor's party with their
wives and children, and they brought so many supplies that the Spaniards
were well provisioned. The Indians were left in quite a peaceful state due to
the good treatment and payment the Governor extended to them.

That entire land is a cheerful place, well furnished with water and trees.
The people of the towns sow cassava, corn, and other seeds, and three kinds
of sweet potatoes—white, yellow, and red, all thick and delicious.[2] They
raise ducks and chickens, and they extract a lot of honey from the hollows
of the trees.

On the first day of the month of January of the year of Our Lord 1542,
the Governor and his party left the villages of the Indians and began traveling across mountainous country and through dense canebrakes. It was
slow and tough going, and until the fifth day of that month they found no
sign of settlements. In addition to this hardship, they found themselves
quite hungry, going on only by dint of laborious effort as they continued
to cut swathes through the canebrakes.

In the small flutes of the canes there were some little white worms, as thick and long as a finger.[3] These the Spaniards fried up to eat. When heat was applied, so much fat came out of them that they cooked up very nicely indeed. Everyone ate them and thought they were quite tasty. Out of other lengths of cane came sweet water, which all the party drank and were glad to find.

The Spaniards began looking for this new sort of food and drink all along the road, and by finding it they were able to sustain themselves and relieve their hunger and thirst in that empty land. Along this same road the party also crossed two mighty rivers with a great deal of effort.[4] Their current flowed to the north.

On another day, the sixth of January, the company traveled through the interior without finding a single town. They paused to sleep along the banks of another voluminous river bursting with mighty currents and lined with canebrakes. Here the party again extracted worms from the canes for their dinner, with which they fortified themselves. Thus refreshed, the Governor and his people set off again.

A few days later the Governor found himself crossing some nice country with good water, offering abundant game—javelinas and deer. They killed some of these and shared them out amongst the party. That same day they crossed a couple of small rivers. It pleased God that no Christian should become ill, and everyone marched along hopeful that the expedition would soon arrive at the city of Asunción, where they would find the Spaniards whom they had come to help.

So, from the sixth to the tenth of January they passed through a number of Guarani towns, where the inhabitants peacefully and happily came out with their chiefs to greet the party of Spaniards. These Indians and their wives and children all brought provisions, which were really quite helpful to the Spaniards. However, fray Bernaldo de Armenta and fray Alonso, his companion, went ahead of the party to collect all these items, and so when the Governor and the rest of the party came up the Indians had nothing left to give them.

Some members of the party began to complain to the Governor about this, as the friars had done it before a number of times. The Governor had warned them not to do this and not to take along as part of their retinue certain useless Indian people, both adults and children, whom they would have to feed. But the padres had no intention of minding the Governor, which made everyone think about shooing off these people for them if the

Governor did not stand in the way. The question became this: What action would be of the best service to God and Your Majesty?

Well, the upshot was that the friars went off again, leaving behind the people they had picked up and following their own path against the Governor's wishes. He told them to bring back news of the Indian settlements they visited, and traveling anywhere in that country would have been very hard for the main party had they not done so.

Setting off again on the tenth of January, the Spaniards went across many rivers and streams and through several terrible passes in the vast mountain ranges as well as through hummocky canebrakes awash in water. Every range they went through had a valley with excellent soil, as well as its own river and springs and groves of trees. There is a lot of water throughout that country, as it lies below the Tropic of Capricorn.

The route the party took over those two days lay to the west.

CHAPTER TEN

The Indians Are Afraid of Horses

B Y THE FOURTEENTH OF JANUARY, WE WERE TRAVELING THROUGH THE SETTLEMENTS OF THE GUARANI TRIBE. THESE PEOPLE HAD ALL GREETED us with great pleasure and had come out to meet us with corn, chickens, honey, and other provisions. The Governor always paid them as a gesture of goodwill, and consequently they brought us so much that the surplus was just left along the roadsides.

All these people go about stark naked, the men as well as the women, and they were dreadfully afraid of the horses. They begged the Governor to tell the horses not to get angry with them, and to keep the animals happy they brought fodder for them.

And so the party eventually came to a wide river with a tremendous current—the Iguatu, a beautiful stream with a lot of fish and groves of trees. On its banks, there is a town of Indians of the Guarani tribe, who sow their corn and cassava just as we had seen everywhere else we traveled. These Guaranis came out to greet us as though they had already heard of our arrival elsewhere and of our good treatment of their neighbors. They traded with us for a lot of provisions, with which they were very well supplied.

In that land there are a lot of pine groves of different kinds, and they bear nuts, as mentioned earlier.

The Indians served our Spaniards well throughout the country, because the Governor always treated *them* well.

Well, this Río Iguatu lies in the western band of the country at 25 degrees south latitude, and it may be about as wide as the Guadalquivir. Along its banks (as related to us earlier by the locals and as the Governor saw with his own eyes) there is quite a population of Indians, and they are the richest people in their province (and in the entire country) because of their hard work and cultivation. They raise large numbers of chickens, ducks, and other birds. They also hunt pigs and deer, tapirs and partridges, and quail and pheasants.[1] The river is a great fishery, and the Guaranis plant and harvest a lot of corn, sweet potatoes, cassava, peanuts, and many other fruits.[2] From the trees they get a great quantity of honey.

The Governor wished to write Your Majesty's officials in Asunción from one of these towns to tell them—as well as the captains and other people residing in the city—that by order of Your Majesty he was on his way to help them. This he did, sending off two local Indians with the letter.

One night while the company was still on the Río Piqueri, a dog bit the leg of one Francisco Orejón, a citizen of Ávila. And another fourteen Spaniards, worn out from our long route, were suffering there alongside him. These men all stayed behind with this Orejón fellow when we left to continue our journey, the idea being that they would come along behind us little by little. The Governor charged the Indians of the place with their care. "Watch over them," he said, "and send them on their way as soon as they are well." To motivate the Indians, he gave a number of trade goods and trinkets to the chief of the town and to several of the other natives of the place. The chief and his men were well pleased with these presents.

All along the road and throughout the countryside the Governor and his men traversed as they explored the province, there is considerable open country and very good water—rivers, streams, and springs, groves of trees and sown fields, and the most fertile land in the world, all ready to be worked and planted. A large part of it could be made into sugarcane plantations.

The land is good for hunting, and is peopled by the Guaranis. They eat human flesh, but they are also all farmers and raise ducks and chickens. They are a domesticated people and friends of the Christians. With a little work, they will grow in the knowledge of our holy Catholic faith, as we have seen through experience.

And considering the kind of country it is, we may say with great certainty that if silver deposits are to be found anywhere, it will be here.

CHAPTER ELEVEN

The Governor Travels by Canoe on the Río de Iguaza, and the Men Carry their Canoes on Their Shoulders for a League to Bypass a Bad Stretch of the River at Some Rapids

THE GOVERNOR LEFT THE INDIANS OF THE RÍO PIQUERI PACIFIED AND VERY MUCH HIS FRIENDS. HE AND HIS MEN TRAVELED ON THROUGH THE country, visiting many other towns of the Guarani Indians. These people all came out to the roadway with a lot of provisions, showing a great deal of pleasure and contentment at the Governor's arrival, and the Governor handed out considerable quantities of trade goods and trinkets to the lordly chiefs of these towns. Even the old women and children came out to welcome the party, bringing corn and sweet potatoes.

It was much the same in the other settlements of that country, one of which was a day's journey further on and another, two days' journey. People came by in the same way and brought along provisions. The Spaniards traveled long stretches at a time, and the Indians always cleared off and cleaned up the roads before they arrived. The Indians danced and leapt for joy at the sight of the Spaniards. And what the Governor and his men took the greatest pleasure in—what made them happiest—was that the old women were so pleased to see them. This was because the Indians are ruled by what the old women say, and they mind them. They're not so attentive to the old men.

On the last day of the month of January, while traveling through the province, the Spaniards came to a river called Iguazú.[1] They had gone on for eight days through empty country, finding no settlements of Indians. This Río Iguazú is the first river they had passed when they went inland from the coast of Brazil. It is also called the Iguazú there, and it runs from the east to the west. Along the Iguazú there are no towns whatsoever. It lies at 25 ½ degrees south latitude.

Arriving at this river, the Governor was told by the local Indians that the Iguazú flows into the Río Paraná, which is also called the Río de la Plata. In addition, they said that it was between this Río Paraná and the Río Iguazú where some Indians had killed the Portuguese Martín Alfonso de Sosa sent to explore the country.[2] The Indians had attacked and killed these men as they were paddling along in their canoes. Some of these Indians, who lived along the banks of the Paraná—the very same who had killed the Portuguese—told the Governor that the Indians of the Río Piqueri were terrible people and our enemies. They were waiting for a chance to attack these people and slaughter them at the river's narrows.

This made the Governor mindful that he should secure both sides of the river. He resolved to go down the Iguazú himself by canoe with part of his men to reach the Río Paraná and send the rest of his people and horses by land to seize the opposite bank. This approach would frighten the Indians, and the canoes would be able to slip through. So that's what was put into effect. The Governor set off with about eighty men downstream on the Iguazú in a series of canoes he had bought from the Indians. He ordered the balance of the men and horses to set off by land, as we have noted, and everyone was supposed to rendezvous at the Río Paraná.

Well, the current was very strong going down the Río Iguazú, and the canoes shot along furiously. Very close to where the party had launched itself into the river, it plunged in a fall over some high rocks with a great crashing noise that you could hear from quite a distance. The mist where the water dropped off with such force rose up for two or more *lanzas.*[3] Because of this it was necessary to get out of the canoes, lift them from the water, and haul them overland past the falls. The men carried them on their shoulders more than half a league, which was a great hardship.

Once that bad stretch was passed, the men put the canoes back into the water and resumed their journey, going downriver until they reached the Río Paraná. It pleased God that the people and horses who had gone by land, as well as the canoes and their men traveling with the Governor aboard, all arrived at the same time. On the banks of the river there was a very great number of Indians of the same Guarani tribe, all decked out in macaw feathers and smeared with red ochre. They were painted up in many styles and colors. There must have been a squadron of them with bows and arrows in their hands, and it was a great pleasure to see them.

The arrival of the Governor and his men by canoe and by land (as we have just mentioned) scared the Indians. They were baffled by us. So the Governor started to talk to them through his interpreters and hand out lots of trinkets and trade goods to their chiefs. And as they were a very greedy people and fond of novelties, they began to calm down and approach the Governor and his men. Many of the local Guarani Indians helped our party get to the other side of the river. After the Governor's party was all on one side, he ordered his men to make rafts by joining their canoes together two by two. With this accomplished, all the remaining men and horses, in cooperation with the locals, were brought over within the space of two hours from the other side. Our men also helped the local Indians themselves to cross.

This Río Paraná, in the area the party traversed, was as wide as a long crossbow shot. It is very deep, and it carries a terrific current, and one canoe in crossing it overturned with several Christians aboard, one of whom drowned. The current just carried him off, never to be seen again. This river also generates a lot of whirlpools, what with its great depth and the tremendous force of its current.

CHAPTER TWELVE

They Make Rafts to Carry the Sick

T HE GOVERNOR AND HIS PARTY HAD NOW CROSSED THE RÍO PARANÁ. HE HAD EARLIER REQUESTED TWO BRIGANTINES FROM THE CAPTAINS of Asunción, and he was quite puzzled not to find them waiting for him. He had advised these captains of his situation through a letter from the Río Paraná, and he thought his own journey would be made a little more certain with the boats because the Indians would fear him more. The brigantines would also have been useful in carrying the sick and exhausted members of his party, who were worn out by the long road they had traveled.

But because the Spaniards of Asunción now had news of his arrival yet had not come, the Governor was exasperated. The sick were numerous and could not travel. Nor was it very safe to linger in that spot, with so many enemies all around. To be among those people was just to dare them to do something treacherous, as that was their custom. And so, the Governor decided to send his sick men down the Paraná on some rafts in the care of a chief from that same river. This man's name was Iguaron, and the Governor gave him a number of trade goods and trinkets because he had offered to accompany the Governor's men to the home of Francisco, a servant of Gonzalo Acosta.[1] This was done in the hope that along the way the party would come across the brigantines, where they would be well received and taken aboard.

In the meanwhile, the Indian named Francisco, who had been a retainer among the Christians, would be sure to protect them. He himself lived on the same bank of the Río Paraná, and his home, according to the locals, was about four days' journey away from where they had just passed.[2]

So the Governor ordered the party to depart. It consisted of about thirty men, and along with these, another fifty men who were harquebusiers and crossbowmen to guard and defend them. Once he had sent them off, the Governor set out cross-country with the rest of his party for the city of Asunción. The Indians living along the Río Paraná assured him that it lay about nine days' journey ahead.

The Governor took possession of the Río Paraná in Your Majesty's name. His pilots took a reading of the latitude, which was 24 degrees south of the equator.[3]

The Governor and his men continued to travel through the countryside among the settlements of the Guarani tribe, where he was very well received. The people came out to the roadsides with plenty of provisions, as was their usual custom. The party went through some large swamps, as well as some other rough country, and encountered a number of rivers. Making bridges on the spot so that the men and horses could cross these was very hard. And all the Indians of the towns on the other side of the Río Paraná accompanied them from one place to another.[4] The Indians showed them the way and were full of love and goodwill, serving them well, providing food to eat, and assisting the Spaniards as guides. The Governor, of course, paid the Indians or satisfied them in other ways, which left them quite happy.

As the party made its way through that country, a Christian Spaniard from Asunción came up. He had been sent from the town to find out about the Governor's arrival and then carry back the news. The people of the place very much wanted to see him and his men, who were to be the source of their relief, and they couldn't believe they were about to be saved until they saw the party with their own eyes. (All this notwithstanding the fact that they had indeed received the letters the Governor had sent them.)

At any rate, this Christian came up and told the Governor of the perilous state in which the people found themselves, of the deaths that had occurred among the party of Juan de Ayolas, and of the many other killings perpetrated by the Indians of that country. The Spaniards were much pained and feeling very lost, generally because they had abandoned the port of Buenos Aires on the Río Paraná. That, of course, had been the cause of all the ships and men sent out from the realms of Spain to come to their aid, which now might themselves have to be saved.[5]

The colonists had simply lost all hope of salvation, had abandoned the port, and had then suffered untold other dangers in that country.

CHAPTER THIRTEEN

The Governor Arrives at the City of Asunción, Where He Finds the Christian Spaniards He Had Come to Help

THE CHRISTIAN SPANIARD ALREADY MENTIONED HAD COME TO THE GOVERNOR AND TOLD HIM OF THE DEATHS OF JUAN DE AYOLAS AND HIS PARTY. Ayolas had gone exploring in the interior, but other Christians had been killed in that country as well. The visiting Christian spoke also of the terrible needs of the people in Asunción and of the abandonment of Buenos Aires, to which place the Governor had earlier ordered his flagship with its 140 men from the island of Santa Catalina.

Now, the Governor had kept his men on Santa Catalina for safety's sake. He had feared they would be in great danger if they arrived in Buenos Aires and found the land around it lifeless and empty, as that was a country of many dangers, full of hostile Indians. Furthermore, he had wanted to send them quickly to the aid of the colonists at Asunción, where they could also calm the fears of the friendly Indians—who, of course, are the vassals of Your Majesty.

So the Governor made his way down the road in his usual, painstaking manner, passing many settlements of the Guarani tribe as he traveled. These people—and many of their relatives from villages at some distance from the Governor's path—soon began to appear with all kinds of provisions for the party. Why, you may ask? Well, it was because the fame, as it were, of the good treatment and many gifts already meted out by the Governor to the native people had spread ahead of the party. The Indians arrived of their own volition and with much affection to see the Spaniards and offer them supplies, and they brought along their wives and children, too. That, of course, was a sign of the great faith they had in the Governor. The Indians also swept the pathways before his party.

All the Indians from the villages the party encountered during this exploration made their houses of straw and wood. Among these people were a number of natives from the countryside surrounding Asunción. These people came to speak to the Governor one by one in our Castilian tongue, saying that he had come just in time. They said the same to the other Spaniards, displaying much pleasure in our arrival.

These Indians showed by their behavior that they had spoken with Christians, mixing with them, and coming as they did from the lands around Asunción. And as the Governor and his men approached the settlement, the people acted as the earlier Indians had—they kept the roads clean and well swept. The men, the old women, and the children lined up in an orderly way, as though they were in a procession, awaiting our arrival with many foodstuffs—corn wine, bread, sweet potatoes, chickens, and fish. They also brought honey and venison, already cooked and seasoned. They graciously shared all this with us, and as a sign of love and friendship they held their hands up high. They welcomed the Governor and his people in their own language, and a number of them did the same in ours. They were familiar and chatty all along the road, just as if they had known us for some time and had been born and raised in Spain.

Traveling along like this, it pleased Our Lord, as they say, that at nine o'clock in the morning on the eleventh day of March, a Saturday, in the year 1542, they came to the city of Asunción. Here were the Spaniards whom the Governor's party had come to assist, living on the bank of the Río Paraguay at 25 degrees south latitude. As the party approached the city, the captains and their men came out to greet them in great, joyous relief. It was incredible, actually. The Spaniards said they never thought they would be rescued, because the road that led to them was so dangerous and hard. Actually, they believed that no one knew anything about a road, as all of them had left Buenos Aires—the port where they had once had a hope of being rescued.

Once the Spaniards had abandoned Buenos Aires, the local Indians had become very daring and impudent, launching a number of murderous attacks. This had happened, of course, because considerable time had passed with no Spanish force coming to the aid of our people in the province.

Following this exchange, the Governor rested himself in their company, chatting with them and receiving them fondly, assuring them that he was there to assist them by order of the king. He then presented foodstuffs gathered from the whole country and brought by canoe on the river, as well as many provisions and his credentials, to Domingo de Irala, the lieutenant governor of the province. The other officials with Irala were Alonso de Cabrera, the inspector, a native of Loja; Felipe de Cáceres, the auditor, a native of Madrid; Pedro Dorantes, a merchant and native of Béjar; and other captains and residents who lived in the province.[1] The Governor's letters of authority were read out in front of these people and the other churchmen and soldiers who were present. The Spaniards of Asunción received the Governor and gave him the allegiance due to a captain-general of the province who would be governing in the name of the king. His powers of justice had, of course, been given him by the king, and in his turn he conferred these instruments of governance once again upon the men who in the name of His Majesty had been exercising both civil and criminal legal authority in that country.

CHAPTER FOURTEEN

The Spaniards Who had Fallen Ill on the Río de Piqueri Arrive in the City of Asunción

T HIRTY DAYS AFTER THE GOVERNOR HAD REACHED THE CITY OF ASUNCIÓN IN THE MANNER I HAD MENTIONED, THE CHRISTIANS HE HAD EARLIER sent off on rafts down the Río Paraná arrived. Some were healthy and some were ill, these latter having fallen under the weather while on the river, but they were *all* road-weary. And of all these fellows, only one was dead, killed by a jaguar.[1]

From these men fresh off the Paraná, the Governor learned for certain that the Indians along the river had come together and sent out a general call to arms all across the country. The tribesmen went out on foot along the banks of the river and by canoe on the river itself. From the river's shores, other Indians had come out to meet them, an enormous number of men on rafts going downstream, and then with tremendous shouts and much beating of drums they had attacked our men, showering them with thick waves of arrows.

The Indians converged on the Spaniards with more than two hundred canoes, aiming to slip in among the Spanish rafts, seize them, and kill our men. And for fourteen days and their nights the fighting raged without a stop. There weren't even small breaks in the action, and the Indians on land shot volley after well-coordinated volley of arrows at our men, following the lead of the warriors who were attacking by canoe. Then they brought out some big grappling hooks. They tried to snag the Spanish rafts with these and drag them to shore so that they could fight our men hand to hand.

With all this action, the uproar and howling from the Indians was so terrible that it seemed heaven and earth had joined together. Some of the Indian troops on shore and those in the canoes switched places; some rested while others fought, and it was so well planned they never stopped, creating a lot of hardship for our Spaniards.

The Spaniards suffered about twenty wounds—just small scratches, nothing dangerous. And while all this fighting was going on, the rafts continued, day and night, to make their way downstream. The river's current was so strong it simply carried them along, with our men doing very little steering. They just kept their craft away from the shore, where all the trouble was. However, the river's grasping whirlpools put them in danger many times, spinning the rafts around freely. Had the men in charge not guided them with a firm hand, the whirlpools would have run them ashore, where the Spaniards would have been captured and killed.

And so, with no chance of help or shelter of any kind, the Indians chased our men for fourteen days in their canoes, shooting arrows at them and fighting with them day and night. They finally came close to the homestead of the Indian we mentioned earlier named Francisco (who was a slave and the servant of some Christians in those parts), who, with certain of his own people, had set out upstream to help our Spaniards. He conducted them to an island in the river close to his own town, where he brought them provisions. With all the hardships of their continuous battle, they had arrived very tired and hungry, and on the island their wounded were able to rest and recuperate.

The hostiles withdrew and never dared attack them again.

And just then, two brigantines we had sent to help them arrived, and our men boarded them and were brought back to Asunción.

CHAPTER FIFTEEN

The Governor Sends Help to the People Who Had Gone in His Flagship to Buenos Aires to Assist in the Resettlement of That Port

T HE GOVERNOR EXERCISED DILIGENCE AND ORDERED A NUMBER OF BRIG-
ANTINES TO BE READIED. HE OUTFITTED THEM WITH PROVISIONS AND
general necessities and staffed them with men recruited in Asunción who
had formerly been residents of Buenos Aires. This crew was familiar with
the Río Paraná, and he sent them to the aid of the 140 Spaniards who had
sailed from the island of Santa Catalina in the flagship of his fleet.[1]

The men in the flagship were in great peril because the port of Buenos
Aires had been abandoned. The Governor wanted the port reestablished,
and these men were just the fellows to accomplish that end. They could
pick the area in or around Buenos Aires that seemed most appealing to
settle in, but they knew that the place absolutely had to be reclaimed. If
they were not successful, all the Spanish people who had been part of the
original conquest and who still resided in the province would be in grave
danger and might be lost.

You see, the ships that had made their way along the customary route
must have made port on the Paraná, and the men, once there, had likely
crafted a number of brigantines to go upriver for 350 leagues to Asunción.[2]
It is hard and dangerous sailing.

As it was, two of the brigantines left on April 16 of that year, and the
Governor also ordered two new launches to be built.[3] Once they were pro-
visioned and staffed, they also set off to relieve the distressed colonists of
Buenos Aires and effect the resettlement of the place.

The Governor ordered the captains of the brigantines to treat the Indians along the banks of the Río Paraná well and trade with them peaceably in obedience to Your Majesty. The captains were instructed to exercise reason and clearly report their actions so that we might keep Your Majesty well informed of the situation. "Should you do all this," said the Governor, "His Majesty will indeed have a clear idea of everything that has been done in his name and in the service of God to bring about the pacification of the natives of the province. You will allay their fears."

To better serve both God and Your Majesty, the Governor ordered a conference of all the clerics then residing in the province as well as those whom he himself had brought to the place. In front of Your Majesty's officials, the Governor's captains, and the people of the province, whom he had also called together, he pled in good and loving words to this effect: "Take special care in the indoctrination and teaching of the native Indians, these most recent vassals of His Majesty."

He ordered to be read out to them a number of chapters of Your Majesty's charter for the province dealing with the treatment of the Indians. The Governor charged the friars, priests, and other clerics, especially, with the responsibility of seeing that the Indians not be mistreated. He asked the clerics to inform him of anything done to the contrary so that he might review the situation and set it right straightaway.

"I offer to provide anything necessary to achieve this just end," said the Governor, "and furthermore to furnish whatever might be needed to properly administer the sacraments in the churches and monasteries of the province." Accordingly, he gave out supplies of wine and flour as well as sacramental objects that he had brought along that would be of service to the churches and the worship of God. To this end, he furnished the churchmen with a cask of wine.

CHAPTER SIXTEEN

They Kill the Enemies They Capture, and Then Eat Them

A LITTLE WHILE AFTER THE GOVERNOR HAD ARRIVED IN THIS CITY OF ASUNCIÓN, THE SETTLERS AND CONQUISTADORS LIVING IN THE PLACE peppered him with complaints and a general outcry against Your Majesty's officials.

He ordered all the native Indians of the place, who were vassals of Your Majesty, to gather together. Once they had done this, with the clerics also present, the Governor made an official speech. He said, "His Majesty sent me to show favor to the Indians, to let you know that you must get to know God and become Christians. This will happen through the teaching and training of the clerics I have brought along, as the ministers of the Lord, for that purpose.

"You must obey Our Majesty," he said, "and become his vassals. You'll be better treated once this happens than you have been and shown more favor."

In addition, the Governor took them to task for eating human flesh. "You have to stop doing this," he said. "It's a grave sin and an offense to God." The padres and the other clerics all chimed in, admonishing the Indians. Then, to leave the tribesmen in a somewhat happier state, they shared out a number of trade goods and trinkets, as well as shirts, other clothes, and bonnets, which did indeed please the Indians.[1]

This tribe of Guaranis is a people whose language is understood by all the other tribes in the province.[2] The Guaranis eat the flesh of any other tribe they take to be their enemy if they are at war with them. They will take captives back to their Guarani villages and do many things to please them, with a lot of celebrating, dancing, and singing. This will last until the captive is fattened up, because from the moment of his capture they begin to feed him, and they keep it up, giving him as much as he wants to eat. They will also give him their wives and daughters so that he may have his pleasures with them. In regard to the fattening-up business, only the Indians' wives—and then only the most important of the wives—may take on this sort of responsibility and care.

The ladies sleep with the captive. They also dress him up, as is their custom, in a number of ways: they will put feathered contraptions and white beads on him, for instance. The Indians make these latter from bone and white stone, which they hold in quite high esteem. And as a captive gets fatter, dances and songs are his greatest pleasures.

At this stage, the Indians put their heads together and pick three young boys of six or seven, whom they will make up and dress. Then they place copper axes in their hands. One of the Indians whom everyone thinks of as the bravest among them carries a sort of wooden spade in his own hands. The Guaranis call it a macana.[3] They take the captive out into the plaza, where they make him dance for an hour. He finishes his dancing, and the man with the macana steps up and gives him a two-handed whack on the back and then another on the shins to knock him down.

It may happen that the six-odd blows they give him on the head will not bring him down. It is astonishing to see the great head wounds they inflict, as the wooden spade is tough and heavy, quite black. Using both hands with such a weapon, a strong man could dispatch a bull with a single blow. But our captive is only done in with many whacks.

At last, however, he *is* done in. Then the kids with their axes show up, either the oldest of them or their leader, the chief's son, and again they give the captive a number of blows on the head until the blood spurts out. As they are doing this, the other members of the tribe tell them to be brave and to show it. "Be ready to kill your enemies," the tribesmen say. "You need to go off to battle with courage in your hearts. Remember, that man before you there has murdered your own people. Avenge yourselves!"

Once the captive is dead, the man who gave him the first blow takes on his name. And from that day on he is known by the dead man's name as a sign of his valor.

Then the old women cut the dead man up and cook him in their pots. They divide up the pieces among themselves and make a meal of him. They are very fond of this particular dish. After all this, they go back to their dancing and other pleasures, which will last for many more days. They say that the enemy who killed their relatives is now quite dead at their hands, and they can accordingly rest and take pleasure in his demise.

CHAPTER SEVENTEEN

The Governor Concludes a Peace with the Agaces Tribe

O N THE BANKS OF THIS RÍO PARAGUAY, THERE IS A NATION OF INDIANS CALLED THE AGACES.[1] THIS IS A TRIBE MUCH FEARED BY ALL THE NATIONS of that country. Above and beyond their being very brave men, much used to war, they are quite treacherous, dishing out havoc and death to the other tribes even as they give their word to keep the peace. They do this even to their own kinfolk, just to make themselves the lords of the earth. So we might say that you cannot trust them.

These are well filled out people, with huge bodies and the limbs of giants. They travel the river in canoes formed up as pirate corsairs, and they leap out onto the banks to steal from the Guaranis and take prisoners from among them. They consider these people to be their primary enemies. The Agaces sustain themselves by hunting on the land and fishing in the water. They do not plant, and it is their longtime custom to take Guarani captives, whose hands they tie as they whisk them off in their canoes, heading for their own lands. The relatives of the captured Guaranis will come along to rescue them, and in front of these parents and children, wives and other kinfolk, they lash their captives cruelly and tell the relatives to bring along something for the Agaces to eat or the men will die.

So the Guaranis bring in a lot of food for them—enough to fill their canoes. And the Agaces then return to their houses, carrying off the prisoners anyway. They do this frequently, as very few of their captives are actually ransomed. When they get tired of carrying around and whipping the Guarani unfortunates in their canoes, they just cut off their heads and leave them along the riverbank impaled atop tall poles.

The Spaniards of the province had waged war on these Indians before the arrival of the Governor, killing large numbers, but they subsequently made peace with them. This peace, however, was broken by the Agaces, as was their habit, by all the damage they continued to inflict on the Guaranis, whose stores of provisions they looted.

It was only a few days after the Governor came to the city of Asunción that the Agaces again broke their peace treaties, taking by surprise and plundering certain towns of the Guaranis. And every day they came to Asunción, too, spreading unrest and causing alarm.

The Agaces knew about the Governor's arrival, and the greatest chiefs among them—Abacoten and Tabor and Alabos—accompanied by many others of their tribe, came in their canoes and disembarked at the city's port. Once onshore, they made their way to the Governor's presence. "We have come to declare our obedience to His Majesty and make friends with the Spaniards," they said. "If we have not kept the peace till now, it is because of the rashness of a few crazy youngsters who have raised a ruckus without our permission. That's what has given rise to this idea that we have purposely broken the peace. These same young men have now been punished."

They asked the Governor to receive them favorably and assist in striking up a peace between themselves and the Spaniards. And in the presence of our clerics and Your Majesty's officials, they pledged to observe and preserve a new compact.

The Governor heard their plea and lovingly welcomed them. In answering the Indians, he said, "I am happy to receive you as vassals of His Majesty and friends of the Christians on condition that you keep the terms of our peace and not break them as you've done at other times in the past. I warn you that if you do violate them I'll hold you to be my capital enemies, and I will make war on you."

Well, that was how the peace was concluded. The Agaces became friends of the Spaniards and the Guaranis, and the Governor ordered his people to treat the Agaces favorably from that time forward and give them provisions. Among the ongoing conditions and agreements that formed the peace were the following: neither the aforesaid chiefs of the Agaces, nor any others of their fellow tribesmen, together or separately, might under any circumstances sail their canoes along the Río Paraguay and step out on its banks within the territory of the Guaranis except in the clear light of day. The same was true for the city of Asunción and for any other stretches of the river where the Guaranis and the Spaniards might have farms and towns. No night landings were allowed: the Agaces simply *couldn't* land.

Beyond this no-landing provision, they had to stop their war against the Guaranis and do them no further harm or evil, as the Agaces were

now, after all, vassals of Your Majesty. They had to return certain captive Guarani men and women in this new peacetime, as these latter were
Christians and their relatives had been complaining. In addition, the Agaces
were not to harm the Spaniards and Guaranis when they went down to the
river to fish and out to the country to hunt. The Agaces were not to obstruct
P40these people at all.

The wives, daughters, and other female relatives of the Agaces who
had joined the company of the Spaniards to be indoctrinated needed to
remain for purposes of this holy work. The Agaces had to leave them
where they were and not carry them off, make them want to go, or cause
them by any means to absent themselves.

"If you can do all this, we'll consider you our friends," said the
Governor. "If you don't follow through, we will think of you as our enemies again, and we will proceed against you."

The conditions and terms of the peace were now well understood by
the Agaces, and they promised to honor them. And that was how peace
was indeed concluded with them and how they pledged their obedience.

CHAPTER EIGHTEEN

The Settlers Complain About Your Majesty's Officials to the Governor

A FEW DAYS AFTER THE GOVERNOR ARRIVED AT ASUNCIÓN, HE NOTICED THERE WERE A NUMBER OF POOR AND NEEDY PEOPLE IN THE TOWN. HE provided them clothes, shirts, shoes, and other things, which remedied their problems. He also provided arms, which they didn't have, to a number of the residents—all at his own expense and at no interest. He also asked Your Majesty's officials to cease the aggravations and vexations they had been visiting and continued to inflict upon the residents of Asunción up to that point.

All the conquistadors and settlers complained bitterly about the local government officials. There were many difficulties regarding the taxes owed to Your Majesty and over new taxes that these officials invented and put into effect. These included taxes on fish and fat; on honey, corn, and other foodstuffs; and on the cured skins in which the settlers dressed themselves, bought from the native Indians.

The bureaucrats reviewed the many reasons they needed to continue the collection of these taxes with the Governor, but he did not agree with them. A great deal of ill-will and hostility came from this, and the local officials decided to cause him as much indirect harm as they could—fueled, of course, by their jealousy. The upshot was that he arrested them and held them prisoner because of the evidence he had taken against them.

CHAPTER NINETEEN

They Complain About the Guaycuru
Indians to the Governor

T HE CHIEFS ALONG THE RIVER'S EDGE AND IN THE REGION NEXT TO THE
Río Paraguay—PEOPLE WHO LIVE CLOSEST TO THE CITY OF ASUNCIÓN
and are vassals of Your Majesty—all got together and complained about
another tribe of Indians who lived nearby.[1] These latter people are quite
stouthearted and warlike, maintaining themselves by deer hunting and on
fat and honey. They also eat fish from the river and pigs they kill, and they
and their women and children consume nothing else.[2]

These people kill game every day and hunt as their single bit of work.
They are so light and sturdy that they *run* after the deer. They don't get
winded, and they hold up so well under these long-distance runs that they
tire the deer out and simply grab them with their hands. They also kill many
other deer with their arrows, as well as jaguars and other ferocious beasts.

They are much inclined to treat women well, and not just their own
women, either. Among them, women have considerable preeminence. And
if they capture women in the course of their wars, they set them free and
never harm or mistreat them.

All the other tribes are terribly afraid of them.

They never stay more than two days in one place. When the time
comes, they pack up their homes, which are made of mats, and go a league
or two away from the place they were before. They do this because the
game animals, which they continually harass, flee and run away, and the
Indians follow along behind, killing as they go.

This tribe and others make their living by fishing and from some
carob beans that grow in that land. These they search out all at one time
in the forests where these trees grow, foraging for them like swine looking for acorns in the woods. This happens during the month of November
and the early part of December, and from the carob they make a kind of
meal as well as wine. The wine comes out so strong and hearty that they
do get drunk on it.

CHAPTER TWENTY

The Governor Asks for More
Details About the Complaint

ND SO THE CHIEFS OF THE GUARANIS COMPLAINED TO THE GOVERNOR ABOUT THE GUAYCURUES, SAYING THAT THEY HAD DISPOSSESSED THEM of their lands and had killed their parents and sisters and other relatives.[1] "We are Christians and vassals of His Majesty," they said, "and you should protect us and restore the lands that have been taken from us and occupied by the Guaycurues." The Guaranis noted that these were the woods and lakes and rivers where they hunted and fished, where they robbed the bees of their honey, with all of which they supported themselves and their children and wives and brought in to the Christians. It was after the Governor had passed through their territory that these outrages and deaths had occurred.

The Governor reviewed the complaint brought before him by these Guarani chiefs, whose names were Pedro de Mendoza, Juan de Salazar Cupirati, Francisco Ruiz Mairaru, Lorenzo Moquiraci, and Gonzalo Mairaru, as well as other Christians recently converted.[2] In order to proceed in accordance with the law, he wanted to find out whether the complaint was true, and so through his interpreters he asked the chiefs to produce evidence of what they had been saying.

Well, they gave it to him. They brought in a number of witnesses who were Christian Spaniards. These men had been present in the Guarani lands and had witnessed the depredations committed by the Guaycurues and the ejection of the Guaranis from their own territory. The Guaycurues had depopulated one of their towns—a place called Caguazu that was quite large and surrounded by a strong palisade.[3]

Having heard their testimony, the Governor convened the padres of Asunción, including Commissary fray Bernaldo de Armenta and his companion fray Alonso Lebrón, as well as the Bachelor Martín de Armenta and Francisco de Andrada, both clerics, so that they might review the evidence and offer their opinions.[4] Should a just war be allowed against the Guaycurues?

They did give their opinion, and they signed their names to it. And it was, namely, that the Governor might proceed with his forces against the said Indians and wage war against them. The Guaycurues were judged capital enemies.

The Governor ordered two Spaniards who understood the Guaycuru tongue and Father Martín de Armenta, accompanied by fifty additional Spaniards, to go in search of the Guaycurues. This force was to require them to swear allegiance to Your Majesty, stop waging war against the Guaranis, and leave the Guaranis alone in their own territories, where they could once again enjoy their hunting and fishing. If they did this, the Governor would accept them as his friends and be favorably inclined toward them. If they refused, following an opposite course, he would wage war against them as his capital enemies.

The aforesaid party departed, instructed to take special care in delivering these warnings a first, a second, and a third time, with a bit of temperance added.

They came back after eight days, saying that they had delivered the Governor's warnings to the Indians. They also said that, having done that, the Guaycurues took up arms against them. These people did not want to swear allegiance to nor become friends of either the Spaniards or the Guaranis. The Guaycurues told the Spaniards to get out of their territory. Then they started firing off volleys of arrows, and the Spaniards came back quite wounded as a result.

Well, once the Governor heard all this, he outfitted a force of two hundred troops, harquebusiers and crossbowmen, along with twelve cavalrymen, and with them left the city of Asunción on Tuesday the twelfth of the month of July in the year 1542. As the army had to pass over to the other side of the Río Paraguay, he ordered up two brigantines to ferry the men and horses across.

He wanted his men to guard a settlement of Indians who were on the banks of the Paraguay. Its name is Tapua, and its chief is named Mormocen, a very brave Indian who is feared in that country.[5] He was already a Christian, and they called him Lorenzo. He came from a place called Caguazu, which had been seized by the Guaycurues.

At any rate, all the men and horses had to travel by land to that place. On the road that same day, they were about four leagues from the city of

Asunción when they passed big squadrons of Guaranis. These men had to assemble in the place called Tapua to go along in the company of the Governor. It was quite something to see their war gear and how they carried themselves in good order. Their outfit consisted of a lot of feathers, especially those of macaws; their bows, painted in different styles; and their war instruments, which were scattered about among them, including kettledrums, trumpets, cornets, and other pieces.

That same day everyone on foot and horseback arrived at Tapua, where a great number of Guarani Indians were staying. They were both inside and outside the settlement, as well as among the groves of trees beside the Río Paraguay. And this fellow Mormocen, the chief, along with some other chiefs—his relatives who were there, too—came out with his men to greet the party of Spaniards an arrow shot outside the village. They had killed and brought in a large catch of deer and ostriches, which the Indians had taken both that same day and in the several days preceding.[6] There was so much of this game that everyone got some, and there were still leftovers.

Afterward, the chiefs held a council and said that it was necessary to send out Indians and Christians as scouts into the country where the party had to go. These men would take a look at the enemy's headquarters and find out if they had heard of the coming of the Spaniards, and whether they set a watch by night. The Governor thought this was good advice and accordingly sent out two Spaniards with this Indian fellow Mormocen and two other brave Indians who knew the country. They left, but they came back the next day, on Friday night. They said that the Guaycurues went out hunting through the forests and fields, as was their custom, and they set fire to the countryside in a lot of places. They also reported that from what they could tell, the Guaycurues had broken camp that same day and gone hunting with their wives and children. They do this to settle in some new place where they can keep up their hunting and fishing.

It seemed to our scouts that the Guaycurues had no inkling of the coming of the Spaniards. From where the scouts were to the Guaycuru camp was maybe five or six leagues, as our people could see the fires burning where they were hunting.[7]

CHAPTER TWENTY-ONE

The Governor and His People Cross the River, and Two Christians Drown

T HAT SAME FRIDAY, THE BRIGANTINES ARRIVED TO CARRY THE PARTY AND THEIR HORSES OVER FROM THE OTHER SIDE OF THE RIVER. THE INDIANS had also brought a number of canoes. The Governor was well informed about the best thing to do. Having spoken with his captains, he agreed that on the following Saturday morning the company would cross the river to continue their journey in search of the Guaycuru Indians. He then ordered rafts to be made out of the canoes to carry over the horses.[1]

The day of the crossing came, and all the party were waiting in good order. The Spaniards began to embark on the boats and rafts, with the Indians in their canoes. There were so many people that the rush and commotion of the passage and the shouting of the Indians were quite a thing to behold. The crossing lasted from six o'clock in the morning until two in the afternoon, considering the fact that there were two hundred canoes undertaking this work.

And a very sad thing happened. As some Spaniards scrambled to get aboard before others, one boat became loaded too heavily along her side and was thrown off balance. She keeled over, and all the people on board were thrown out into the water. Had they not had a bit of help, they all would have drowned. You see, there were a lot of Indians on the riverbank, and they threw themselves into the water and righted the little boat. The current was strong in that part of the river, and it carried off a couple of Christians who could not be saved. Some time later, we found them drowned downstream. One was named Diego de Isla, a citizen of Málaga, and the other Juan de Valdés, a resident of Palencia.

After all the party and the horses had crossed the river, a number of the Indian chiefs came up to the Governor to tell him that it was their custom to make a present to their commander whenever they were about to engage in a war. Following this tradition, that was what they proposed to do with the Governor, and they asked him to accept their gift.

Well, the Governor wanted to please them, so of course he agreed to their request. Then all the chiefs, one by one, gave him an arrow and a painted bow, both very nicely turned out. After that, each of the rest of the Indians brought him a painted arrow, fletched with parrots' feathers, and the giving of presents went on until nightfall.

Because of all this we had to sleep on the riverbank that night, and we posted a good watch and sentinels and did so.

CHAPTER TWENTY-TWO

Spies Go Out by Order of the Governor to Follow the Guaycuru Indians

T HAT SAME SATURDAY, THE GOVERNOR AGREED TO SEND OUT A NUMBER OF THE INDIAN CHIEFS TO FIND THE PATH THE GUAYCURUES HAD TAKEN and where their settlements might be before his party continued into the interior. He did this with the consent of his own captains and clerics.

What were the Guaycurues' encampments like? He needed to know this, of course, in order to attack these Indians and then eject them from the Guarani territory they occupied.

So off went his various Indians, spies, and Christians, and they returned just as we were nodding off. They told us that the Guaycurues had spent the day hunting. Their women and children were moving along in front of them, and no one could say where they might settle down for the night.

Given this state of affairs, it was agreed that the party would keep moving as inconspicuously as possible, just behind the Guaycurues. "No daytime fires," said the Governor, not wanting the Guaycurues to spot the army while they were hunting, "and our own Indians should be kept well under control and not go off hunting themselves or pursuing their other business."

With this order in place, the company moved out in good form on Sunday morning, traveling across plains and then through groves of trees to be under better cover. They kept going like this, sending Indian scouts out in front to look over the land (all these men were light and fast and especially selected for these reasons), and they came back frequently to pass on their intelligence. In addition to these scouts, the Governor's spies, very stealthy types, set out after our enemies to find out where they might be camped.

The Governor's marching instructions extended to a squadron of Guarani Indians, spread out over an entire league, who were traveling with us. These men were dapper, painted-up warriors, with their parrot feathers and bows and arrows, quite orderly and harmonious. They formed the vanguard, and just behind them, in the center of the army, were the Governor and his cavalry. Further back came the Spanish infantry with its harquebusiers and crossbowmen and the baggage train with the women, who were lugging the Spaniards' munitions and supplies. The Indians also carried their own supplies in the middle of their party.

The party went along like this until noon, when we decided to pause in the shade of some copses of trees. All the Spaniards and Indians ate a meal and rested there. Then they took up the trail again, skirting the edges of the forests and the groves of trees where the Indians who knew the country guided them. And all along this trail and throughout the countryside there was abundant game—deer and ostriches. They were really something to see. Neither the Indians nor the Spaniards did any hunting, though, for fear that the Guaycurues might discover their presence.

So with this firm command in place they marched on, with the Guaranis in the vanguard (as we have noted) and formed into a neat squadron, in very good order. There must have been ten thousand of these men, and what a sight they were, all painted up in red ochre and other colors, with many strings of white beads around their throats, feathered crests on their heads, and copper plates dangling with the sun glinting off them. Great quantities of bows and arrows on their backs. So resplendent, and marvelous to see!

CHAPTER TWENTY-THREE

Following the Enemy, the Governor is Advised that They Are Just Ahead

THE GOVERNOR AND HIS MEN TRAVELED ALL THAT DAY AS A RESULT OF THE EARLIER MARCHING ORDER. AFTER SUNDOWN, AT THE HOUR OF THE AVE María, there was a raucous disturbance among the Indians in the army.[1] As it happened, a number of Indians were squeezing in among the others, and a minor riot ensued with the arrival of a spy who was perhaps sent by the Guaycurues. It made the Governor suspect that our Indian friends might wish to withdraw from sheer terror of the Guaycurues.

The spy told them that the Guaycurues had been pressing forward ahead of us and that he had watched them as they hunted all day long across the countryside. Their women and children were still marching along in front of our party. "The Guaycurues believe that they'll be able to camp tonight," he said.

The Guaranis were advised about some female slaves whom the Guaycurues had captured a few days before, members of another tribe called the Merchireses. The spy also said that some of the Guaranis might have heard the story of the Guaycurues fighting with a tribe called the Guatataes.[2] The Guaycurues thought that the Guatataes might be coming to tear up their towns, and that was why they had been traveling cross-country at so hectic a pace.

Our own agents had been going along watching to see where they stopped and bedded down for the night, so that they could come back and let us know.

The Governor pondered everything the spy said. Then, seeing that it was a good, moonlit night, he ordered everyone to continue to move forward carefully, the crossbowmen with their crossbows at the ready, and the harquebusiers with their pieces loaded and the fuses lit (which in this case was the best thing to do).[3]

You see, the Guaranis may have been already in our company and our friends, but we had every right to be cautious and as alert as if they were our enemies. They were quite capable of treachery and general nastiness if we were careless or if we put a little too much faith in them.

Well, all right, then: *now* let them go ahead and try some of their tricks.

CHAPTER TWENTY-FOUR

A Jaguar Causes an Uproar Between the Spaniards and the Indians

As NIGHT WAS APPROACHING, THE GOVERNOR AND HIS PARTY WERE TRAV-ELING ALONG THE EDGE OF A THICK FOREST. SUDDENLY, A JAGUAR JUMPED into the middle of the Indians, causing a tremendous commotion. The Spaniards quickly took up their arms, believing that the Indians were about to attack them, and charged, yelling, "Santiago!"[1] They injured a number of the Indians in the ensuing fray.

The Indians fled into the forest after wounding the Governor with a couple of shots from their harquebuses that went through the lower part of his face. They shot him quite maliciously, and it was clear they were trying to kill him just to please Domingo de Irala, whom the Governor had replaced as commandant of the province. (You see, Irala had gotten used to being in command.)

At any rate, all the Indians ran off into the woods. The Governor knew he would have to placate them and make amends for this whole disgraceful business, and he would have to do so by himself. He got down from his horse and strode off through the forest into the midst of the Indians, telling them to take heart, that the jaguar lay behind all the confusion and uproar and the Spaniards were their friends and brothers and fellow vassals of Your Majesty. "Everyone," he said, "must now move forward to throw our enemies out of the country. By the way, they're just ahead."

When the Indians saw the Governor himself among them, they listened to his words and settled down. Then they walked out of the forest with him. The case in point in those dire straits was that we were certainly about to lose the field. If the aforementioned Indians had fled to their homes, neither they nor their friends or relatives would ever have trusted the Spaniards again.

So, the Indians emerged from the forest, with the Governor calling all the chiefs by name. The chiefs, of course, had fled to the jungle with the other tribesmen, and they had all been very frightened. The Governor told them they might come back to the rest of the party with nothing to fear at all.

"However, if the Spaniards wanted to kill you just now," he said, "you yourselves were the cause. You took up your arms so quickly, you know, and they believed themselves to be under immediate threat of death. But, as everyone now knows, it was that jaguar jumping into the middle of you that created all this turmoil and frightened people out of their wits."

Well, everybody became friends again, and the Indians returned to the party. But it began to dawn on them that this war we were about to wage would touch them quite personally. And it was the Spaniards who were about to fight it on their behalf. The situation was this: the Guaycurues had never seen the Spaniards nor had anything to do with them, had never expressed any anger toward them or done them any harm. But to protect and defend the Guaranis and keep them out of harm's way, the Spaniards were now campaigning against the Guaycurues.

Beseeched by the Governor and persuaded with honeyed words, they finally put themselves into his hands and emerged trembling from the forest. They were much traumatized, thinking at first that their enemies, for whom they had just recently been searching, had sprung out of the woods to ambush them. They had rushed around intending to take refuge among the Spaniards, and that had been the sole cause of the entire altercation.

With the Guarani chiefs calm at last, the rest of the Indians came back. Not a single person had been killed. With them all together, the Governor then ordered that the Indians take the rear guard, while from that point on the Spaniards would be in the vanguard. The cavalry would interpose itself between the Spaniards and the "Spanish Indians." Everyone was to march along in this order to make the Guaranis a little happier, and we would all see how this would improve their spirit when it came to facing the Guaycurues. "They'll likely forget their recent fears this way," said the Governor.

You see, if we had broken faith with the Indians, with no chance of patching things up, all the Spaniards living in the province would no longer have been able to sustain themselves or live there at all. They would of necessity have had to abandon the place.

And so the Governor marched along that night for two more hours, when he at last paused with all his people under some trees and cooked supper from the provisions they carried with them.

CHAPTER TWENTY-FIVE

The Governor and His Men Catch Up with the Enemy

I T WAS ELEVEN O'CLOCK AT NIGHT, AND THE SPANIARDS AND THEIR INDIAN ALLIES HAD BEEN RESTING IN THEIR CAMP. THE GOVERNOR HAD KEPT THE men from lighting any fires so that the Guaycurues would not sense their presence. One of the spies or scouts whom the Governor had sent out to reconnoiter the enemy came into camp, saying he had just left the Indians resting quietly in their own town. The Governor was very glad to hear this, as he had feared the Indians might have heard the blasts of the harque-buses during the tremendous commotion earlier that evening.

"Where are they?" asked the Governor.

"About three leagues from here," said the spy.

Weighing this, the Governor ordered everyone to break camp. They marched along their way little by little, going slowly so as to be in place to strike a blow as soon as the dawn began to smile. This tactic would prove useful in protecting our Indian allies, whom we also distinguished with crosses painted on their chests in gypsum. We marked their backs with these crosses too, so that our Spaniards would know them and not kill them thinking that they were the enemy.

However, even though our allies carried these distinguishing marks as a form of security and protection from danger, the gypsum lines might not be enough to protect them from the fury of the Spanish swords when we went into the houses of our enemies at night. In such a case, we might kill friend and foe alike.

Our party traveled along until dawn began to break. We were close to the enemy town and were just waiting for it to be light enough for us to attack. The Governor did not want them to hear us or know that we were around, and so he ordered the horses gagged with grass stuffed in their mouths over their bits to keep them from whinnying. He also ordered our Indian allies to encircle the town, taking care to leave our enemies an escape route so they could flee into the woods. You see, we didn't want to slaughter them wholesale.

We were biding our time, waiting, and our allies the Guaranis were just petrified with fear. The Governor could never persuade them to attack the Guaycurues. While he was coaxing and cajoling them, you could hear the drums of the Guaycurues as they began to beat. They started to sing, calling out to all the tribes. *Come and join us,* they sang. *We are few, but we are braver than all the other people of this country. We are the lords of this place, the lords of the deer and all the other animals of the wilderness, lords of the rivers and of the fish that swim in them.* That's how that tribe thought of itself: they were the people who kept watch through all the nights the world has ever known.

As day was beginning to break, the Guaycurues crept out of their town a little way and threw themselves on the ground. Then they saw shadowy figures before them, the hulks of men, and the smoldering wicks of our harquebuses. So many hulks, and so many sparking wicks.

They recognized us and realized they were looking at our guns, and they shouted out, "Who are you who dare to come here to our houses?"

A Christian who knew their language said, "It's Héctor (as that was the name of the interpreter who was talking), and I'm here with my friends to do a little trading with you (which meant seeking vengeance in their language) for the Batates you killed."[1]

Then our enemies said, "You've come at a very bad time. You'll get the same treatment they got."

Finishing these comments, they flung the firebrands they had been carrying at us and ran back to their houses. They grabbed their bows and arrows and returned to fall so furiously on the Governor and his men it seemed nothing could stop them. The Indians who had come along with the Governor fell back and would certainly have fled had they dared to do so.

But the Governor saw all this coming. He had given command of the artillery to don Diego de Barba and command of all the Spanish and Indian infantry, comprising two squadrons, to Captain Salazar. So he ordered the horses to be armored with their breastplates, which were festooned with jangling bells.

Once everyone was in order, the Spaniards charged the enemy, calling out the name of our lord Santiago. The Governor raced out ahead on his horse, trampling everyone he found in front of him.

And as the enemy Indians got a look at the horses, which they had never seen before, they were so frightened they fled toward the forest immediately, hoping to hide themselves in it. They raced through their town, setting a house on fire. Now, the houses of the Indians are made of rushes, cattails, and mats, so it began to burn fiercely, and the flames rapidly spread to all the other houses of the place. There were about twenty of these, all raised above the ground, and each one was some five hundred paces in length.[2]

The Guaycurues had about four thousand warriors, all of whom retreated behind the heavy smoke produced by the burning houses. There, veiled by the smoke, they killed two Christians and beheaded twelve of the Indian allies they had carried off with them in the following way: they grabbed them by their hair and used clubs inlaid with three or four teeth of a fish they call the *palometa*.[3] This fish can even cut *fishhooks* with its teeth.

Well, the Guaycurues hold their prisoners by the hair, marking their skin three or four times with their clubs; next, they run their hand down a man's neck, twisting it a little, and cut sharply. The head comes off, and they carry it around by the hair. They can do this while they are running, and so easily you would think it was nothing at all.

CHAPTER TWENTY-SIX

The Governor Breaks His Enemies

THE INDIANS WERE BROKEN AND SCATTERED, AND THE GOVERNOR AND HIS MEN WERE IN HOT PURSUIT. ONE OF THE GOVERNOR'S CAVALRYMEN found himself closing in on one of the enemy warriors, who suddenly grabbed the neck of the mare on which the horseman rode and pushed home three arrows. He wouldn't let go until they killed him. Had the Governor not been present during this engagement, our victory would have been very dubious indeed.

These Indian people are tall but slight, very courageous and quite strong, and they live a heathen existence. They have no fixed homes, and they support themselves by hunting and fishing. No nation but the Spaniards could ever conquer them. Their custom is to give themselves as slaves to anyone who overcomes them. Their women have a custom, too: if their menfolk have taken one of their enemies prisoner, expecting to kill him, the first woman to see him will set him free. He then will not die, nor will he be a captive. Any captive might like to be such a man, living among these people where they would treat him and love him as though he were one of their own.

And yes, it's true that these Indian women have more freedom than our queen, doña Isabel, our lady, once gave to the women of Spain.[1]

But the Governor and his men eventually grew weary of pursuing the enemy, and so they returned to their camp.

The Governor got his men into good order and began to march back to the city of Asunción. As they went along their way, the Guaycurues followed them and attacked them several times. This made it hard for the Governor to keep all his own Indians together to prevent any Guaycurues who had escaped the skirmishes from picking them off. Much of this was due to a Guarani custom practiced by the men in his service: if they came into possession of a feather or an arrow or a mat owned by one of their enemies, they left with it to go back to their own lands, by themselves, without waiting for anyone else. And this was the way twenty Guaycurues killed a thousand Guaranis, picking them off divided from their companions and all alone.

The Governor and his men took about four hundred prisoners during that trek—men, women, and children. As the party traveled along its route, the cavalrymen took many deer with their lances. The Indians were amazed that the horses were light and quick enough to catch the deer, and they themselves killed a lot of these with bow and arrow. At four o'clock in the afternoon the hunters all came back to rest in the shade of some large groves of trees, where they slumbered that evening, their sentries posted and their spirits peaceful.

CHAPTER TWENTY-SEVEN

The Governor Returns to the City of Asunción with All His Men

THE FOLLOWING DAY, BRIGHT AND CLEAR, THE PARTY LEFT IN GOOD ORDER, HUNTING AS THEY TRAVELED ALONG. THE SPANIARDS WERE ON HORSEBACK and the Guaranis on foot, and they killed a lot of deer and ostriches. At the same time, a number of the Spaniards who were afoot, using their swords, killed deer running toward the squadron that had been scared up by the men on horseback and the Indians. It was quite a thing to see—a great pleasure, really, all the game taken that day.

An hour and a half before sunset they came to the banks of the Río Paraguay, where the Governor had left the two launches and the canoes. And on that same day some of the men and their horses began to cross. The next day from morning to noon everyone else got across. Traveling on, the Governor arrived at the city of Asunción with all his men. He had left 250 men as a guard in the place, and Gonzalo de Mendoza as captain.

Mendoza held as prisoners six men from a tribe called the Yapirues—a large people, of great stature.[1] These are valiant men, warriors and terrific runners, and they neither farm nor raise livestock. They maintain themselves by hunting and fishing, and they are enemies of the Guarani and Guaycuru Indians.

The Governor spoke with Gonzalo de Mendoza, who told him that these Indians had come the day before and crossed the Río Paraguay. "Our tribe has heard of the war that you have come here to wage," they said. "You've already campaigned against the Guaycurues, and we and all the other tribes are much frightened by this. Our chief has sent us to let you know how greatly we wish to be friends with the Christians. If any help against the Guaycurues becomes necessary, we'll come."

Mendoza thought that underneath all these blandishments the Indians had likely come under false pretenses and they might well have wanted to look around his camp. "So I took a few men prisoner until I could become a little better informed and know what the truth of the matter might be," he said.

The Governor listened to all this. Then he ordered the men freed and brought before him. This was done, and the Governor sent for an interpreter—a Spaniard—who knew their language. "Ask them," said the Governor to the interpreter, "why they came. Each one."

The Governor treated these men well, knowing that considerable advantage and service to Your Majesty would be the natural consequences of his actions. He gave the warriors a lot of trade goods and trinkets for themselves and their chief, while welcoming them as friends and vassals of Your Majesty. "I'm going to treat you well and shower you with favors," he said. "With this in mind, you need to stop the ongoing war you've had with the Guaranis, who are already vassals of His Majesty. Don't do them any more harm." He let them know that the sort of mischief they had visited upon the Guaranis had been the principal cause of the Spanish war against the Guaycurues.

So the Governor dispatched his captives, and they left quite pleased and contented.

CHAPTER TWENTY-EIGHT

The Agaces Indians Break the Peace

GONZALO DE MENDOZA HAD ALREADY REPORTED ON OTHER MATTERS TO THE GOVERNOR, AS MENTIONED IN THE PREVIOUS CHAPTER, AND NOW HE told him about the Indians of the Agaces tribe. Mendoza had concluded a peace treaty with them on the night of the very day that Álvar Núñez had left Asunción to wage war on the Guaycurues, but the Agaces had later returned fully armed to Asunción to burn the place down and make war on the Spaniards. Our sentinels had seen them coming and raised the alarm.

The Agaces realized this, and they began to run away. They sped through the houses and farms of the Spaniards, which were scattered about the countryside. Here they kidnapped a number of women of the Guarani tribe, just recently converted to our Christian faith.

And from that time on, having broken the peace, they came back every night to ambush and rob people in the territory, doing a great deal of harm to the natives of the place. They earlier had given us some of their women as hostages to ensure peaceful relations. But these women fled the night the Agaces first appeared, and they told the warriors that very few people remained in the place. "It's a good time to kill off the Christians," they said. Following the advice of these women, the Agaces came back to crush the peace and wage war, as was their old custom. And so, they had now robbed the Spaniards' farmhouses in the countryside, where they had stored all their provisions, and spirited all these off along with the Guarani women.

The Governor listened to Mendoza's tale. Then he called together his captains and clerics and Your Majesty's officials, let them know his understanding of the affronts the Agaces committed in breaking the peace, and begged them to give him their opinions of the situation. In fact, he *ordered* them to do so on behalf of Your Majesty. (Your Majesty will remember that he has commanded the Governor to do this, and to use the opinions gained as he might see fit.) Each of the assembled worthies signed the council's conclusions with his own hand, and, with everyone of the same mind, the Governor proceeded to do as his advisors had recommended. They talked the matter through, all of them, and looked at it from all sides. They were entirely in agreement, advising the Governor to wage war with blood and fire against the Agaces to punish them for the terrible damage and destruction they continued to wreak across that country.

All this being the council's true opinion, and all the advisors being in agreement, they signed their names to it.

To further codify the crimes of the Agaces, the Governor ordered that a lawsuit be brought against them. Having done this, he also ordered that this action be combined with four other suits that had been filed earlier against the Agaces.

The Governor might well begin a new campaign, but the Christians in the province had already killed more than a thousand of these Indians because of the outrages they had continually perpetrated in the place.

CHAPTER TWENTY-NINE

The Governor Sets One of the Guaycuru Prisoners Free and Sends Him to Fetch the Others

AFTER THE GOVERNOR CONCLUDED EVERYTHING WE HAVE RELATED CONCERNING THE AGACES, HE CALLED IN THE GUARANI CHIEFS FROM THE war against the Guaycurues. He instructed them to bring in all the Guaycuru prisoners from that campaign. Then he told the chiefs that the Guaranis could not hide any of these prisoners or spirit them off elsewhere. "Anyone who does so will be severely punished," he said.

So the Spaniards collected all these men together. The Governor then told them this: "His Majesty has ordered that none of the Guaycurues be made a slave, as certain fine points of conduct on our part have not yet been observed." Furthermore, it was simply better for everyone that they be freed.

Among these Indian prisoners there was a certain well-proportioned gentleman. Noticing him, the Governor immediately ordered him set free. Then he sent the man off to fetch the rest of his tribe. "I wish to speak with them on behalf of His Majesty and receive them in his name as his vassals," he said. Once this was done, the Governor intended to shelter and protect them and would always give them trinkets and trade goods and other things.

Well, the Governor did give this gentleman a number of these items with which he set out quite happily for his own people. Four days later, he came back with his entire tribe, many of whom were badly wounded. So that was how they all came to Asunción, with no one left behind.

CHAPTER THIRTY

The Guaycurues Come to Give
Their Allegiance to His Majesty

F OUR DAYS AFTER THE PRISONER LEFT CAMP, HE CAME BACK TO THE BANKS
OF THE RÍO PARAGUAY WITH HIS WHOLE TRIBE. THEY STOPPED IN THE
shade of a grove of trees at the edge of the river, on the other side.

The Governor heard of this. He dispatched a considerable number of
canoes with several Christians and some interpreters to bring the Indians
into the city and find out who they were.

The canoes came back from the far side of the river with about twenty
Indians from that tribe, and they all came before the Governor. They
squatted down over one foot, as is their custom, and told him they were the
chiefs of the Guaycurues. They said they and their ancestors had warred
with all the tribes of that country, including the Guaranis as well as the
Imperues, Agaces, Guatataes, Naperues, Mayaes, and many others.[1] "The
Guaycurues have always won," they said, "and then shown no mercy to
all the other tribes. We have not yet been conquered by any tribe, nor
would any of the tribes even think of vanquishing us.

"But now," they continued, "the Guaycurues have come upon a
people who are braver than they. We have come back to put ourselves
under your power and be your slaves. We now intend to serve the Spaniards." As the Governor, with whom they were speaking, was the chief of
the Spaniards, would he tell them how best they could be of service as
his obedient subjects?

The Guaranis well knew that by themselves they could not make war
upon the Guaycurues, as the Guaycurues didn't fear them in the least,
and the Guaranis had no edge over them. The Guaranis would not even
dare look for the Guaycurues while spoiling for a fight if it weren't for
the Spaniards.

The women and children of the Guaycurues were waiting on the other side of the river, and they came across to us to offer their loyalty just as their menfolk had. "It was on their behalf, and in the name of all the Guaycuru tribe," said the chiefs, "that our men have come to offer their services to His Majesty."

CHAPTER THIRTY-ONE

The Governor, Making Peace with the Guaycurues, Returns His Prisoners

LISTENING TO WHAT THE GUAYCURUES HAD TO SAY ABOUT HIS MESSAGE TO THEM, AND CONSIDERING THE FACT THAT A PEOPLE SO DREADED throughout the country had come so humbly to present themselves and be placed under his power (which had struck terror throughout the land), the Governor ordered his interpreters to tell them he had arrived by order of Your Majesty so that the natives of the province might grow in knowledge of Our Lord God.

"I am here to make you all Christians and vassals of His Majesty, and to endow you with peace and quiet, to show you favor and treat you well. If the Guaycurues will simply discontinue all the wars and harm you have indulged in against the Guaranis, I will shield you, defend you, and consider you my friends. I will always treat you better than the other tribes. I'll give you back the prisoners of war I have taken—both my own and those of the men under my command." The Governor also intended to give back all the Guaycuru captives the Guaranis in his company had taken (and they had a lot of them).

Putting all this into effect, the Governor had brought before him all the prisoners who were within his control as well as those the Guaranis held. He then handed them over—he gave them back. And once they were in the hands of the Guaycurues, the tribesmen affirmed again that they wished to be vassals of Your Majesty. From that time forth, they offered—and reaffirmed—their obedience and subservience. They quit all their wars with the Guaranis. They said they would bring back to the city everything they had taken and give it all as supplies for the Spaniards.

The Governor was most grateful. He gave the chiefs a lot of jewels and trinkets. The peace was cemented, and both sides intended to guard it carefully from then on. The Guaycurues from that time forward came to visit every time the Governor sent for them, and they were most mindful of anything commanded of them. They came every eight days to visit Asunción, loaded with barbecued venison and pork from wild pigs.[1] This barbecue is like a grill, two palm-widths above the ground, made of narrow sticks. The Indians place the slabs of meat on top of these, and that's how they cook them.

They also bring in a lot of fish and other foods, chunks of fat and other things, and many linen cloths they make from a thistle. These are painted nicely. They carry in skins of jaguars, tapirs, and deer, and those of other animals that they kill. The trading and contracting for these foodstuffs lasts for two days, and they contract for other foods that are still at their farms along another part of the river. This kind of trade is extensive, and the Guaycurues are quite gentle with the Guaranis, to whom they give in barter a considerable amount of corn, manioc, and peanuts, which is a fruit like filberts or groundnuts that is grown beneath the ground. They also trade bows and arrows.

For purposes of this trade, a fleet of two hundred canoes, all loaded with these goods, plies the river. It's the most beautiful thing in the world to see them in action. Because they go about in such a hurry, they will at times run into each other. All the merchandise and the canoes themselves will then go into the water. The Indians to whom this happens, and the others who are waiting for them on shore, laugh so much at the sight of all this that the chuckling about it goes on for two days. The Indians engaged in this business are completely painted up and decked out in feathers, and the feathers are all carried off downriver.

They also sometimes die when some canoes dock before others; we find that this happens quite often.[2]

They all shout while conducting this sort of business, so that they can't hear each other, and everyone is happy and in good spirits.

CHAPTER THIRTY-TWO

The Aperues Indians Come to Make Peace and Give Their Allegiance

A FEW DAYS AFTER SIX APERUES INDIANS HAD RETURNED TO THEIR PEOPLE, FOLLOWING THEIR RELEASE AS ORDERED BY THE GOVERNOR TO REASSURE the other Indians of their tribe, a squadron of Indians came into view.[1] This was on a Sunday morning, on the other side of the Río Paraguay and well within view of Asunción. They signaled the city that they wanted to come across. Once the Governor saw this, he sent out canoes to find out who they were. And as the Indians had come by land, they climbed aboard the canoes and passed over from the far side of the river into the city. They came before the Governor, said they were the Aperues, and—as men seeking peace— squatted down on the ground on one foot, following their custom.

From their sitting position, they said, "We are the chiefs of the tribe called the Aperues, and we have come to meet the chief of the Christians. We want to have you as our friend and do what you tell us to do. The war you have been waging with the Guaycurues is well known throughout the land. Because of it, all the tribes were afraid that the Guaycurues would be attacked, conquered, and dispersed by the Christians. And they are the most valiant and feared warriors in the land!"

As a sign of the peace they wanted to establish and then preserve with the Christians, they had brought with them certain daughters of theirs. "Would the Governor please accept them?" they asked. So that the Christians might be assured that they and the Spaniards were indeed friends, they handed over the young women as hostages.

The Spanish captains and clerics the Governor had in his party were present as this was happening. So were Your Majesty's officials. The Governor said, "I've come to this land so that its inhabitants might be led to understand that they must become Christians and learned in the faith. They must give their allegiance to His Majesty and establish peace and friendship with the Guaranis, who are natives of this country and already vassals of His Majesty. If you keep the peace and do the other things I ask of you on behalf of His Majesty, I'll receive you as his vassals. And as such, I will protect you and defend you against all comers.

"But you must indeed keep the peace and work to be friends with all the natives of this country. I also will order the other Indians to show favor toward the Aperues and cultivate your friendship."

So we took them to be friends from then on.

"Whenever the Aperues want to come to Asunción," continued the Governor, "to trade and contract with the Christians and the Indians who live here, you may do so with our assurances for your safety. The Guaycurues have been doing this since concluding their own peace with us."

As a surety on the part of the Aperues, the Governor accepted the wives and daughters the chiefs gave him. He also did this so that the Aperues might not become angry with him—all of them thinking that if he did not accept their gift the Governor would not let them into the city. The Governor handed over the women and children to his clerics so that they might indoctrinate them in the ways of Christianity, teach them good customs, and put them to good use.

The Indians were pleased by this, happy to have become vassals of Your Majesty, and as such from then on to obey the Governor and fulfill their obligations as he might order. The Governor gave them numerous trinkets and trade goods, which pleased them greatly.[2] They left very happy.

These Indians of whom we have been speaking never stay more than three days in one place. They move every third day, looking for game and forests and fish to sustain them, and they take along their wives and children.

The Governor wished to attract them to our Holy Catholic Faith. He asked his clerics if there might be a way to indoctrinate the Aperues and make them industrious. The padres replied, "There is really no way, as the Indians have no permanent place of residence, and day after day slips by with them spending all their time looking for something to eat. It takes so much of the Aperues' time for them to scare up food that we would never be able to do anything but search for them and their wives and children." The padres thought that if the Aperues should ever try to do one more thing, they would die of hunger. "These additional chores would be too much: neither the men nor the women with their children would be able to come to church school.

"Nor can we clerics go among them," they said, "because our feelings tend toward very little safety and even less trust when it comes to these people."[3]

CHAPTER THIRTY-THREE

*Sentence Is Passed on the
Agaces, with an Opinion Offered
by the Clerics, the Captains, and
Your Majesty's Officials*

AFTER THE GOVERNOR RECEIVED THE INDIANS' OFFER OF OBEDIENCE TO
YOUR MAJESTY (AS YOU HAVE HEARD), HE ORDERED UP THE CASE THEY
had brought against the Agaces with all its evidence.[1] In light of this case
and the other suits that had been brought against them, it did seem that
the Agaces were guilty of various robberies and deaths that they had perpetrated across the land. The trial clearly showed both their culpability *and*
the way in which Your Majesty's instructions were being carried out by the
clerics and religious orders in front of Your Majesty's officials and captains,
who were also present during these proceedings.

And the considered opinion of all those present, with no disagree-
ment in any respect, was this: they told the Governor to wage war on the
Agaces with fire and blood. "That will best serve God and His Majesty,"
they said.

The result for the Agaces of being tried for their crimes was that, in
accordance with the law, the Governor condemned to death thirteen or
fourteen men of their tribe whom he held prisoner. The *alcalde mayor*
and his men went into the jail to take these men out.[2] The Indians began
stabbing away at the alcalde's men with some knives they had hidden and
would have killed them had not several other fellows come to their aid.
These other men were forced to draw their swords to defend themselves,
and they jumped in at a time of great need, killing two of the Indians and
dragging the others out to the gallows to execute the sentence.

CHAPTER THIRTY-FOUR

The Governor Again Helps the People of Buenos Aires

As things were now peaceful and quiet, the Governor sent help to the people who were in Buenos Aires and to Captain Juan Romero, whom he earlier had sent off with two brigantines and a crew to provide the same kind of aid. For this latest effort, he decided to dispatch Captain Gonzalo de Mendoza with another two brigantines loaded with supplies and a hundred men.[1]

With all this set in motion, he called together the clerics and Your Majesty's officials and told them that nothing now stood in the way of the further exploration of the province. "Perhaps we can shed a bit of light on the proper road into the interior, a route with the least danger and loss of life as we begin our incursion," he said. "We need to find settlements of Indians with plenty of provisions and stay well away from the empty quarters and deserts of this place." (There were plenty of these in this country.)

The Governor begged his assembled worthies to mull over what would be most useful and advantageous along these lines. "What do you think?" he asked.

They all gave him their opinion, all the clerics and friars. Present were the commissary fray Bernaldo de Armenta and fray Alonso Lebrón of the Order of St. Francis, as well as fray Juan de Salazar of the Order of Mercy and fray Luis de Herrezuelo of the Order of St. Jerome. Francisco de Andrada, the Bachelor Martín de Almenza, the Bachelor Martínez, and Juan Gabriel de Lezcano, as well as other clerics and chaplains of the church in the city of Asunción, were also present. He also asked for the opinions of his captains and the officials of Your Majesty.

Having discussed the matter among themselves, they all agreed that the Governor should proceed quickly to search for some populated area where his explorations might continue, for all the reasons he had laid out. And that was how matters were settled on that particular day.

The Governor thought the fastest and best way to proceed with the expedition would be to summon the most prominent of the Guarani chiefs and elders. Once they were assembled, he said, "I would like to explore the settlements of the interior, with which I've had a fair number of exchanges over time. Before I do this, I want to send a few Christians out to see with their own eyes what the proper route might be for us to take. You are also Christians and vassals of His Majesty, and as such, would you kindly give us men from your tribe to guide us? This will ensure good relations with the Indians we meet." This was intended to serve Your Majesty well, and it would gain the Indians advantages above and beyond any payments and rewards the Governor might have made to them.

The chiefs said they themselves would go and that they would provide as many men as might be necessary whenever the Governor asked. And they actually offered quite a few men to go along on the expedition. The first of these was a chief from upriver called Aracare, along with others we will talk about later. Seeing that the Indians were willing to do all this, the scouting party prepared to leave soon with its three Christian interpreters, men fluent in the language of that place. With them would go the Indians repeatedly offered to the Spaniards by the chiefs and elders—Guaranis and other tribesmen, all of whom had asked the Governor to give them the job of carrying out this expedition. The Governor charged them to be true to their word. "Take every pain to find the proper path, the results of which would be of such great service to God and His Majesty," he said.

Then, with these Christians and Indians ready to search for their route, the Governor ordered three additional brigantines to be made ready and outfitted with provisions and other necessities. In these he put ninety Christians, with Domingo de Irala, the Biscayan, as their captain. "Go up the Río Paraguay as far as you can sail and explore over the course of three-and-a-half months' time," he said. "See if you can find some Indian towns along its banks, and if you do, ask the locals about the extent of their settlements and the kinds of people to be found in the country."

These three ships sailed on the twentieth of the month of November in the year 1542. In them were the three Spaniards and their designated guides, who would be searching for the best land route into the interior from a port they called Piedras, seventy leagues up the Río Paraguay from the city of Asunción. Eight days after the ships left on their expedition, Captain Vergara wrote the Governor a letter as follows:[2]

The three interpreters have left the port of Piedras with more than eight hundred Indians to pursue their explorations and look for a path into the interior. Piedras lies below the Tropic of Capricorn at 24 degrees south latitude.[3] The Indians were very cheerful and eager to show the Spaniards the way forward.

Captain Vergara reminded the Indians of their duty and then sailed off upriver on his own exploration.

CHAPTER THIRTY-FIVE

Three Christians and Some Indians Come Back from Their Explorations

TWENTY DAYS AFTER THE THREE SPANIARDS HAD LEFT ASUNCIÓN TO FIND THE ROUTE THE INDIANS HAD OFFERED TO SHOW THEM, THEY RETURNED to the city. They said that Aracare, their primary guide and a great chief of that country, had taken them into a port town they called Piedras. About eight hundred Indians, perhaps a little more or less, had gone into the town with them.

The party marched about four days' journey in the Piedras country, guided by this same Aracare, who was a leader much feared and respectfully obeyed by the locals. From the very start of their expedition, he ordered these people to set fire to the countryside as they traveled along. The idea was to notably announce their presence to the Indians of that land, who were his enemies, so that they would show up along the road and be killed. Aracare and the Indians of our party were doing this against our custom and the normal order of things; it certainly went counter to the orders given to anyone attempting similar expeditions. It was, however, customary among the Indians.

Furthermore, this confounded Aracare then told the Indians of the party to go back home. He did not want them to continue with our men and show them the way to the settlements of that country. "The Christians are evil," he said. He said a lot of other harsh and nasty words, much alarming the Indians who were with him.

Nevertheless, our men implored these Indians to continue on in good faith and stop burning all the clearings along the trail. This they were not of a mind to do. Four more days passed, and the Indians came back to Asunción. Our men were abandoned, lost in the wilderness and in very great danger. And so they, too, were forced to return, as all their guides and Indian companions had already done so.

CHAPTER THIRTY-SIX

Boards Are Cut for
Brigantines and a Caravel

T HE GOVERNOR THEN ORDERED HIS MEN TO FIND TIMBER THAT COULD BE
SAWN INTO DECKING AND BOND BEAMS SO AS TO MAKE SOME BRIGANTINES
to explore the country. He also needed to construct a caravel to send word
to Your Majesty about everything he encountered during his exploration
and conquest of the province.

And the Governor himself went out into the woods and plains of the
country with Your Majesty's officials, the captains of the brigantines, and
the lumberjacks. Within three months, they cut what seemed to them to
be enough timber to build the caravel as well as ten launches with oars,
which they would use to sail up the river and carry on with its exploration.[1]
They hauled all the wood to Asunción by using the local Indians, whom
the Governor instructed to be paid for their labors.

Then they diligently set themselves to turn the logs into lumber to
build their brigantines.

CHAPTER THIRTY-SEVEN

The Indians of the Countryside Return to Be of Service

THE CHRISTIANS SENT OFF BY THE GOVERNOR AS SCOUTS TO EXPLORE A WAY INTO THE PROVINCE HAD RETURNED WITHOUT ANY KNOWLEDGE AT all that might be useful to him. However, certain chiefs of the Indians who were natives of the banks of the Río Paraguay, several of the newly converted Christian Indians, and many other tribesmen all offered to go and explore the settlements of the interior. In addition, they wanted to take along a few Spaniards to have a look at the land. These men might well bring back an account of the routes they had taken.

The Governor talked over the matter with the chiefs, whose names (among others) were Juan de Salazar Cupirati, Lorenzo Moquiraci, Timbuay, and Gonzalo Mayrairu. In light of their enthusiasm and willingness to undertake the exploration of that new land, the Governor expressed his appreciation for their offer and said that Your Majesty, and he himself in Your Majesty's name, would compensate and reward them. At that point, he asked around for four Spaniards who knew something of that country, as he wished to engage them in the enterprise of exploring it. He proposed that they go along with the Indians and throw themselves into the task of discovering the proper route with all the pluck that such a task might require.

Several men volunteered for the task, and the Governor proceeded to assign it to them.

And so, the Governor's Spanish volunteers and the chiefs—along with about fifteen hundred Indians whom they raised from the surrounding countryside—left on the fifteenth of December in the year 1542, paddling upstream in their canoes on the Río Paraguay. Other members of the party went overland toward the port of Las Piedras, where they would launch their venture into the interior.[1] Our men had to go through the territory of

Aracare, the fellow who earlier had obstructed the Indians in their efforts to find a route, and here they were approaching him once more. Our party did not want him to seduce the Indians again with all his talk of mutiny, because they would likely want to quit their explorations. So the Spaniards went along in the van to thwart him.

They got to Las Piedras with their many Indians, including several acting as guides who said they knew the route to the interior. They then traveled some thirty straight days through empty country, suffering a great deal of hunger and thirst. Some of the Indians died, and the Christians with them became so dizzy and confused from lack of food and water that they lost their feel for the thing and couldn't figure out which way to go. For these reasons, they decided to return and *did* return, eating wild thistles all the way back. For something to drink, they squeezed juice out of the thistles and other weeds they found, and after forty-five days they arrived at the city of Asunción.

As they came back down the river, this man Aracare whom we earlier mentioned pounced on them while they marched and did them great harm, showing himself to be a capital enemy of the Christians and their Indian friends. He waged a continual war on them all. So both the friendlies and the Christians arrived in Asunción gaunt and very much worn out.

Well, in light of the grievous damage this fellow Aracare had inflicted on us and *continued* to inflict on us, and as he had declared himself our capital enemy, the Governor ordered a new campaign to be carried out against him. This, of course, was with the advice and consent of the clerics and Your Majesty's officials. The proper legal papers were drawn up, and the Governor directed that Aracare be notified of this action. He was indeed notified, at great risk and through the considerable efforts of the Spaniards the Governor sent to carry this out.

You see, Aracare actually came out to meet the Governor's envoys fully armed, calling them names and intending to kill them. And he called on all his relatives and friends to aid in the effort.

But the writ was executed according to law, and Aracare was sentenced to death. This sentence was carried out—Aracare was executed—and the just reasons for this action and its causes were explained carefully to the Indians.

Twenty days into December, the four brigantines the Governor had sent off to the Río Paraná appeared in the port of the city of Asunción.[2] These launches were dispatched to help the Spanish colonists he earlier had sent in their nao from the island of Santa Catalina to Buenos Aires.

Along with them came the nao itself, a small sailing ship—in all, five vessels with their men, and they all disembarked.

Pedro Estopiñán Cabeza de Vaca, whom the Governor had appointed captain of the nao and its party, reported that he had arrived at the Río Paraná and gone looking for the port of Buenos Aires. There, at the entrance to the port, next to where the town was, he found a small vessel covered with tree growth and stuck in the ground, with some script carved into it that said, "Here is a letter." The men probed about, digging a few holes, and found it. When they opened it, they saw it was signed by Alonso Cabrera, the Inspector for the Establishment of Towns, and Domingo de Irala, the Biscayan, who styled and named himself the lieutenant governor of the province.

The letter told how the Spaniards had abandoned the port of Buenos Aires. The people who lived there had been transported to the city of Asunción for reasons stated in the letter. Because Pedro Estopiñán found a settlement in turmoil and revolt, he came very close to losing all the people he had brought in the nao. The place was consumed by hunger and the raging war with the Guarani Indians. Twenty-five Christians had fled the country in a skiff from the nao in an effort to escape starvation, heading toward the coast of Brazil.

The simple truth of the matter was that if the Spaniards did not quickly get help—if relief had been delayed by as much as a single day—the Indians would have killed them all.

So, on the very night when help arrived in the form of the 150 abovementioned Spaniards who had been sent to that country, the Indians attacked (at the crack of dawn) and set fire to the camp. They managed to kill or wound five or six Spaniards. But, as there was such a great force of ships and men, the Indians found themselves in considerable peril.

Therefore, we might say that all the Spaniards who had arrived at the settlement in the nao would have been slaughtered had not reinforcements arrived, with which they reformed and armed themselves to save all the colonists.[3] In addition to this, the Governor's men with considerable devotion to duty attempted to refound and seat the town and port of Buenos Aires on the Río Paraná at the confluence of a river called the San Juan.[4] They were unable to do this because it was winter, a very wearing time, and all the building walls they put up were destroyed by the rains. So, they were forced to abandon their efforts, and it was agreed that everyone would sail upriver, finding their way to the city of Asunción.

Poor Captain Gonzalo de Mendoza: it seemed that always on All Saints' Eve or Day something disastrous happened to him.[5] At the mouth of the San Juan on that very day, he lost a nao loaded with provisions and full of people, who all drowned. It was a strange thing that happened as he was sailing. On All Saints' Eve, his heavily laden ships were anchored along the riverbank under some high cliffs, and the galley that Mendoza sailed in was tied up to a tree. Suddenly, the earth shook. This caused the land to jump, and a tremendous wave came up and crashed into the cliffs. The trees fell into the river and the bluffs caved in on the brigantines, and the tree the galley was tied to fell on it with such a heavy blow that the ship turned upside down. The water then carried it off downstream for half a league with the mast underneath and the keel on top.

Out of this storm, fourteen people—men and women—were drowned. According to the survivors, it was the most frightening thing that had ever happened to them.

Coming out of these hardships and tribulations, the colonists arrived at the city of Asunción, where they were given good lodgings and provided with all their necessities. The Governor along with all the people of the town gave thanks to God for having brought them to salvation in Asunción and for their escape from the awful dangers of the Paraná.

CHAPTER THIRTY-EIGHT

The Town of Asunción Burns

Early one Sunday morning in the following year, three hours before daybreak on the fourth day of February of 1543, a straw house in the city of Asunción caught on fire. From there the flames jumped to many other houses. There was a cool breeze that morning, and the fire spread with such force that it was frightful to see. The Spaniards were distraught and unsettled, as they believed the Indians were doing it to drive them out of the country.

The Governor issued a call to arms to deal with the threat. He ordered people to take up their weapons to defend themselves and their interests in the country.

The Christians ran out with their arms and escaped the flames. However, all their clothing was burned, and more than two hundred houses went up in smoke. No more than fifty houses were left intact, and that was only because they were located in the middle of a stream. More than four or five thousand fanegas of corn kernels were burned.[1] This corn is the wheat of the country, of course, and a lot of meal made from it was also lost.

The flames wiped out other foodstuffs such as chickens and pigs in great quantity and left the Spaniards so stripped naked, lost, and destroyed that they had nothing to cover their bare skins.

And the fire was so big that it lasted for four days. It burned underneath the surface of the ground for a fathom, and the walls of all the houses collapsed with the force of it.[2]

We later found that an Indian woman in the service of a Spaniard had touched off the conflagration. Her hammock had caught on fire, and, shaking it to and fro, she tossed a spark into the straw walls of the house. As they themselves were made of straw, the place burned down.

Well, since everything was lost to the Spaniards and their houses and possessions burned to bits, the Governor assisted them with what was left of his own belongings. Being of considerable service, he gave food to those who had none, buying supplies from his own store of provisions. He then helped them build new houses with real walls so that they would not burn so easily on an everyday basis.[3]

The Spaniards found themselves in a great fix, and because of it they had everything rebuilt in just a few days.

CHAPTER THIRTY-NINE

The Return of Domingo de Irala

Sᴏᴍᴇ ꜰɪꜰᴛᴇᴇɴ ᴅᴀʏꜱ ɪɴᴛᴏ ᴛʜᴇ ᴍᴏɴᴛʜ ᴏꜰ Fᴇʙʀᴜᴀʀʏ, Dᴏᴍɪɴɢᴏ ᴅᴇ Iʀᴀʟᴀ ᴀᴘᴘᴇᴀʀᴇᴅ ɪɴ ᴛʜɪꜱ ᴛᴏᴡɴ ᴏꜰ Aꜱᴜɴᴄɪᴏ́ɴ ᴀʟᴏɴɢ ᴡɪᴛʜ ᴛʜᴇ ᴛʜʀᴇᴇ ʙʀɪɢᴀɴtines he had taken on his exploration of the Río Paraguay. He came ashore to give the Governor an account of his excursion. He said that since the twentieth of October last, when he had left the port of Asunción, until Twelfth Night, the sixth of January, he had traveled up the Río Paraguay, trading and studying the Indians along the riverbanks.[1]

Irala had come to a land of Indians who farmed and raised chickens and ducks, which they kept to fend off all the annoyance and damage done to them by crickets. It seemed that no matter how many blankets these people had, the crickets gnawed away and ate them up. These crickets proliferated in the straw covering of their roofs. "The Indians kept a number of big jars in which they stored their clothes," said Irala. "They placed both blankets and skins inside these containers and sealed them with clay lids, and that's how they protected their clothing. Many crickets fell out of the high ceilings of the houses looking for something to gnaw on, and the ducks were on them very fast, gobbling them all up.

"This sort of thing went on two or three times each day when we went out to eat," said Irala. "It's a beautiful thing to see the ducks feeding themselves like this."

These Indians have their houses right on the shores of some lakes and near others. They call themselves the Cacocies Chaneses.[2] They advised Irala that the way to the towns of the interior lay along a certain route. So Irala made three trips of discovery into the interior. "The country seemed to be very good," he said. "The Indians gave me a good account of these lands."

In addition to this, there are a lot of foodstuffs in these Indian towns, things with which our Spaniards were able to provision themselves in preparation for a journey of discovery and conquest.

Irala had seen signs of gold and silver among the Indians. They had offered to guide him and show him the route he should follow. "In all the journeys of discovery I've made along the entire river," he said, "I have never had clearer news of any place I had intended to explore." So, he had gone off into the country the Indians described from his camp on the river—the place he had arrived at on that same Twelfth Night. He called this jumping-off place Puerto Reyes, and he left its inhabitants with a keen desire to meet other Spaniards.[3] "Perhaps you might wish to meet them," he said to the Governor.

And so Domingo de Irala finished his report to the Governor of what he had found and brought back.

The Governor then summoned his clerics, the officials of Your Majesty, and the army captains. Once they were assembled, he had read out to them the report of Domingo de Irala. The Governor asked them to accept the report and its contents. In addition, this group gave the Governor their opinion of what should be done to further explore Irala's new territory in the service of God and Your Majesty, in response to a question the Governor had asked earlier. "It might well serve His Majesty that we now have a certain route of exploration, the best found up to this time," said the Governor.

The upshot of this was that, with everyone present—leaving no one out—the group gave their opinion: it was indeed in Your Majesty's best interest that we begin our exploration with all speed at Puerto Reyes. That's what the official group said, and they all put their signatures on their opinion.

After this, the expedition could begin with no need at all for any modifications, as the countryside was brimming with provisions—the foodstuffs and other items needed for its own exploration. Comprehending the views of the clerics, the monks, and the captains, the Governor followed them strictly, thinking all the while that in this way he was performing a service for Your Majesty. He ordered the ten brigantines he had already constructed for this expedition to be readied and brought around for service. To outfit the brigantines and canoes we assembled for this new exploration, he also ordered the Guarani Indians to sell us the supplies they had. The situation was that the recent fire in Asunción had wiped out the supplies the Governor had earlier stockpiled, and he was now forced to buy new provisions for the expedition at his own expense.

The Governor gave the Indians a lot of trade goods in exchange for their supplies, not waiting for his own possessions to be replenished. This was because he wanted to send the expedition off with the greatest possible dispatch.

In order to make all this happen fast, he didn't want the Indians to bear the burden of transporting all the necessary supplies. To this end, the Governor sent Captain Gonzalo de Mendoza with three brigantines up the Río Paraguay to the lands of the Indians who were Your Majesty's loyal vassals and our friends to pick up everything. He ordered the Spaniards to pay the Indians and treat them very well. "They will love trinkets," he said, so Mendoza took a great abundance of these. The Governor emphasized to Mendoza's interpreters that they *had* to pay the Indians for their provisions; they *had* to treat the Indians well. Under no circumstances were they to wrong the Indians or use force with them or they would be punished. "Our forces must follow these instructions and fulfill them all," he said.

CHAPTER FORTY

What Gonzalo de Mendoza Wrote

A FEW DAYS AFTER GONZALO DE MENDOZA LEFT WITH HIS THREE SHIPS, HE WROTE THE GOVERNOR A LETTER. MENDOZA LET THE GOVERNOR know that he had arrived in a port called Giguy.[1] He had sent a party inland to the places at which the Indians were supposed to give him supplies. Mendoza said that a number of chiefs had come in to see him and had begun to bring him provisions.

He said his interpreters had suddenly come running up to take shelter in the brigantines because the relatives and friends of a certain Indian who had risen in revolt wanted to kill them. This Indian had run around the countryside raising a considerable ruckus against the Christians and those Indians who were our friends. The Indians were now saying they would not give our men supplies.[2] Many chiefs had come to ask Mendoza's help in defending their towns from two other chiefs, Guacani and Atabare, with all their relatives and supporters. He said:

> These men were waging a raw war of blood and fire. They burned towns to the ground and rampaged through the countryside, saying that they would kill people and tear the place up completely if the locals did not join them in murdering the Christians and throwing them out of the country.

Mendoza was engaged in entertaining and stalling the Indians until he got to know what was happening. He did this so he could work out what to do next. More to the point, the Indians had not actually brought him any provisions, having taken steps to the contrary, and all this while our Spaniards in their ships were suffering great hunger.

Well, that was Mendoza's letter. The Governor sent for the friars, the priests, Your Majesty's officials, and the captains, all of whom then assembled, and he had the letter read to them.

"What do you think we should do?" he asked. "Give me your opinion, following the intent of His Majesty's instructions to us." He then had the instructions read out to the group.

They gave him their opinion, keeping in mind, of course, the best way to be of service to Your Majesty.

The assembled worthies all agreed that the aforesaid Indians had begun a war against the Christians and the Indian vassals of Your Majesty. Their considered opinion, which they all signed, was that we should send out a battle force against them. First, we would demand that they make peace, warning them that they must reaffirm their obedience to Your Majesty. Should they not do so right away, we would persist and ask them again once, twice, or three times—or as many times as it might take, putting them on notice that the blame for all the murders and burnings and damage that might take place across the land would rest squarely on their shoulders. If they still did not come around, we would consider them enemies and make war on them while defending and sheltering our other Indian friends in the country.

A few days after the priests and friars and other officials gave the Governor their opinion, this same Captain Gonzalo de Mendoza wrote another letter to the Governor. In it, he said:

> The chiefs Guacani and Atabare are waging a cruel war against our Indian friends, running them down, robbing and killing them all across the land. Our friends fled cross-country until they came to the port where our Christians were defending the provisions they had gathered.

Our friends among the Indians were much fatigued, streaming in every day to ask Gonzalo de Mendoza for assistance. They warned him that if help were not forthcoming, the whole country would rise up because of the cruel war and the damage it continued to wreak among them.

CHAPTER FORTY-ONE

The Governor Helps
Gonzalo de Mendoza's Men

W ITH THIS SECOND LETTER AS WELL AS THE OTHER COMPLAINTS THE
NATIVES HAD GIVEN HIM IN HAND, THE GOVERNOR CONFERRED WITH
the clerics, the monks, and the other officials, and with their concurrence
sent Captain Domingo de Irala to show Spanish favor to the friendly
Indians. He was also to bring the war that had broken out to a peaceful
end, and to support the natives who had been harmed by their enemies.

To accomplish this, the Governor sent four brigantines with 150 men
to be added to the soldiers Captain Gonzalo de Mendoza already had
there. He also ordered Domingo de Irala and his men to go straight to the
ports of Guacani and Atabare and prevail upon the people of these places
in the name of Your Majesty to cease their fighting and not resume it.[1]
"These Indians should return to the fold and once again give their allegiance to His Majesty," said the Governor. "They must make friends with
the Spaniards."

The Governor told Irala to compel and admonish them once, twice, or
three times—or as many times as it might take. "Should war be unavoid-
able, you are instructed to wage it with the least damage possible," he said
to Irala. "Murders, robberies, and other acts of malfeasance are excepted
from this direction." Irala was instructed to pressure them to stop fighting
and return to the peace and friendship they once enjoyed. And he was to
pursue these goals with every means at his disposal.

CHAPTER FORTY-TWO

Four Christians Die of Their Wounds in a War

DOMINGO DE IRALA LEFT ON HIS JOURNEY, AND ONCE HE GOT TO THE INDIANS' TERRITORY HE SENT FOR ATABARE AND GUACANI, THE CHIEFS responsible for the war, to reprimand them. They had plenty of warriors ready to fight. Irala's interpreters arrived to let them know our demands, but they would have none of that. They had already challenged a number of other Indians friendly to us, robbing them and doing them a great deal of harm.

As our men defended our friends and withdrew with them, they were involved in a number of skirmishes. Several Spaniards were hurt as a result, and Irala sent them to get their wounds tended in Asunción. Four or five of the wounded men who came back died, but this was largely their own fault. It was because of their own carelessness, as their wounds were quite small and neither dangerous nor deadly.

In one of the cases, the man died from a little glancing scratch on his nose made by an arrow. You see, the arrows in that country are poisoned, and those wounded by them must be careful thereafter not to indulge in excesses with women.[1] Otherwise, there is nothing to fear from any poison in that land.

The Governor wrote again to Domingo de Irala:

Make peace and ensure friendship with our enemies by every means at your disposal, he said, *as that is how we will best be of service to His Majesty.*

Meanwhile, the country was at war, and there was no end to general disturbances and commotions of all kinds, not to mention killings, robberies, and tremendous unease—all of which were a disservice to Our Lord and Your Majesty. So, along with his orders to Irala the Governor sent off an abundance of trade goods and trinkets for him to distribute among the Indians who were in the service of Your Majesty, as well as any others who in his opinion might settle down and agree to a peace.

With these things in hand, Domingo de Irala began his negotiations. And as the Indians by then were all worn out and hard up from the furious war the Christians had been waging on them, they did indeed wish to make peace. The Captain General had bestowed upon them quite a number of gifts, including a lot of novel items from his own stores, and so they agreed to a new peace and once again offered their obedience to Your Majesty.[2] They fell in line with all the other Indians of the land.

Their chiefs, Guacani and Atabare, along with many of their followers, came to see the Governor to proclaim their friendship and service to Your Majesty and to restore the peace.

The Governor told the chiefs' warriors, "In ending the war, you've done the right thing. And in the name of His Majesty, I pardon you for your past disrespect and disobedience. But if you do this again, you will be rigorously and mercilessly punished." Then he gave them presents, and they went away quite contented.

That left the country and its people now quiet and peaceful. So the Governor ordered that the necessary provisions be very carefully taken upriver to load the ships in Puerto Reyes for his new exploration, as that was the place where it would begin. He was quite determined that the expedition should proceed.

Within a very few days, the natives had brought the Governor more than three thousand quintales of manioc flour and cornmeal, and so they completed the provisioning of all the ships.[3] The Governor paid them for all this, which they appreciated and were pleased with, and then he provided arms and other necessities to the Spaniards who were lacking them.

CHAPTER FORTY-THREE

The Friars Flee

T HE BRIGANTINES WERE ALL PRIMED AND READY, LOADED WITH PROVI-
SIONS AND ALL THE NECESSITIES FOR ENTERING AND EXPLORING THE INTE-
rior, as we earlier agreed.

But Your Majesty's officials and the priests and friars had produced
another opinion, which they sealed and enclosed in an envelope they gave to
the Commissary fray Bernaldo de Armenta and his companion, fray Alonso
Lebrón, both of the Order of St. Francis. They did this quietly and under
cover. They induced these clergymen to travel cross-country using the
route that had just been discovered by the Governor through the Indian
settlements all the way from the coast of Brazil.

"You should go back to the coast," said the officials and the clerics,
"and from there carry certain letters to His Majesty."

These, of course, would let it be known that the Governor had ill-used
the powers of governance Your Majesty had seen fit to bestow upon him.
This all came from the terrible jealousy caused by the hatred and hostility
they had for the Governor. It was an attempt to obstruct—really, to block
entirely—the exploration of new lands he was about to undertake (as I
have already said).

These men did this to prevent the Governor from serving Your Majesty
by exploring new areas. They never wanted him to find himself in a new
land or explore it. And, of course, this was because when the Governor
arrived in the province he found it poor, with the Christians disarmed
and everyone who labored in Your Majesty's service broken. The regular
residents of the place had complained to the Governor of the wrongs and
mistreatment done to them by Your Majesty's officials, who in their own
interest had imposed a new tribute and a tax that were both very unjust and
against everything customary in Spain and the Indies. The officials called
this a *quinto*, of which this account duly makes note.[1]

By these means, the aforesaid men were attempting to impede our expedition by sending off their secret note with the friars. One of the padres carried a crucifix under his cloak, and they thought that if he held it tight he would be able to keep his trip across the countryside to Brazil a secret.

But the Indian chiefs knew about the friars; they came before the Governor and asked if they could have their daughters back. They had earlier handed over their girls to these clerics to be taught Christian doctrine. "Afterward, we heard that the friars wanted to go to the coast of Brazil and they were carrying off our daughters by force," they said. "Before they get there, they'll let everyone who is with them die. Our young women didn't want to go and tried to flee, but they are now in the friars' custody and very much locked up."

Well, by the time the Governor learned all this the friars were already gone. He sent men after them, and they were nabbed two leagues from Asunción. He made them come back to the city. The friars had carried off thirty-five girls. The Governor's force also collected some other Christians the friars had carried off; these people were intercepted and brought back. This caused a scandalous uproar throughout the whole country, as much among the Spaniards as the Indians.

The chiefs universally registered great complaints about their daughters being kidnapped, and they brought in to see the Governor an Indian named Domingo from the coast of Brazil, an important man in Your Majesty's service from that country.[2]

With this evidence in hand against the royal officials and the clerics, the Governor ordered them all placed under arrest. He began proceedings against them for the crimes they had committed against Your Majesty. So as not to mix himself up personally in their case, he handed the whole business over to a judge who was asked to familiarize himself with their transgressions and the charges stemming from them. The two friars posted bail, and the Governor took them along with him, leaving the other prisoners in the city. He then suspended the royal officials until such time as Your Majesty might indicate how best he could be served in this case.

CHAPTER FORTY-FOUR

The Governor Takes Four Hundred Men on His Expedition

B Y THAT SEASON ALL THE NECESSARY ITEMS TO CARRY OUT THE PROPOSED EXPLORATION WERE READY TO GO, AS WERE THE TEN BRIGANTINES LOADED with provisions and munitions. So the Governor collected four hundred select men, harquebusiers and crossbowmen, to go with him on the expedition. Half of them embarked in the brigantines, and the others, with twelve cavalrymen, were to go by land, along the riverbank, until the party should reach the port called Guaviaño.

The Spaniards would be traveling through the towns and little settlements of the Guarani Indians, our friends, as that was the best way. The horses left, and so that they might not have to wait around in the ships, the Governor sent them off eight days before the rest of the party. They would be able to sustain themselves on land, and we wouldn't have to waste anything feeding them on the river. The factor, Pedro de Dorantes, and the comptroller, Felipe de Cáceres, went with them.[1]

Some eight days later the Governor embarked, leaving behind in Asunción Juan de Salazar de Espinosa as his lieutenant captain-general, so that in the name of Your Majesty he might sustain the country and govern it in peace and with justice. The Governor left in Asunción two hundred-odd soldiers, harquebusiers and crossbowmen, and everything necessary to guard the place well. There were also six horsemen.

The Governor departed on the day of Our Lady of September, knowing the town's church was newly reconstructed and very well at that.[2] The old church had burned, and he had worked on this new one with his own hands.

The Governor left the port of Asunción with his ten brigantines and 120 canoes, carrying twelve hundred Indians, all warriors, and they looked very smart indeed as they sailed along in these vessels. They had a tremendous stock of bows and arrows, and they were much painted up, with a lot of feathers and crests. They had metal discs, much polished, on their foreheads, gleaming as the sun struck them. The Indians say they wear these discs because they blind their enemies, and these men go forth to do their business with the greatest hubbub and pleasure in the world.

When the Governor left the city, he instructed Captain Salazar to exercise all possible speed and industry in building the caravel the Governor had been planning so that it might be ready when he returned from his explorations. This ship would be used to give Your Majesty news of the Governor's findings, and to this end he made sure everything was perfectly in place.

Making good time, the Governor arrived at the port of Tapua, where the chiefs had come to greet him. He explained to them how he proposed to explore new lands. And to this end he begged them—and on behalf of Your Majesty, *ordered* them—to remain peaceful. For his part, they would certainly find he wanted only friendship and harmony with them—the conditions they had always enjoyed with each other.

Proceeding in this fashion, the Governor promised always to treat the Indians well and be a boon to them, as he had always been. And after this he gave the chiefs and their children and their other relatives a lot of trade goods and trinkets he had brought along, leaving them contented and happy.

CHAPTER FORTY-FIVE

The Governor Leaves Behind the Supplies He Is Carrying

I N THIS PORT OF TAPUA, THE SHIPS WERE SO LOADED WITH SUPPLIES THAT THEY BARELY STAYED AFLOAT.[1] TO SECURE THE BALANCE OF THEIR CARGO, the Spaniards left behind more than two hundred quintales of goods and equipment. This accomplished, they set sail again and went along briskly until they came to a port that the Indians called Juriquizaba, where they pulled up during the night.[2]

The party stayed in talks with the local Indians for three days, during which time quite a number of other Indians came to see the Governor, bringing provisions. These they distributed among the Spaniards as well as the Guaranis the Spaniards had brought along as part of their company.

The Governor received everybody with good words, because these people were always friends of the Christians and valued this friendship. He gave trinkets and trade goods to the chiefs and others who brought in supplies and told them he was on his way to explore the country. "It's a good thing," he said, "and it will be useful to you."

Meanwhile, people wanted peace everywhere the Governor turned. They also wanted peace with the Spaniards who remained in Asunción. The Indians promised the Governor peace. And so with the locals quite happy, the party sailed upriver, making good time.

CHAPTER FORTY-SIX

He Pauses to Talk with the
Natives of That Port

O N THE TWELFTH DAY OF THE MONTH, THE GOVERNOR ARRIVED AT
ANOTHER PORT CALLED ITAQUI, IN WHICH HE DROPPED ANCHOR AND
brought the brigantines to a halt. His intention was to talk to the natives of
the port, who are Guaranis and vassals of Your Majesty.

That same day, a large number of Indians appeared who were laden
with supplies for our people. Along with them came their chiefs, to whom
the Governor reported—as he had done to others in the past—that he had
come to explore the country. He implored them to continue the peace and
harmony now established between themselves and the Spaniards who
remained in the city of Asunción until he returned. But he also *ordered*
them to do so. And in addition to paying them for the provisions they had
brought, he shared out among the most important chiefs and their families
many gracious gifts, with which they were very pleased. They felt well
rewarded. The Governor spent a couple of days with them before leaving.

He traveled for a day and came to another port named Itaqui, which he
passed, finally casting anchor in a place belonging to the chief Guacani.[1]
Guacani had risen up with Chief Atabare to make war against us, as I have
related earlier. The people of the place were living in peace and harmony.
And then, because they knew the Governor had come, they swarmed in
to see him—lots of them, along with other Indians allied to them or with
whom they were friendly. The Governor received them all with great love,
as they had complied with the terms of the peace arrangements he had
concluded with them.

All the people who came in with these Indians arrived happy and
reassured. That was because just having these two fellows, Guacani and
Atabare, now living peacefully and securely in friendship with us had
made it possible to pacify the entire countryside.

When the people came in again a few days later, the Governor greeted them lovingly and politely gave them a number of trinkets and trade goods, doing the same for everyone's relatives and friends—in addition to paying all those Indians who brought in supplies for barter. The upshot was that everyone was happy. And as the principal chiefs of the natives of the area were among the visitors, the Governor spoke as lovingly as he could, imploring them to promote peace throughout their lands. "The obligation is yours," he said. "You must take care to visit the Christian Spaniards in the city of Asunción, and follow any orders they might give you in the name of His Majesty."

The chiefs answered that after they had agreed to peace and given their allegiance to Your Majesty, they were determined to keep it and actively pursue it. "You'll see," they said.[2] And so that the Governor might believe even more strongly in their earnestness, this character Atabare would go along with them in their explorations because he was the most useful in case of war, while the other fellow, Guacani, would be pleased to remain in his country to keep an eye on it, thus assuring the Governor of local peace and harmony.

This was all fine with the Governor. He took the chiefs' offer seriously, as it seemed to him to be a good start toward their compliance with the new peace they were offering. He thought the country would be safe and secure with Atabare leaving in his company. "I very much appreciate your gesture," he said to Atabare, "and I accept your offer to accompany us." He then gave Atabare more trade goods and trinkets than he had ever given any chiefs along that river.

It was certain that if Atabare were happy the whole country would be peaceful. No other Indian would dare rebel for fear of his wrath.

The Governor charged Guacani with the safety of the Christians, and he in turn promised to live up to all the terms of the peace.

So in all, the Governor spent four days talking to these Indians, making them happy, and giving them presents out of his stores, and with that he left them quite pleased.

As the party left that port, the factor Pedro Dorantes's horse died. Dorantes told the Governor he found himself in no position to continue the exploration and conquest of the province without his mount. In light of this, and as he wished to return to the city of Asunción, he named in his place his son, Pedro Dorantes, whom he also designated to serve as factor. The Governor and the contador agreed with this and allowed the

younger Dorantes to serve in his father's position in the party of exploration and conquest.

So the aforesaid Chief Atabare left in the company of the Governor
with about thirty of his relatives and servants, in three canoes. The Governor set sail from Guacani's port, traveling up the Río Paraguay, and on
Friday, the twenty-fourth of September, he arrived at the port they call
Ipananie.[3] Here he ordered the launches to pause and drop anchor so that
he might talk to the natives of the country, who are Your Majesty's vassals.
He wanted to find out if there were anyone in this port of the Guarani tribe
who had been a long-time captive of the Payaguaes Indians and knew
their language. This sort of person would also know the Payaguaes' country and where their towns might be located. The Governor was thinking to
take a Guarani along to talk to the Payaguaes (who were the people who
had killed Juan de Ayolas and other Christians). And as a means to cement
peace with the Guaranis, he might be able to recover the silver and gold
the Payaguaes had stolen from Ayolas.

Well, seeing the Governor in port, the people of the place came out
with pleasure, loaded with provisions. He received them warmly and
treated them well, and he ordered them to be paid for everything they
brought. To the chiefs he politely gave many trade goods and trinkets, and
he began to talk with them. "I need an Indian who has been a captive of the
Payaguaes," he said, "as an interpreter for the country through which we
propose to travel. We intend to entice those people into peace and harmony
with us, and the armada needs to know what route to take to reach their
towns." So, listening carefully to this, the Indians of the port sent off to certain Indian places that they knew in the backcountry for just such a person.

CHAPTER FORTY-SEVEN

He Sends for an Interpreter
for the Payaguaes

THREE DAYS AFTER THE NATIVES OF THE PORT OF IPANANIE SENT FOR AN INDIAN INTERPRETER, THE MAN CAME TO WHERE THE GOVERNOR WAS. HE offered to go along with the Governor's party and show him the country of the Payaguaes.

Having contented the Indians of the port, the Governor set sail up the Río Paraguay. He arrived four days later at a port they called Guayviaño, which is where the Guarani settlements end.[1] He told his party to drop anchor here so that he might speak to the natives of the place. These people indeed appeared, and their chiefs brought along a lot of supplies for the Governor. The Spaniards received them happily. The Governor treated the Indians well, ordering his party to pay them for everything.[2] He graciously gave the chiefs in return a large number of trade goods and trinkets and other things.

The Indians told the Governor that the horsemen who had gone on into the interior had already arrived in their towns, where they had been well received, with their needs taken care of. The Indians had guided them and directed them some distance ahead to a place close to the port of Itabitan, where the horsemen said they would await the arrival of our brigantines.[3]

Armed with this knowledge, the Governor hastily ordered the party to set sail, leaving the port of Guayviaño. The brigantines caught a good wind upriver, and they arrived at the port of Itabitan that same day at nine in the morning. The Governor found that the horsemen had all arrived hale and hearty. These troops told the Governor they had passed through the towns in the district in peace and harmony and had shared out in these places numerous gifts of goods and trinkets they carried along for that purpose.

CHAPTER FORTY-EIGHT

The Horses Embark from the Port

THE GOVERNOR WAS IN THIS PORT OF ITABITAN FOR TWO DAYS, DURING WHICH TIME THE PARTY LOADED THE HORSES ONTO THE LAUNCHES AND GOT all the paraphernalia of the armada into the sort of order he liked. As the country of the Payaguaes Indians was just a short way ahead, very close, the Governor ordered that the Indian from the port of Ipananie who knew the language of the Payaguaes as well as their territory should go along with the party in the lead brigantine. The Governor wanted his good advice on what needed to be done as they advanced.

The Governor sailed with a good wind from Itabitan. He declared that the brigantines should proceed together in a tight body so that the Payaguaes would not be able to do any harm to the Guaranis who were traveling in the Governor's company. "No one sails apart from the brigantines," he said, and the armada did travel along in proper form. At night he ordered everyone to cast anchor along the riverbank, and posting a good guard he slept on land. The Guaranis positioned their canoes next to the brigantines, and the Spaniards and the Indians occupied more than a league of land downstream. The firebrands and campfires were so extensive that it was a great pleasure to see them.

And for as long as the ships sailed on this exploration, the Governor gave the same rations to the Indians as the Spaniards. The men were so well provided for and full that it was a great thing to see. The fishing and hunting were excellent to excess. Contributing to this was the pursuit of a quantity of wild pigs, bigger than those of Spain, that go about continually in the water.[1] These pigs have a blunter and larger snout than others brought here from Spain. The people call them "water pigs." They stay on land at night, but by day they are always in the river. When they see people, they immediately plunge into the water, going deep and staying down for quite some time. When they surface again, they are a crossbow shot away from where they dove under.

No one can hunt these pigs with fewer than a half dozen canoes manned by the Indians, who, like the pigs, are ready to plunge into the water. Three canoes go upstream and three down, and the men in the canoes divide themselves up into three groups. The Indians make themselves fully ready, with the arrows drawn back in their bows. As a pig comes up to the surface, they shoot him with their arrows very quickly, three or four times, before he can go under again. Then they follow him until he bobs back up, dead from his wounds.

Of course, they have a lot of meat to eat, which the Christians accept willingly, although they actually have no need of it.

All up and down this river there is an abundance of these types of pigs. All our people got so fat and stout on this trip that they looked like they had just come from Spain. The horses were fat, too, and many days our riders took them out into the countryside to pursue game, as there were many deer and tapirs and other wild game. And a lot of otters.

CHAPTER FORTY-NINE

How They Killed Juan de Ayolas and His Companions When They Came to This Port

O N THE TWELFTH DAY OF THE MONTH OF OCTOBER, THE GOVERNOR CAME TO THE PORT THEY CALL CANDELARIA, WHICH IS IN THE COUNTRY OF THE Payaguaes Indians.[1]

Captain Juan de Ayolas once came through this port with his men, and this was where he and his Spaniards began and later returned from their explorations. Ayolas had left Domingo de Irala there to wait for him with the brigantines that the party had brought along, and when he came back they were nowhere to be seen. Ayolas and his men then waited in Candelaria for the boats for more than four months, during which time he suffered greatly from hunger.

The Payaguaes could see that the Spaniards were wasting away and lacked arms, so they began to treat them familiarly. "As your friends, we would like to invite you to our houses to share our hospitality," they said. They then led them off into some canebrakes, where two Indians grabbed each Christian while a number of their friends ran up with clubs and began beating the Spaniards' brains out. That's how they managed to kill Captain Juan de Ayolas and the 80 men who were still with him, out of the 150 who had started out on the exploration of the interior.

And who was responsible for the deaths of these men? None other than the man who had remained in Puerto Candelaria with the brigantines and men posted there—the same man who had abandoned the port and gone off downstream to wherever he pleased. Had Juan de Ayolas found his men and launches where he had left them, he and the other Christians would have been able to sail away and the Indians would not have killed them.

Domingo de Irala did this dirty business with malice aforethought. He *wanted* the Indians to kill those men, and they certainly did so when they rose up in that country. And some time after this, it indeed became obvious that Irala rebelled against God and his king, and he is *still* rebelling. He has ruined and devastated that entire country, and it is now twelve years that he has ruled there as a tyrant.[2]

The Governor's pilots measured the latitude at Candelaria, saying that the port lay at 21 degrees minus ⅓ south.[3]

Having arrived in the port, all the men of the armada gathered together. "See if you can speak with these Payaguaes to find out where their towns are," said the Governor. The next day, at eight in the morning, about seven of the Payaguaes appeared on the banks of the Río Paraguay. The Governor ordered only a few of the Spaniards to go out and palaver with them, along with the interpreter (which made a very good impression on the Indians). So, our men walked up to where they were, fairly close to them, so that the two parties might talk and understand one another. The interpreter said, "Come closer so we can talk to you." Our men wanted to parley and conclude a peace with them.

We also wanted to be sure that their chief had not come for some other reason.

Well, they began speaking. "Have you Christians come back in your launches?" they asked. "Are you the same men who marched cross-country in the past?"

Hearing this, the Spaniards said, "No, we're not those same people on foot. We have only recently come to this place."

Once they heard this, one of the Payaguaes came over to the Christians and was taken back to the Governor. The Governor asked questions through the interpreter. "Who ordered you to come here?" he said.

"My chief has heard of the arrival of the Spaniards," said the Payagua. "So he sent me and my companions to see if it was true that the newcomers were the men who had come here before on foot. 'Tell them I want to be their friend,' he said. 'Everything I took from Juan de Ayolas and his Christians I have collected and guarded in order to give it back to the chief of the Christians. I want to conclude a peace with them, and I would like them to forgive me for the deaths of Juan de Ayolas and the other Christians who died in the war.'"

The Governor asked, through the interpreter, "How much gold and silver might it be that you Payaguaes took from Juan de Ayolas and his Christians?"

The Payagua said, "About sixty-six loads that the Chaneses Indians were carrying, all of it in plates, bracelets, crowns, and hatchets, and in little vessels of gold and silver."

Through the interpreter, Cabeza de Vaca said, "Tell your chief that His Majesty has sent me into your country to secure a peace with the Payaguaes and with any other people who may wish to be included, and that wars now past will be pardoned. As your chief wishes to be a friend and restore everything he's taken from the Spaniards, let him now come and speak with me. I have a very great wish to see him and treat him decently. I will conclude a peace with him and receive him as a vassal of His Majesty. Let him come, and he'll be very well treated."

As a token of his word, the Governor sent along with the man a number of trade goods and trinkets as well as other things to take to his chief. "When might you and the chief be back?" he asked.

This chief, although a fisherman and the lord of these abject people (as they are all fishermen), is very somber, and his people fear him and make a big fuss over him. If one of his men makes him angry about something, he grabs a bow and shoots him with two or three arrows. After he dies, the chief sends for his wife (if he has one) and reports the facts to her. And this is enough to defuse her anger over her husband's death. If the chief does not make a direct report to the wife, he sends her two feathers.

When the chief has to spit, the man who finds himself closest to him cups his hands together and awaits the phlegm.

The chief holds drunken sprees and other debaucheries, and up and down the entire Río Paraguay there is no Indian who has what this man has.

The interpreter for the Payagua said that the man and his chief would return the next day, in the morning, and the Governor remained in Candelaria awaiting his arrival.

CHAPTER FIFTY

The Interpreter and the Others Who Were Supposed to Return Fail to Do So

T HAT DAY AND FOUR OTHERS WENT BY, AND THEY DIDN'T COME BACK. THE GOVERNOR SENT FOR THE INTERPRETER WHO HAD COME ALONG WITH the party and asked him what he thought about the tardiness of the Indian envoy. The interpreter said he knew for certain that he would never come back, as the Payaguaes Indians were wary and very crafty. *Of course* they had said that their chief wanted peace. This chief simply would have wanted to sound out and entertain the Christians and the Guaranis so that they would not continue their advance and find the rest of the Payaguaes in their towns. While the Christians and their allies were waiting for the chief, the others would alert their towns and their women and children.

This being the case, the interpreter thought that the Payaguaes had fled into hiding somewhere upriver. He said to the Governor, "You'll have to go after them, and you will certainly catch them, as they'll undoubtedly be very encumbered and loaded down with all their possessions." He also said, "It seems to me, as a man who is quite familiar with that country, that the Payaguaes won't stop until they reach a certain lake in the territory of the Mataraes Indians, all of whom were killed and wiped out by the Payaguaes." These Payaguaes had earlier seized their lands, which were bountiful and full of excellent fishing.

So the Governor ordered the brigantines and all the canoes to hoist sail, and he went on upriver. In the places where he later anchored, there was a great track along the riverbank where the Payaguaes had traveled—or so said the interpreter. "They went along this way because they would not all have fitted in their canoes," he said.

After the party had sailed along for eight days, they came to the lake of the Mataraes, which they entered. No one was there. Half the Governor's party then proceeded by land to make peace with the Mataraes, should they find them. But another day passed, and nobody appeared. So as not to use up their provisions in vain, the Governor called on all the Christians and Guaranís to reassemble. They had by then found some canoes and large stakes belonging to the Mataraes or Payaguaes, who had hidden them under the water, and they also found the trail the Indians had taken when they left.

But the Governor couldn't delay. He resumed his journey, the canoes and the brigantines traveling together. They went upriver, sometimes sailing, sometimes rowing, and at times using a towrope to pull the vessels along. This was all due to the many twists and turns of the river. The Governor continued on his way until he came to a bank covered with *cañafístola* trees, which were very large and imposing.[1] The cañafístola fruit is about a palm and a half in length and three fingers wide. The people there eat a lot of it, and its insides are very sweet. This fruit is no different than that which is brought from many other places to Spain, except in these ways: it is thicker, a little harsh to the taste, and collected from the wild, not grown. Of these remarkable trees there are more than eighty growing in one place along the bank of this Río Paraguay.

Where the Governor was traveling there are many wild fruits eaten by both the Spaniards and the Indians, among which is one much like a tiny Ceuta lemon both in its color and the texture of its peel.[2] With its sourness and smell, it does not differ from the Ceuta lemon of Spain, which looks much like a dove's egg. The tree that produces this fruit also has a leaf like that of a lemon.

There is a great diversity in this country of trees and fruits, and in the variety and strangeness of the fish there are also many distinctions that a person could make. Our Spaniards and Indians catch an unbelievable quantity of fish on days when the sailing is poor. As their canoes are light and they are accustomed to paddling, the Indians also take them out to hunt capybaras and otters (of which there is an amazing abundance). All this is a great pastime.

It seemed to the Governor that with a few days' traveling we would arrive in the country of some Indians called the Guaxarapos, who live on the banks of the Río Paraguay. These people are trading neighbors of the Indians of Puerto Reyes, where we had been. Well, if we attempted to pass their way with all these men in ships, and all our Indians in their canoes, they would have been startled and run away into the interior. To keep them calm and placate them, our party split into two halves. The Governor took five brigantines and half the canoes along with the Indians who had come in them and decided to press forward with these. He ordered Captain Gonzalo de Mendoza with his other ships and canoes to come along behind this first party little by little. The Governor told the captain to exercise his authority over all his charges, Spaniard and Indian alike, lightly and graciously. "Under no circumstances should any of your Indians or Spaniards get out of control in their behavior," he said. Neither on land nor river was any native of the country to suffer any aggravation or act of violence on the part of the captain's party. The Governor instructed Mendoza to pay for any supplies or other items the local people might bring in to trade with the Spaniards and the Guaranis. By these means the Governor intended to preserve the peaceful conditions that would best serve Your Majesty and the good of the country.

So, the Governor set off with the five brigantines and the canoes I have mentioned. And he sailed along until one day, the eighteenth of October, he came to the land of the Guaxarapo Indians. About thirty of these people came out of the brush, and the brigantines and canoes stopped to talk to these Indians and reassure them of our intentions. Our party wanted to find out which tribes lay ahead.

Several Christians went ashore at the Governor's order, as the Indians of that country called out to them and then came for them. Six of these Guaxarapos approached the brigantines and went aboard. The Governor spoke with them by means of his interpreter, and he told them the same thing he had relayed to the other tribesmen downriver: they needed to express their allegiance to Your Majesty, and once they did that he would regard them as his friends. They all did so. Among them was a chief, and the Governor offered him some trade goods and trinkets and said that he would assist him in any way he could.

Close by the place where the Governor was parleying with these Indians, there was another river that flowed in from the interior, about half as wide as the Río Paraguay. But the water rushed along with a frightening force. This river discharged into the Río Paraguay, which itself comes from the direction of Brazil.[3] The old folks say that's the way Garcia the Portuguese came when he fought his way through the countryside.[4] He had entered this country with a lot of Indians and had waged a very great war indeed all through it and torn apart many towns—and all this with no more than five Christians. All his other men were Indians.

The Indians said that Garcia had never come back. They said he had brought along with his party a mulatto named Pacheco, who had himself gone back to the country of one Guacani.[5] This Guacani had killed the fellow there, and this character Garcia had then returned to Brazil. Many of the Guaranis who had accompanied Garcia had been stranded in the interior. "You'll find a lot of them still there," said the Indians, "and from them you'll find out about Garcia's activities. They'll also tell you what the country is like."

They said that country was inhabited by some Indians called the Chaneses. These people had fled from somewhere else into that territory, where they were joined by the Sococies and Xaquetes Indians, who also lived near Puerto Reyes.

Mulling over this account from the locals, the Governor pressed on to see this river from which Garcia had left on his exploration, which was quite near the place where the Guaxarapos had appeared and spoken with the Governor. He found the mouth of the river, which was named the Yapaname.[6] He ordered his men to sound the river, which he found to be very deep, especially in the middle, and it had a mighty current. Both banks were covered with trees. He ordered a brigantine to sail upriver about a league, sounding the bottom the whole way. They found it to be deeper and deeper as they went along. The Guaxarapos told him that the banks of the river were populated with many diverse tribes, all people who planted corn and manioc. They used the river as a great fishery, and it produced all the fish they wanted to eat. Their great catches yielded considerable fish oil, too.

When the brigantine came back, the men said they had seen a lot of smoke in the country beyond the riverbanks, and that from this it appeared that the riverside was heavily populated. As it was growing late, the Governor ordered his party to cast anchor at the mouth of this new river, which lay at the outskirts of a mountain range called Santa Lucía.[7] Garcia had crossed this range.

A day or so later, in the morning, the Governor asked his pilots to take our position at the mouth of this new river, which they found to be 19 ⅓ degrees south latitude.

That night we were much troubled by a shower of rain that dropped a great deal of water and brought bitter winds. Our people lit big fires. A lot of men got off the boats and slept on land, though some stayed on the brigantines, which were protected by awnings made of mats and the hides of deer and tapirs.

CHAPTER FIFTY-ONE

The Guaxarapos Parley with the Governor

THE NEXT MORNING, THE GUAXARAPOS WHO HAD VISITED THE GOVERNOR THE DAY BEFORE CAME BACK IN TWO CANOES. THEY BROUGHT FISH AND meat, which they gave to our people. After they had spoken with the Governor, he paid them out of his trade goods and trinkets, bade them farewell, and said he would always consider them friends and would do them any favors he could.

Coming along behind the Governor were a number of his men in ships and also many canoes filled with his friends the Guaranis, so he asked politely that the Guaxarapos receive them graciously and treat them well when they appeared. "If you do that, they won't harm you or cause you any sort of damage," he said. The Guaxarapos promised him they would do just that, but they didn't keep their word.

And you may take it for a fact that a Christian was the cause of all this and must accept the blame, as I will relate directly.

So, the Governor took his leave of these Indians and went upriver with a good wind in his sails that whole day. At sunset he came upon the towns of some Indians of the same tribe, all of whom were settled right along the bank of the river, next to the water. So as not to lose time, which he thought a very good idea, he went on by them without stopping.

The people here are peasants. They plant corn and other roots, and they are much given to fishing and hunting, as fish and game are wildly abundant here.[1]

They and their women run around quite naked, except for a few who do cover up their privates.

They carve stripes on their faces with quills, and their bulging lower lips and earlobes are pierced. They travel the rivers in canoes that do not hold more than two or three people. These canoes are so light, and the

Indians so skillful, that they move along quite briskly upriver or down using just their paddles. They look like they're flying. Not one of our brigantines (although there these little launches are made of cedar), whether rowed or under sail, no matter how light or what good time it might make, nor considering the fact that it has a dozen oars and the canoes only two, can ever catch them.

Well, the Indian tribes wage war with each other up and down the river on land and in these canoes. Among themselves the Indians also have various trade agreements. The Guaxarapos provide canoes to the Payaguaes, who provide things to them in return, as they give the Guaxarapos bows and arrows in whatever quantity is needed. They also make a number of other trade goods that they are ready to barter. And so, sometimes these tribes are all good friends, and at other times they become enemies again and carry on their hostilities and wars.

CHAPTER FIFTY-TWO

The Indians of That Country Come to Live Along the Banks of the River

ONCE THE FLOODWATERS GO DOWN, THE INDIANS OF THE INTERIOR RETURN TO LIVE ALONG THE RIVERBANK WITH THEIR CHILDREN AND WIVES. Here they enjoy the rich fisheries, because they do indeed take a lot of fish, and very fat ones at that. They live a good life dancing and singing day and night, like people who are sure of where their next mouthful will come from. And when the waters begin to rise again, which happens in January, they move to more secure parts. The floodwaters, you see, rise more than six fathoms above the cliffs along the river, and across that wide land they will cover the plains for more than a hundred leagues into the interior.[1] The whole place looks like a sea, and the water will rise over the palms and other trees scattered across the land; boats can pass over them.

Ordinarily, this happens every year the world has ever known at the season when the sun leaves the Tropic of Cancer and returns to the Tropic of Capricorn, which lies directly over the mouth of the Río del Oro.[2] When the water rises above the cliffs along the river, the local natives are ready with the very large canoes they have set aside for this particular season. They throw two or three loads of clay into the middle of these canoes, where they make up a hearth. Once this is done, an Indian will set out with his wife and children and house, floating along wherever the crest of the water may take them. They light a fire on the hearth, with which they cook up things to eat and warm themselves, and that is how they go about during the four months of the year that this flood lasts.

The floodwaters take them to various unflooded islands, where they hop out and hunt deer and tapirs along with other wild creatures that have fled there from the rising water. And as the waters begin to recede and follow their old courses, the Indians return to fish and hunt in these places. They will not leave their canoes until the cliffs where they customarily make their houses start to appear again.

It's quite a thing to see the huge numbers of fish the water leaves behind on the drying land as the floods recede. And when this happens, which is toward the end of March and in April, a terrible stench rises over the whole countryside due to the land being poisoned with all the muck.

In that season, all the natives, and we Spaniards with them, became so ill we thought we would die. And as it was still summer, the place was simply insufferable. But toward the end of April, everyone who had been sick began to feel well again.

The Indians of the place spin the thread they need to make their fishing nets from the fibers of some thistles. They crush these thistles and throw them into a bog. After fifteen days, they pull them out and scrape them with some clamshells. At this point the material is quite cured, and the fibers are whiter than snow.

These people had no chief, but there are chiefs within the larger tribe as a whole. The Indians are fishermen, wild men, and bandits—frontier people. As the Governor traveled through their country by boat, as well as past other towns located along the edge of the water, he would not consent to a single Spaniard or Guarani stepping ashore. He didn't want any of his party to stir them up. He also simply wanted to leave them happy and peaceful. He gave the local Indians a lot of trade goods and trinkets and told them that other boats were coming, bearing Christians and Guarani Indians, friends of his.

"Please see them as your friends and treat them well," he said.

And traveling on one Friday morning, the party came upon a very strong current that flowed between some jagged rocks in the river. Down in the flow we saw tremendous numbers of a fish called the *dorado*.[3] An infinite number of these fish just swam by in the strongest currents we had yet found in the river, something we were only able to get through under full sail and rowing like mad.

Here the Spaniards and the Guaranis made a very big catch of these dorados in the space of an hour. One of our Christians alone caught forty of them. They're sizable fish, each one weighing about half an arroba, and some of the big ones a full arroba each.[4] What a beautiful fish to eat, and the best morsel is the head! It is a very greasy kind of fish, and we got a lot of oil out of it. People who regularly eat the fish cooked in its own oil are themselves fat and shiny. And if you eat broth made from this fish for a month, it will rid you of any mange or leprosy you might have.

In this manner the Governor continued on his way, with a good wind in his sails. One afternoon, on the twenty-fifth of October, he came to a division of the river. It split up into three forks. One of these was a big lake the Indians called the Río Negro, which comes out of the north from the interior of the country.[5] In regard to the other branches, their water is of a good color.[6] These forks come together a little farther downstream.

So, the Governor continued to sail into the interior until he came to the mouth of a stream on the left-hand side, toward the setting sun, that empties into the channel. This was where you lose the top end of the Río Paraguay because of the many rivers and big lakes that here break up into branches and forks. In fact, there are so many mouths and passages into this watery morass that even the native Indians who go there customarily in their canoes only find their way with difficulty, and in reality often get lost.[7]

This river the Governor explored is called Iguatu by the natives of that country.[8] This means "Good Water," and it runs into the lake to our benefit. Up to that point we had been traveling upriver, but once in the lake we began to go downstream.

CHAPTER FIFTY-THREE

They Put Three Crosses at the Mouth of This River

T HE GOVERNOR ORDERED A NUMBER OF FELLED TREES TO BE PLACED AT THE MOUTH OF THIS RIVER AS SIGNALS, AND HE HAD THREE HIGH CROSSES put up, too, for the boats to use as they came into the channel behind him. He didn't want them to miss the entrance to the river.

We went on rowing for three days, at the end of which time the Governor left the river. He tried two other branches that emerged from the lake, both of which were very large indeed. On the eighth of the month, an hour before dawn, the party came across some ranges of hills that lay in the middle of the river. These ranges were quite high and round—in form or outline rather bell-shaped, and turning bloodred toward the top. These mountains are bald, with no trees or other vegetation on them at all, and vermillion in color. We think they contain a lot of metal, because the other, neighboring lands outside the confines of the river, beginning right at the shoreline, are extremely mountainous but with big trees and lots of undergrowth. As the mountains in the middle of the river are nothing like this, it seems to us a sign that they contain a great deal of metal, because where it occurs, trees and other plants will not grow.

The Indians told us that in earlier times their predecessors extracted a white metal from this bald range.[1]

Because the Governor had no miners or foundrymen along, nor the necessary tools to use in prospecting and reconnoitering that country, and due to the terrible illness that had befallen the party, he did not search out the metal. He left this task to his next visit, as these lands lie generally close to Puerto Reyes if you approach them by land.

Traveling upriver, we entered another lagoon through a mouth of the river, and this one was more than a league and a half wide. We emerged via another mouth of the same lagoon. Then we went on up a branch of the

river that ran next to terra firma. That same day, at ten o'clock in the morning, we came to the entry to another lake where the Sacocies, Xaqueses,
and Chaneses Indians had their principal town, the seat of their rule.

The Governor did not want to go further, because it seemed to him
that he should let the Indians know of his presence. So he sent off an
interpreter in a canoe with a few Christians to talk with the Indians on his
behalf and invite them to come to see him and palaver. The canoe and the
envoys left and came back at five in the afternoon, with the news that the
Indians in those towns had come out to receive them with very great pleasure. They told the interpreter they already knew our party was coming
and that they very much wanted to see the Governor and his Christians.
The Indians said the waters had dropped substantially and a canoe would
only find its way to their settlements with great effort. For our boats to
get through the low waters and make it to Puerto Reyes, the Indians said
they should be unloaded and lightened up, as nothing else would work.
The water was not much deeper than the width of a man's palm, and to be
able to sail the ships needed five or six palms' worth of water if they were
loaded. This kind of shallow water, or shoals that were even shallower,
were found near Puerto Reyes.

One morning soon after, the Governor ordered the boats to depart, with
all their crew, Christians and Indians, propelling them by oar until they
reached the shallows the Indians mentioned. Once they arrived, he ordered
everyone to get out—right into the water—which didn't even come up to
their knees. He positioned many Indians and Christians along both sides
of the brigantine called the *Sant Marcos*—all the people he could muster there—and they lifted the boat up onto their shoulders, balancing and
holding it with their arms to keep it from tumbling down.

The river shallows went on for more than one and a half times the
range of an harquebus shot.[2] It was very hard to manhandle a boat along
with your arms. After getting the first boat through the shallows, these
same Indians and Christians hauled other boats in the same way with
less work, as they were not as large as the first.

After we got to deep water again, we proceeded to Puerto Reyes,
where we found a great multitude of Indians waiting, and their wives and
children as well.

The Governor disembarked with all his men, and the people of the
port rushed up to him. "I've come on behalf of His Majesty to let you
know you must become Christians," he said to them. "I would urge you
to listen to our Christian doctrine and to believe in God, the Creator of

heaven and earth. You must become vassals of His Majesty, and once you do, you will be protected and defended by me and my men from your enemies and those who would do you harm. You will be always be well regarded and well protected, as His Majesty has commanded. If you conduct yourselves well, you will be given trade goods and various rewards, as has been the case with others who have done so in the past."

Then the Governor called for the clerics and told them he wished to build a church in Puerto Reyes in which they might say mass and perform the other divine offices, and that might serve as an example to and consolation for other Christians. "Take special care of these Indian people," he said to them.

The Governor had a large cross made out of wood, which was driven into the riverbank below some tall palm trees in the presence of Your Majesty's officials and many other people. And before the notary of the province, he took possession of the country in Your Majesty's name as a newly discovered land.[3]

Having pacified the natives of the place and handed out trinkets and trade goods, the Governor ordered the Spaniards to set up camp along the lakeshore, with the Guaranis next to them. "No force is to be used with the people of this place," he said to them. "They will suffer no harm of any kind. They are our friends and the vassals of His Majesty. Don't go into their towns or their houses under any circumstances."

The Indians abhor the idea of the Christians and other Indians entering their houses, where the intruders may well turn everything upside down and steal the owners' possessions. They are much disturbed and very sensitive about this.

"If you trade with them or barter for anything, pay them out of your own store of goods and trinkets," he said. "And if I hear that you've done anything else, you will indeed be punished."

CHAPTER FIFTY-FOUR

The Indian Farmers of Puerto Reyes

HE INDIANS OF THIS PUERTO REYES ARE FARMERS. THEY PLANT CORN AND MANIOC (WHICH IS THE CASSAVA OF THE INDIES), AND THEY ALSO PLANT mandubies (which are like hazelnuts), and of this fruit there is a great abundance.[1] These people plant twice a year, as the land is fertile and abundant in both game and fish.

The Indians raise a lot of ducks—a huge quantity, really, to defend themselves against crickets, as I have already noted. They raise chickens, which they shut away at night for fear of bats, which chew off their crests. Once this happens, the chickens will surely die. These bats are a very bad and disgusting sort of reptile, and there are many of them flying along the river that are the size of the doves of this country, and sometimes a bit larger.[2] They slice so sweetly with their teeth that the creatures they bite never feel it. They only bite people in the thin, transparent skin between the toes or the fingers of the hand, or at the tip of the nose. Once a bat has bitten someone—even though many other people may be present—he will continue to nip only that same person.

These bats bite by night and do not appear during the day. We have to defend our horses against them by protecting their ears, which the bats love to bite. And when a bat begins to fly among the horses at night, they are wildly disturbed. They'll wake up everyone in the house, and until you kill or chase away these bats flying around among the horses, they won't calm down.

The Governor was bitten by one of these bats while sleeping aboard one of the brigantines. The bat discovered one of his bare feet and bit him in the skin between his toes, and the blood ran all night until morning. He later remembered the coldness he felt in his leg and his bed swimming in blood. "I thought it was a wound of some sort," he said. The other men in the boat tried to find his wound and then laughed, because they recognized what they saw. They had had experience with bat bites. The Governor found that the bat had carried off a slice of the thin flesh between his toes.

These bats only bite where they can find a vein. It's a very bad business they pursue. You know, we brought along six expectant sows on this expedition so that we might create litters, and when they gave birth the piglets tried to suckle and found no nipples! The bats had eaten them all up. The piglets all died, and we had to eat the sows because they had no way to nurse their young.

There are some other nasty creatures in this land—some very large ants that come in two kinds. One sort is dark red, and the other very black. When one of them bites a person, he will spend twenty-four hours crying out and spinning around on the ground. It's a pity to see. For twenty-four hours there is nothing to be done; but once this time is past, the agony is over.

In the lagoons at this Puerto Reyes, there are many stinging rays. When people go down to the water to fish, they see them and they often step on them. The rays swing their tails around and sting them with a barb they carry there, which is longer than a finger. If the ray is large, it's about as long as the distance between your extended thumb and forefinger, and the barb is like a saw.[3] If they sting you on the foot, it goes right through the flesh. The pain is just enormous, about what you feel from an ant bite, but at least there is something you can do about it. The Indians know an herb that is taken once a man is stung. The herb is mashed and placed on the wound, and this cures the pain, although the wound will take more than a month to heal up.

The Indians of this country are medium bodied, and they walk about completely naked, with their private parts showing. Their ears have drill holes, and these are so large that a clenched fist would fit in them. They put medium-sized dry squashes in them and are continually pulling these out and replacing them with larger ones. Their lobes become so big from doing this that they stretch down close to their shoulders. Other Indians from neighboring tribes call them the Big Ears. This is similar to the Incas of Peru, who are also called Big Ears.[4]

When these Puerto Reyes Indians fight, they remove the calabashes and disks from their ears. Afterward, they return the ornaments to their former positions or, if they are not inclined to do so, tie their earlobes down below the backs of their heads.

The women among these Indians do not cover up their private parts. Each Indian lives off by himself with his wife and children. The women are in charge of spinning cotton, and the men plant their own plots of ground. When evening comes and they return to their houses to find a cooked meal, they need not bother themselves with any work about the house. The sole exception is when the corn is ripe, at which time they must harvest the cornstalks and carry them to their houses.

From this place onward, these Indians practice idolatry. They adore idols that they make from wood. And from what they said to the Governor, going onward from Puerto Reyes into the interior the idols are of gold and silver. He was able with some apt words to pry them away from their idolatry. "Burn your idols and get rid of them," he said. "You must believe in the true God, He who made heaven and the earth, men, the sea, the fish, and other things. What you are worshiping is the devil, and he has you well deceived."

And so, the Indians burned a lot of the idols, although their chiefs were terrified, saying that the devil would kill them now as he was very angry.

After the church was finished and the padres said mass, the devil fled from the place, and the Indians went about much more reassured, losing their fear. This town was the first settlement in the countryside to be found for more than half a league; it had eight hundred houses, and all the people were farmers.

CHAPTER FIFTY-FIVE

How Garcia's Indians
Populated This Place

A T HALF A LEAGUE THERE WAS ANOTHER, SMALLER TOWN, OF ABOUT SEV-
ENTY HOUSES, AND OF THE SAME TRIBE OF THE SOCOCIES.[1] AT FOUR
leagues there were another two towns of the Chaneses who settled in
that land, part of those people whom, as I mentioned earlier, Garcia had
brought from the interior of the country. They had taken women into that
land, and many of the Indians came to look at them and get acquainted.
The whole time they said they were very happy and great friends of the
Christians because of the good treatment meted out to them by Garcia
when he brought them from their own country.

Some of these Indians brought along beads, pearls, and other things
they said Garcia had given them when they came along with him. All
these Indians are hard-working farmers, breeders of ducks and chickens.
The chickens are like those of Spain, and so are the ducks.

The Governor treated these Indians well, gave them some of his trade
goods and trinkets, and received them as vassals of Your Majesty. But he
also implored them and warned them, saying to them that they needed to
be good and loyal to Your Majesty and to the Christians. And if they were
to do this, they would be favored and well treated, better than they had
been before.

CHAPTER FIFTY-SIX

The Governor Speaks with the Chaneses

T HE GOVERNOR WANTED TO USE THE CHANESES TO INFORM HIMSELF ABOUT THE INTERIOR AND ITS TRIBES AND ALSO TO FIND OUT HOW MANY DAYS IT might take to go from Puerto Reyes to the first town in that region. The chief of the Chaneses, a man of about fifty, said that when Garcia brought them from their own country they came with him through the country of the Mayaes Indians, finally emerging into the territory of the Guaranis.

The Guaranis had killed a number of them, and the chief of the Chaneses and some others of his tribe who escaped had fled back along the banks of the upper Río Paraguay until they arrived at the village of these Sacocies Indians. They were sheltered here, and they dared not go back along the same trail they had followed with Garcia because the Guaranis would rise out of the bush and kill them.

Because of this, they did not know whether they were close to or far from the towns of the interior. Not knowing that, and not knowing the trail, they have never gone back to their own land. But the Guaranis who inhabit the mountains of that region do know the roads into the interior. They could certainly show the Spaniards the way, because they go back and forth to war against the Indians of the interior along those paths.

The Chanes chief was asked what towns of Indians there were in his country and which tribes other than his own. "How do they sustain themselves, and what kinds of weapons do they use when they fight?" we inquired.

He said, "In my country, the people of my tribe have only one ruling chief. All the people obey him. In my tribe there are many villages with large numbers of residents. They constantly make war against some Indians we call the Chimneys and against others we call the Carcaraes.

"There are a lot of other people in the area who have large towns. These tribes are called the Gorgotoquies, Payzuñoes, Estarapecocies, and

Candirees.[1] They all have their own chiefs, and they all make war against each other. They fight with bows and arrows, and all of them are generally farmers and livestock growers. They plant corn, manioc, sweet potatoes, and peanuts in great abundance, and they raise ducks and chickens like those of Spain. They also raise big sheep, and all the tribes fight continually with each other."[2]

The Indians trade bows, arrows, and blankets with each other and other things for bows and arrows. They also trade women for these items.

Having told us this, the Indians went away quite happy and contented. Their chief offered to go with the Governor as he mounted his expedition into the country. "I'll go back with my wife and children and live in my country again," he said, which was what he wanted most in the world.

CHAPTER FIFTY-SEVEN

The Governor Looks for Garcia's Indians

W ITH THE INDIAN'S REPORT IN MIND, THE GOVERNOR ORDERED THAT SOME SPANIARDS GO OUT WITH A NUMBER OF THE LOCAL INDIANS TO look for the Guaranis who lived in that country and find out what they were doing. Our party would then take them along as guides for the expedition to the interior. Some Guaranis who were already part of the Governor's company were the Indians who would go with the Spaniards.

These men all left, traveling where the guides led them. After six days they came back, saying that the Guaranis of the interior had vanished. Their houses and towns were deserted, and the whole countryside was empty. They had scouted around for ten leagues in every direction and not found a soul.

In light of this, the Governor asked the Chanes Indians if they knew where the Guaranis might have gone. The Chaneses told him that the Indians of a certain interior port had joined forces with the Indians of a nearby island to make war on the Guaranis and they had succeeded in killing quite a number of them.[1] The remaining Guaranis had fled even further into the interior, and the Chaneses thought they would join up with other Guaranis who lived along the border with another tribe called the Xarayes. The Guaranis, of course, were also at war with these Xarayes and several other tribes.

The Xarayes are said to be people who have some gold and silver, which the Indians of the far interior give them. This part of the country reputedly has a considerable population, with perhaps some towns. The Xarayes are also farmers, planting corn and other crops in great quantity, and they raise ducks and chickens like those of Spain.

We asked the Chaneses how many days' journey it was from that port to the country of the Xarayes.[2] A man told us that you could indeed go by land but the road was terrible and very hard to negotiate because of all the swamps and the great lack of sweet water. However, you could make the trip in four or five days. If you wished to make the journey upriver by canoe, it took eight or ten days.

CHAPTER FIFTY-EIGHT

The Governor Speaks to the Officials and Lets Them Know What Is Happening

AFTER THIS THE GOVERNOR CALLED ALL THE OFFICIALS AND CLERICS TOGETHER, INFORMING THEM OF THE ACCOUNT GIVEN BY THE XARAYES and Guaranis who were then on the frontier. He agreed that, just to be safe, some of the Indians who were natives of the port should go along with two Spaniards and two Guaranis to talk to the Xarayes and look over their land and settlements. "These men should then tell us about the towns and people of the interior," he said, "after speaking with the people of the settlements and the residents of the lands beyond. Where does the route lie from their country to the interior? And our Spaniards need to be particularly courtly as they speak with the Guaranis, because through them they will most certainly be best advised of conditions and come to know the truth of what lies ahead."

Well, the two Spaniards, Héctor de Acuña and Antonio Correa, interpreters and translators working with the Guaranis, along with about ten Sococies and two Guarani Indians, left that same day. Their orders were to talk to the chief of the Xarayes.

"Speak with the chief of the Xarayes," said the Governor, "and tell him that I've sent you so that you might converse with him and come to know him and his people. We hope he and his people will accept us as their friends. I would also like to ask him to come and see me."

The Governor wanted the Xaray chief to tell the Spaniards about the settlements and people of the interior and the best route to take to get to them.

The Governor loaded up these Spaniards with a lot of trinkets and trade goods and a scarlet bonnet to give to the chief of the Xarayes. He got together an equal series of presents for the chief of the Guaranis, so that they might also convey his wishes to the Xaray chief.

One day shortly thereafter, Captain Gonzalo de Mendoza arrived back at the port with his men and ships.

The captain and his men said that on the evening of Todos Santos, he was sailing through the country of the Guaxarapos, having talked once with them and come to the conclusion that they were friendly.[1] He had spoken with them first on his way upriver, at a time when the weather was no good for sailing.

Some of the Spaniards in his brigantines had jumped out and were making their way by land, and as Mendoza passed, through some twist or turn of the river the wind caught the sails of the five brigantines in front. The one boat that was left behind, which was a brigantine whose captain was Agustín de Campos, was being towed by all her men, who were ashore. The Guaxarapos suddenly rushed out of the bush, hitting them hard and killing five Christians.

Juan de Bolaños drowned while trying to take refuge in the ship.

All our men had been traveling along safe and secure, thinking the Indians were their friends, trusting them and taking no precautions for themselves. And if the other Christians had not gotten back to the one brigantine, the Indians would have killed them all, as they had no arms with which to defend themselves or cause anyone else any harm.

The death of our Christians caused grave damage to our reputation, as the Guaxarapos freely traveled in their canoes to visit and trade with the Indians of Puerto Reyes, with whom they were friends. The Guaxarapos told them how they had killed five Christians and that we were gutless. They said we had tender heads, and that the Indians of Puerto Reyes should grab us and kill us and that the Guaxarapos would help them do it.

From that point forward they were in open revolt, and they did indeed begin to put bad thoughts into the minds of our Indians in Puerto Reyes.

CHAPTER FIFTY-NINE

The Governor Sends Word to the Xarayes

NTÓN CORREA AND HÉCTOR DE ACUÑA LEFT FOR THE TOWNS AND THE TERRITORY OF THE XARAY INDIANS, ALONG WITH SEVERAL INDIANS AS guides, to speak with those people on behalf of the Governor.

Eight days later they came back to the port to let the Governor know what they had done and what they knew of that country, its people, and its chief—what they had seen with their own eyes. They brought with them an Indian who had been sent by the chief of the Xarayes to act as a guide for the exploration of the back country.

Antón Correa and Héctor de Acuña also said that on the day after they left Puerto Reyes with the guides for their journey, some Indians they called the Artaneses had arrived in the native towns. These are a people large in body who go about totally naked. They're farmers, but they plant very little because they have only a small bit of good land to cultivate. The greater part of their lands is often subject to flooding and full of very dry sands. They are quite poor, maintaining themselves for most of the year by fishing in the lakes that lie next to their towns. The women among these Indians have very ugly faces, because they carve them up with a lot of lines, using the stingers of the rays found in the waters there. They do, however, cover up their private parts.

The faces of the men of this tribe are also appallingly ugly because they perforate the lower lip, inserting in it the husk of the fruit of some trees.[1] This fruit is round like the large knob of a spindle, and the size of one as well. It overloads the lip and enlarges it to such an extent that it is horrible to behold.

The Artaneses received our envoys very graciously in their houses, however, and gave them food to eat out of what they had.

Later, our men had continued on their way with a man of that tribe to guide them. They took drinking water along in calabashes and with an enormous effort traveled all day through the swamps. They had to put one foot in front of the other while sinking up to the knee with each single step, pulling their legs out only with a great struggle. And all that slime was so hot, and the sun so boiling, that their legs were affected by the temperature and erupted in ulcers, which caused the men untold pain. As if this weren't enough, they were about to die for certain that same day of thirst, because the water the Indians carried in the calabashes didn't last even half a day's journey. They slept that night on the ground between those swamps only after much hardship—hungry, worn-out, and thirsty.

On the following day, at eight in the morning, they came to a little pool of water, which they drank although it was very dirty. They filled up the calabashes the Indians carried and traveled all day through flooded spots, just as they had the day before, except that they found pond water in some places, which refreshed them. They came across a tree that gave them a bit of shade, where they dozed and ate their provisions. But they saved nothing for the road ahead.

The guides said that a considerable journey still remained before they came to the settlements of the Xaray Indians. As night had come, they slept until daybreak. Then they started out again, heading into swamps from which they never expected to emerge, considering the harshness and dif-ficulties they found in them. Their legs not only ulcerated again with the heat, they sank into the morass up to their belts, and they couldn't turn their feet around to extract themselves. These swamps lasted more than a league, and then they found a better path, well situated.

By an hour past noon that same day, our party had eaten nothing, nor did they have anything left to eat. They suddenly saw coming along the path toward them some twenty Indians, who approached expressing great pleasure and joy, loaded with cornbread, roasted ducks, fish, and corn wine. These fellows said their chief had known that the Spaniards were on their way to the Xaray lands via this road, and he had sent them to greet our men on his behalf and take them something to eat. The Xarayes were also to take them to where the chief and his party were staying, very happy to hear about the visit of our men.

With what these Indians had brought, our men were able to remedy their sore lack of provisions.

On that same day, an hour before nightfall, they approached the towns of the Xarayes. And before they came within a crossbow shot of these places, more than fifteen hundred of the Xaray warriors came out to greet them with delight, all looking very smart as they were made up with lots of macaw feathers and aprons with white beads, which covered their privates. Our men were carried off in the middle of this throng into the town, at the entrance to which a large number of women and children awaited them. All the women had covered up their private parts—many of them with the long cotton shifts that they often wear. (They call this sort of clothing *tipoes*.)

Well, after coming into the town our men went to see the chief of the Xarayes, accompanied by about three hundred well-disposed Indians, the majority of them older men. The chief was seated in a cotton net in the middle of a big plaza; all his people were standing with him in their midst.[2] When everyone had finished filing into the plaza, they formed an open street for our men, who made their way up to the chief. The chief's men brought up two small tree trunks to serve as benches, and the chief indicated through signs that the Spaniards should sit down.

The chief ordered a man from the Guarani tribe to come forward. He had been among the Xarayes for a long time and had married a woman of that tribe. They all seemed to love him, and they considered him to be a member of their tribe. Through the Guarani the chief said, "Welcome, and I'm very glad to see you. I have wanted to see what the Christians were like for some time. I've had little news about you since Garcia came through this country. I think of you as relatives of mine and my friends."

He also said he wanted to see the chief of the Christians, because he knew that he was a good man and very much a friend of the Indians—a man who was generous with his possessions, not stingy. "If he were to ask me for anything here in my own country, I would give it to him," said the chief.

Through the Guarani interpreter, our men said, "The Governor sent us to ask you to tell us about the road to the back country and its settled areas from your territory and any towns or people lying between your lands and the interior. He would also like to know how many days it might take to reach the Indians with gold and silver.[3] And in addition to this, the Governor would hope that the chief realizes how much he would like to make his acquaintance and count him as a friend."

The Governor had earlier asked our men to relate a few other things to the chief as well.

The Indian said, "I am delighted to have you as friends. The Governor should know that he is my lord, and he needs to let us know what he wishes."

As far as the road to the settlements of the interior was concerned, the chief knew nothing of it. "We have no news of any such road," he said. "We've never gone to the back country because the whole place is inundated during the time of the floods," which was two moons away. "Even after the rains pass, the country is such a mess that you can't travel there at all.[4]

"However," said the chief, "this interpreter through whom we've been speaking is a member of the Guarani tribe, and he has indeed visited the settlements of the interior and knows the road to take. I'll send him along to please the chief of the Christians as he accompanies him and shows him the route."

A little later, in the presence of the Spaniards, the chief ordered the Guarani interpreter to go with them, which he agreed to do quite willingly.

Well, the chief had denied the interior route to the Spaniards, offering a number of plausible cautions and reasons. It seemed to them from what they had already seen of the country that what he said might actually be true. They believed him. "Could you then allow us a guide to the country of the Guaranis?" they said. "We would like to pay them a visit and speak with them."

The chief suddenly changed. He was tremendously scandalized. But he regained his composure and with a sly bearing said, "The Guaranis are my enemies, and we are at war. We go on killing each other every day. I am a friend to the Christians, so kindly don't go looking for my opponents to make them your friends. However, if you still wish to visit these Guaranis, my men will take you one of these mornings to speak with them."

By then it was night, so the chief took our men to his house, ordering something for them to eat and many cotton hammocks to sleep in. He also offered them a girl each. "I'll give them to you," he said. But the men didn't want the girls. "We're tired," they told the chief.

The next day, an hour before dawn, a tremendous racket—drumming and shouting—started up, drowning the town in sound. All the Indians began to gather in the plaza in front of the chief's house. They were decked out in feathers and equipped for battle, with all their bows and many arrows. "Open the door," ordered the chief inside the house. "I want to see them."

There must have been a good six hundred warriors in the plaza, and the chief said to the Spaniards, "Christians, look at my people. Here's how you'll be escorted to the Guarani towns. Go with them, as they will get you there and bring you back. If you just went by yourselves, they would simply kill you because they know that you've been in my country and you're my friends."

Well, the Spaniards knew that would be no way to talk to the chief of the Guaranis and that it would be a fine opportunity to lose the friendship of the Xarayes. "We've decided to return to the Governor and tell him about everything we have seen so far," they said. "We'll see what he asks us to do once we've reported to him."

That was how they calmed down the Xarayes. All the Xarayes, it seemed, were in the plaza that day, and there must have been a thousand of them. At a league and a half from that town you also would have found another four settlements of the same tribe, all of which owed their allegiance to that chief, who was named Camire.

These Xarayes are large people, and good-natured. They are farmers, and twice a year they plant and harvest corn, sweet potatoes, manioc, and peanuts. They raise ducks in enormous quantities and some chickens like those of our own Spain.

The Xarayes pierce their lower lips like the Artaneses. Each man has his own house off by itself, where he lives with his wife and children. The men cultivate and sow. The women harvest and carry the produce back to their houses, and they are tremendous spinners of cotton.

These Indians raise a lot of ducks to kill and eat the crickets, as I noted earlier.

CHAPTER SIXTY

The Interpreters Return from Seeing the Xarayes Indians

T HESE XARAY INDIANS FIND THEMSELVES THE POSSESSORS OF GREAT FISH-
ERIES WITH THEIR RIVERS AND LAKES. THEY ALSO HAVE GOOD DEER HUNT-
ing. The Spaniards were with their chief all day. They gave him a number
of trade goods and trinkets as well as the scarlet bonnet the Governor
had sent along. The bonnet made him very happy, and he received it with
an air of tranquility that was a marvel to behold.

The chief sent for a quantity of headdresses of macaw feathers and of
other types and gave them all to the Christians to take back to the Governor.
These were dapper indeed. The Spaniards took their leave of this Camire
so as to return to Puerto Reyes, and the chief sent along twenty of his warriors to accompany them. So, our men left, and the chief's men went along
with them until they got to the towns of the Artanés Indians, where they
went back to their own country.

But the guide whom Camire had given them stayed with the Spaniards,
and the Governor welcomed him with warm affection. With his interpreters from among the Guaranis, he began to question this Indian to see if
he knew the way to the settlements of the interior. He asked what tribe he
belonged to and of what part of that country he was a native.

The man said that he was a Guarani and a native of Itati, which is on
the Río Paraguay. When he was very young, the people of his tribe had
sent out a broad call for a meeting of the Indians from all across his country, and they afterward traveled into the interior. He went along with his
father and his relatives to make war against the natives of the place, and
they had robbed those people of the plates of gold and silver and jewels
set in the same that they had.

After the Guaranis got to the first settlements of the interior, they began
fighting with the locals and killed a lot of those Indians. They depopulated

quite a few towns whose residents fled to some settlements even deeper in the interior for refuge. But all the tribes of the interior eventually collected themselves to fight the Guaranis, and they scattered and destroyed a large number of them. The Guaranis fled in different directions, and their enemies followed them, capturing the passes over which they were fleeing and killing them all. The man from Itati made signs that some two hundred of those Guarani Indians who had swarmed around the battlefields never escaped. Among those who got away, he had been saved. The greater part of the escapees had stayed in the mountains through which they had fled, and they still lived there. They didn't dare leave because they were afraid that the Guaxarapos and Guatos and other tribes who stood in their way would kill them.

The man from Itati hadn't wanted to stay in those hills, and he had gone back toward his own land with some men of his party who had wanted to press on. They had been surprised by hostile tribesmen as they went along their way, and one night his party engaged some of them and was slaughtered. The man from Itati had escaped into the thick undergrowth of the mountains. Traveling through them, he had come to the land of the Xarayes, who kept him under their control and nurtured him for quite some time. They ended up loving him dearly, and he them, and he eventually married a woman of their tribe.

He was asked if he had a good knowledge of the road he and his fellow tribesmen had followed to the settlements of the interior. He replied, "It's been a very long time since I passed that way."

When he and the others of his tribe had gone along that route, they had to open up the path: they cut down trees and leveled the ground, which was uneven and rough. "Now," he thought, "the paths would all be closed in again by brush and undergrowth. I've never gone back to look at them or walk along them. However, it seems to me that if I started along that way again everything might come back to me." He would know where to go. You could make out this path from a high, round mountain that was within view of Puerto Reyes.

We asked him how long it might take to reach the first settlement of the interior. He said about five days, from what he could remember, and the place would have a lot of provisions. "The people are great farmers," he said, although when he and his fellow tribesmen were fighting them they had destroyed everything. The Guaranis wiped out a lot of villages. "But they have probably reestablished themselves by now," he said.

"Are there strong-flowing rivers or springs along the way?" we asked.

He said he had seen rivers, but they were not particularly mighty. "However," he said, "there are some other rivers that *are* strong flowing, as well as springs, lakes, hunting grounds full of deer and tapirs, and a lot of fruit and honey."

"Back when you and your fellow tribesmen were making war on the people of the interior, did you notice if they had any gold and silver?" we asked.

"Well, in the towns we plundered they had quite a few plates of gold and silver, as well as *barbotes*, earrings, bracelets, crowns, hatchets, and little vessels.¹ We took all that when we laid waste to those places."

The Guaranis, who themselves later fled, carried along some silver plates, barbotes, and beads, which the Guaxarapos took from them as the Guaranis were passing through their country. The Guaxarapos had killed many of them, but the Guaranis remaining in the mountains still had a certain quantity of gold and silver. The man from Itati said that the Xarayes had some of it, too. When the Xarayes had marched out to war, he had seen them display plates of silver from their hoard, all of which came from the Guarani plunder of the interior.

"Would you come along with the Governor and his company to show the Christians the way to the interior?" we asked.

"Yes, I'll go freely," he said. "My chief sent me for that exact purpose."

The Governor cautioned him to tell the truth about what he knew of the road. "Nothing else," he said, as much harm would likely come to this Indian otherwise. If he told the truth, a lot of good fortune would be his.

"I've told the truth about what I know of the route," he said. "I want to go along with you to show you the way."

CHAPTER SIXTY-ONE

The Governor Resolves to Set Off on His Exploration

T HE GOVERNOR HAD IN HAND THIS REPORT FROM THE FIELD AS WELL AS THE OPINIONS OF THE CLERICS AND HIS CAPTAINS. WEIGHING THESE, HE decided to launch an expedition to explore the settlements of that country. He called for some three hundred harquebusiers and crossbowmen to assemble. And considering the empty country they would have to traverse before arriving at towns of any sort, he ordered up provisions for twenty days. He also ordered a hundred Christian men along with about two hundred Guarani Indians to stay in Puerto Reyes and guard the brigantines. The Governor appointed Juan Romero as their captain, as he was familiar with that part of the country.

So, the Governor set out from Puerto Reyes on the twenty-sixth of November of the year 1543, and for that entire day we traveled underneath the arching branches of the trees. The land was cool and nicely shaded and our route little used. Our guide, of course, steered us on, and that night we rested next to some springs of water. The next morning, a little before daylight, we started out again, pushing our way forward with some twenty of our men up front to break trail with the guide. We had to do this because the farther we went down the path the more it closed in on us with its high and very thick trees and brush. We traveled along like this with tremendous difficulty.

That same day, about five o'clock in the afternoon, we stopped to spend the night beside a big lake. Here the Christians and the Indians caught fish with their bare hands.

As we went along, the Governor sent our guide up various trees and mountainsides to make sure we were on the right track and not veering off somewhere. He climbed, looked around, and assured us that it was indeed the right road into the settled country we had been looking for.

The Guarani Indians the Governor had taken along as part of his company sustained themselves with the supplies he had given them out of respect. They also supplied themselves with honey they extracted from the trees and from their hunting of wild pigs, tapirs, and deer. There seemed to be quite an abundance of this sort of game in that country. But as there were a lot of people in the expedition and they made quite a racket as they traveled, the game fled, and for that reason the Guaranis did not kill much.

The Indians and the Spaniards ate a great deal of wild fruit from the trees, of which there were quite a few. Remarkably, none of these fruits made anyone ill, with one exception. One of the trees resembled a myrtle and its fruit the same sort of thing that a myrtle would produce in Spain (where they say *murta*).[1] The latter is a little thicker, though, and of a very good flavor. Well, this forest fruit made some of those who ate it vomit and gave others diarrhea. This didn't last long, and it caused no further difficulty.

Some of our people also took advantage of palm fruits, of which there was a great quantity in that land. They did not exactly eat the dates; they just split open the pits. Inside these stones, which are round, the pith is almost like a sweet almond. The Indians make flour from this to eat, and it is a very good food indeed—as are the young palm shoots, which also are tasty.

CHAPTER SIXTY-TWO

The Río Caliente

O N THE FIFTH DAY OF TRAVELING ALONG THE ROUTE SHOWN US BY OUR
GUIDE, WHERE WE ONLY MADE OUR WAY THROUGH ARDUOUS EFFORT,
we came to a little stream that flowed down off a mountain. Its water was
very hot and clear and good. Some of the Spaniards began to angle in it
and pulled out some fish. Our guide began to babble foolishly at this warm
spring, telling us that it had been some time since he had been this way
and that he therefore was not sure of his route, as none of the old paths he
knew had reappeared.

The Governor left the warm spring the next day, traveling along a
route suggested by our guide. It was very difficult going, as we broke trail
through the continual forests, jungles, and canebrakes of that country. At
about ten o'clock that morning, two Indians of the Guarani tribe came out
of the brush to speak to the Governor. They told him they belonged to the
people who had remained in that deserted wilderness after the past wars
their people had engaged in with the Indians of the interior. They had gone
to the forest after their tribesmen had been scattered and largely killed off.
These men had stayed in the woods where we found them. Out of fear of
the local Indians, they and their wives and children had hidden themselves
in the thickest and hilliest part of the forest.

The grand total of people in hiding was only about fourteen souls, and
they confirmed what we had heard before: that two days' journey away
there was another small hut occupied by these same people—perhaps up
to ten souls. The brother-in-law of the two Guarani men lived there. In
the land of the Xarayes there were also other Guaranis who belonged to
the same band as our two men, and those Guaranis and the Xarayes were
at war.

The two Indians were made very uneasy by the sight of the Christians
and their horses, so the Governor instructed our interpreter to reassure

them and calm them down. He also wanted the interpreter to ask where their house was.

"Very near here," they said.

Just then, up came their wives and children and some of their other relatives—about fourteen persons.

The Governor obliged them to say how they kept themselves alive in that country and how many of them there were.

"Well," they said, "we grow corn, which we eat." They also sustained themselves by hunting and by gathering honey and the wild fruits of the trees, which are found in great abundance in that place. "Very few of us remain from the time when our parents were killed and scattered to the winds." This is what the oldest people of the tribe said, who from looking at them appeared to be about thirty-five years of age.

We asked them if they knew the road that went from their lands to the interior and how long it would take to reach a populated place again.

"We were very small when we last came down that road," they said. "We never went back to it, we haven't seen it since, and we remember nothing of it." They didn't know how far it went nor how long it would take us to get there. "But our brother-in-law (who lived in that other small house some two days' journey from their own house) has been along that road many times. He knows it well and can tell you where it goes."

Seeing that these Indians knew nothing of the road that would take us farther along on our exploration, the Governor told them to go home. He gave all of them—men, women, and children—trade goods and trinkets, and with these they returned to their homes very happy.

CHAPTER SIXTY-THREE

The Governor Sends Men to Look for a House That Lies Ahead

THE NEXT DAY THE GOVERNOR ORDERED AN INTERPRETER TO GO OUT AHEAD OF OUR PARTY WITH TWO SPANIARDS AND TWO INDIANS (WHO HAD COME from the house they were saying was ahead of us) to find out whether anyone knew the road and how much time it might take for us to reach the first inhabited district in that part of the country. The Governor wanted this scouting party to report back as quickly as possible so that he might be prepared for whatever might be needed. The day after the scouts had left, he mustered the company out to go little by little along the same route taken by the interpreter and his companions.

They had been traveling along this way for three days when an Indian who had been sent by the scouting party came back to the Governor. He handed over a letter from the interpreter that said they had arrived at the house of the Indians for whom they had been searching and had spoken with the Indian who knew the way into the interior. This man was saying that from his house the next settlement lay near a hill they called Tapuaguazu, which is a high rock.[1] A person climbing this hill might see a great deal of populated country.

From his house to Tapuaguazu, you would have to travel for sixteen days through the wilderness, and the road was simply terrible. It was choked off by trees and other vegetation, all of it very tall, and there were horrendous thickets. The trail the scouting party had followed to find the house of this Indian after taking leave of the Governor was also rife with difficulties and unimaginably overgrown, and it had been very hard work to traverse it. The interpreter and his companions had gone most of the way on all fours.[2] The Indian they had found was saying that the trail they were about to follow was worse than the one they had just come on.

Our men said they would bring along with them their new Indian informant so that the Governor might benefit from his knowledge.

Well, that's what was in the letter. The Governor left to go to wherever the Indian messenger had come from, and he found paths so overgrown and hilly, with such giant trees and massive thickets, that the party could only go less than the distance of a crossbow shot after hacking and cutting all day. The rain fell endlessly during that season of the year, and so as not to drench and ultimately lose all his men and their munitions, he told everyone to withdraw to the small farmsteads they had left earlier that morning. There they would be able to shelter themselves in a number of small huts.

CHAPTER SIXTY-FOUR

The Interpreter Comes Back from the Little House

THE NEXT DAY, AT THREE IN THE AFTERNOON, THE INTERPRETER AND THE INDIAN WHO HAD SAID THAT HE KNEW THE WAY CAME BACK. THE Governor welcomed the Indian and spoke happily with him, and he gave him a number of trade goods and trinkets. This pleased the man. The Governor then said to the interpreter, "Tell this man—ask him—to truthfully describe to me the way to the settled territory of the interior."

But the man said, "It's been many long days since I've traveled that path. However, I still know it, and I've walked it many times on my way to Tapuaguazu, where I've seen the smoke of the fires burning at the towns in the interior. I used to go to Tapua for arrows, which they have in those parts." It took many days to make the trip for them, and he could see well before he arrived the rising smoke of the fires lit by the Indians. "When I saw that, I knew the people who used to live in that country had begun to repopulate the place." They had left the land empty after the last set of wars. "I haven't dared travel down that old road for fear of the local Indians killing me," he said. "That path is so closed up now that only by very great effort could a person follow it. It might take sixteen days of cutting trees and clearing off the road again to get to Tapua."[1]

We asked him if he wanted to go along with the Christians to show us the road.

"Yes," he said, though he was very afraid of the Indians of the interior. "I'll go willingly."

Well, taking into account the tale of this Indian, and the difficulty and inconvenience posed by the path before us, as he told it, the Governor convened a council of Your Majesty's officials, his clerics, and his captains. "Let's have your opinion," he said, "as well as a general discussion of what should be done regarding our proposed exploration in light of this Indian's stories."

The assembly said they had noticed that most of the Spaniards lacked provisions: they had not eaten for three days, and they had not dared ask for much of anything due to their earlier disorderly consumption of food rations. "The first of our guides swore to us that we would find a lot to eat on the fifth day of our journey, in a country full of people with abundant provisions. And with this assurance, and believing that it was the truth, both the Christians and the Indians had exercised very little caution and less care regarding the supplies of food they had brought along." You see, each Christian had with him two arrobas of flour.[2] Seeing as how the remaining provisions would not last six days, and we were well past that, the people now had nothing to eat.

It seemed to them a very dangerous business to go on without anything to sustain us, especially as the Indians never told us anything that was certain. It might well be that where the guide said sixteen days it could be many more. We would find ourselves so far along that if we had to turn back we would not be able to do so. Everyone would die of hunger, as had happened so often in the explorations we undertook in all those parts. The Governor's council thought that, considering the safety and lives of all the Christians and Indians in the party, he would be well advised to turn back to Puerto Reyes, where he had started and where he had left his ships. In Puerto Reyes, the Governor could refit the party and collect new supplies to continue his exploration.

That was their opinion, and if need be, they would require it to be followed on behalf of Your Majesty.

CHAPTER SIXTY-FIVE

The Governor and His Men Return to the Port

THE OPINION OF THE CLERICS, THE OFFICIALS, AND THE CAPTAINS WAS OBVI-OUS. THERE WAS THE CLEAR NEED OF OUR PEOPLE, AND EVERYONE'S WISH that we should turn back, although the Governor made plain the great danger that they would face by doing so. In Puerto Reyes, it would be impossible to find enough supplies for so many people and outfit the expedition all over again. The corn would not be ready to harvest, and the Indians had none to give us. And everyone should remember that the natives had said the river waters would soon rise, creating much hardship for our party and for them, too.

All these and other arguments the Governor mentioned were still not enough to sway the council, but he himself was not of a mind to return. He knew, however, what the overwhelming general opinion was, and he had to give in so as not to show disrespect or have to castigate anyone.

The Governor would just have to humor them. He ordered everyone to get ready to return to Puerto Reyes the next day. And on the following morning he sent Captain Francisco de Ribera to the interior with six Christians and the guide who knew the way. He also sent along eleven Indian chiefs with Captain Ribera to accompany the party and keep it safe. These Indians were under strict instruction not to leave Ribera's company until they all returned to wherever the Governor was, and he advised them that if they did so he would punish them forthwith.

And so the little party went off toward Tapua, taking with them their guide who knew the route. At that point the Governor also left with all his people for Puerto Reyes. He got back to the port in eight days, thoroughly displeased at not having been able to continue his exploration.

CHAPTER SIXTY-SIX

How They Wanted to Kill the Men Who Had Stayed Behind in Puerto Reyes

T HE GOVERNOR RETURNED TO PUERTO REYES, WHERE CAPTAIN JUAN ROMERO, WHO HAD REMAINED BEHIND AS HIS LIEUTENANT, TOLD HIM MOST assuredly that the natives of the port and those of an island that lies about a league away had tried to murder all the Christians in the place and steal their brigantines only a short time after the Governor had left. The locals had sent out a call across the land to all the Indians, and then the Guaxarapos, who are our enemies, had joined together with many other tribes to strike the Spaniards by night.

The Indians had come to see our men under the ruse of trade, but they brought no supplies as they had done before. And when they did come in with something, it was only to spy on our men. They told Romero clearly that they would be back to slaughter the Christians. "We'll destroy you," they said.

With this in mind, the Governor called the local chiefs to a meeting. He ordered them to talk to their men and admonish them on behalf of Your Majesty to calm down and not break the peace they had made with us. "I myself and indeed all the Christians have done you numerous good works as your friends," he said. "We've shown no signs of anger or displeasure with you. I have given you a lot of things and at any time would defend you against your enemies.

"But if you persist in your warlike ways, I will consider you my enemies and make war on you," said the Governor. He warned them against this with the clerics and Your Majesty's officials present.

Then he made presents to the Indians of some scarlet bonnets and other things, and they again promised to consider the Christians their friends and throw out of their lands those Indians who had assembled against the Spaniards—namely the Guaxarapos and some other tribes.

The Governor found Puerto Reyes full of large numbers of Spaniards and Indians, and two days after he had arrived he realized he would have to deal with the gnawing reality of hunger. He had to find something to eat for everyone, and in the whole place there were no provisions other than those he had aboard the brigantines moored at the port. These supplies were scanty, and he only had enough of them to feed all the people for ten or twelve days. Between Christians and Indians, this throng amounted to more than twenty thousand people.[1]

Seeing so much need, and in light of the danger of everyone dying on him, he assembled all his interpreters and told them to go out and look for foodstuffs in the surrounding area. These they would pay for with trade goods and trinkets, and for this purpose he gave the interpreters a lot of these items.

They went out and found nothing.

So the Governor called the chiefs together again and asked them where he might barter for provisions with his trade goods. The chiefs said that at about nine leagues from the port some Indians called the Arianicosies lived along the banks of several large lakes. "They have provisions in great abundance," they said, "and they should be able to give you what you need."

CHAPTER SIXTY-SEVEN

The Governor Orders Captain Mendoza to Search for Provisions

A FTER THE GOVERNOR UNDERSTOOD THE SITUATION WITH THE INDIAN CHIEFS OF PUERTO REYES, HE CALLED TOGETHER ALL THE LOCAL OFFI-cials, clerics, captains, and other persons of some experience to ask their counsel and opinions regarding what he should do. The people in the place were begging for a morsel to eat, the Governor had nothing to give them, and they were ready to scatter off into the interior to find something to devour.

With the officials and clerics assembled, he said, "You've seen the hard need and hunger here, very widespread, that our colonists are suffering. I must expect nothing less than wholesale death if the order is not given very soon to come up with some kind of remedy. I've been told that some Indians called the Arianicosies have provisions. Can you give me your opinion about what you think I should do?"

The assembly thought the Governor should send the greater part of the population to the Indian towns, as much to let them get something to eat right away and save themselves as to buy provisions. "Then the people we send out should bring back food to those who have remained behind with you in Puerto Reyes," they said. "And if the Indians do not want to part with any provisions that we pay for, we should take them by force. Furthermore, if the Indians try to resist these actions we should attack them until they give us what we need. Our need is enormous: everyone is dying of hunger, and we would snatch food off an altar if it came to that."

They issued this opinion signed with their names.

So it was agreed to send out Captain Mendoza to search for provisions, with these instructions:

"Captain Gonzalo de Mendoza, you're about to visit a number of towns in your search for supplies to sustain our people and keep them from dying of hunger. As you negotiate for rations, what you must do is pay the Socorinos and Sococies to their satisfaction. You must do the same with the other Indians in the surrounding territories and tell them on my behalf that I am amazed they have not yet come to see me as have all the other tribes of the area. Tell them I have heard that they are good people, and that's why I would like to see them and make them my friends. When they come, I'll have presents for them from my own possessions.

"They also need to come and declare their obedience to His Majesty, as all their neighbors have done. If they will do that, I will favor them and assist them against anyone who may be angry with them.

"You must exercise the greatest discretion and care with our friends, the Indians who accompany you in your task. You cannot allow them to enter the houses of the Indians you visit nor commit violence of any kind against them. They cannot mistreat them in any way. As you think about giving the people you visit trinkets or trade goods, or if they give you something, pay them until they are happy. That way, they'll have nothing to complain about.

"Once you arrive in their towns, ask the Indians to give you provisions out of their stores to feed your own people. Do offer to pay them; ply them with sweet words. If they aren't inclined to give you anything, ask them again, once, twice, or three times. Or more than that—however many times you believe you must. Keep on offering to pay them. If they still are not forthcoming, you must take what you need by force. And if they arm themselves for defense, by all means attack them. Our overwhelming hunger will suffer nothing else.

"Remember this: in everything that may happen in this endeavor you need to conduct yourself with the sort of moderation that suits our service to God and His Majesty.

"And so, I place my confidence in you as a servant of His Majesty."

CHAPTER SIXTY-EIGHT

The Governor Sends Captain Ribera
in a Brigantine to Explore the
River of the Xarayes

HE GOVERNOR HAD SENT OFF CAPTAIN GONZALO DE MENDOZA WITH HIS
INSTRUCTIONS. THE CAPTAIN ALSO CARRIED WITH HIM THE WRITTEN OPIN-
ion of the clerics, officials, and captains. He took along 120 Christians
and 600 Indian archers—a force that would have served for a much greater
purpose. He left on the fifteenth of December of that year.[1]

But the Indians of Puerto Reyes had also advised the Governor that
people could now go up the Río Igatu in brigantines to the country of
the Xarayes because the waters had started to rise. "Boats should be able
to sail well," they said, "and the Xarayes and the other people along the
banks of the river have a lot of provisions." At the same time, they noted
that there were other roiling tributaries pouring out of the interior that
came together in the Río Igatu, with large Indian towns along them, and
that these places also had an abundance of food supplies.[2]

Accordingly, the Governor dispatched Captain Hernando de Ribera
with fifty-two men in a launch to uncover the secrets of the river. He had
orders to go upriver to the towns of the Xarayes. "Confer with the chief of
the Xarayes and find out what lies up-country from him," said the Governor.
"Then explore it yourself; see it with your own eyes. Under no circumstances should you or any of your men go ashore, except for the interpreter
and two men. See if you can find the Indians along the river and set up treaties with them. Hand out presents and make peace with the people so that
when you come back you can give me a full account of their country."

To assist in this effort, the Governor included in addition to his instructions a large number of trinkets and trade goods. The Governor let Captain
Ribera know through his written and spoken comments everything that he

might accomplish by way of service to Your Majesty and for the good of the country.

And so the captain set sail on the twentieth of December of that year.

Captain Gonzalo de Mendoza wrote a letter to the Governor several days after he had left with his men to buy provisions. In it, he said that he had sent out an interpreter soon after he arrived in the country of the Arianicosies to let them know that he had come to ask them to sell him foodstuffs out of their stores. The captain proposed to pay the Indians to their hearts' content out of his stock of trade goods, including beads, knives, and wedges of iron (of which the captain had many), and he also intended to give them a lot of fishhooks.

The captain's interpreter carried these items along with him so that the Indians might see them. "We had no intention of deceiving them or doing them any harm, nor did we wish to take anything by force," said the captain in his letter.

The interpreter went off on his task but soon returned in full flight. "They came at him to kill him," said the captain. "They shot a lot of arrows at him."

"We don't want you Christians in our country," they said, "and we won't give you a single thing!"

They were about to kill everyone in the captain's party, and for that very purpose the Guaxarapo Indians had arrived as their allies. These latter Indians are quite brave. They've killed Christians before. "You Christians have tender heads," they said. "You're not tough fellows."

Captain Gonzalo de Mendoza sent the interpreter back to the Indians. "Ask them again for provisions," he said. "Tell them they must be forthcoming." With the interpreter he sent along a number of his Spaniards to observe the proceedings.

All these men had to flee from the Indians, too. "They all came out at us armed to the teeth," they told Mendoza. "Lots of arrows, and they were yelling at us to get out of their country. 'No provisions for you,' they shouted."

After that, Mendoza had pressed forward with all his men to talk to the Arianicocies and reassure them. But as he got close to their settlement, all the Indians of that country came out to fight him, firing off volleys of arrows and trying to kill our men without wanting to hear what they had to say or entertaining any of the captain's propositions. To defend themselves, the Spaniards had blown down a couple of the Indians with shots from their harquebuses, and seeing this, the others fled to the hills.

The Christians went into their houses, where they found no end of rations of corn and peanuts, as well as other vegetables and roots and things to eat. After this, Mendoza sent off one of these Arianicocies whom he had taken prisoner to tell the others to come back to their houses. "Tell them I promise to be their friend," he said. "Assure them of my intentions. I'll do them no harm at all, and I would like to reimburse them for the foodstuffs we took from their places after they fled."

They were having none of this. Rather the Indians returned to attack the Spaniards where they had pitched camp, and they set fire to their own houses. They burned a great part of their own settlement. Then they called on a large number of the neighboring tribes to join them in making war on our men. That was their reply to Mendoza. "We'll never stop doing all the damage we can to you," they said.

The Governor sent an order back to Captain Mendoza to work hard to get all the Indians to go back home. "I won't consent to your harming the Indians or waging war against them until you have paid them for all the provisions you took from them. Leave them in peace now and search for food somewhere else."

The captain wrote back that he had tried once more to talk to the Indians, reassure them, and urge them to return to their homes. "I'll treat you as friends," he had said, "and I'll do you no harm. I'll treat you well."

But they wouldn't hear of it. They returned again and again to attack Mendoza and do him all the mischief they could, and they had their allies with them. Other tribes, including the Guaxarapos and Guatos, who were enemies of ours, had by then joined forces with them.

CHAPTER SIXTY-NINE

Captain Francisco de Ribera
Returns from His Expedition

O N THE TWENTIETH OF JANUARY 1544, CAPTAIN FRANCISCO DE RIBERA
RETURNED WITH THE SIX SPANIARDS THE GOVERNOR HAD SENT WITH
him, as well as the guide he had taken along. He also brought back the
three Indians who were left of the eleven Guaranis the Governor had
sent with him. As I have said before, the Governor had dispatched this
entire party to explore—to see with their own eyes—the settlements lying
beyond the point from which he himself had earlier returned.

They had gone off down the road in search of Tapuaguazu, where the
guide was saying that the Indian settlements began for the whole region.

When Ribera arrived in Puerto Reyes with the six Christians, all
wounded, everyone in our company rejoiced and gave thanks to God that
they had escaped that perilous road.

Truth be told, the Governor had given them all up for lost, as eight
of the eleven Indians who had gone with Ribera and his party had earlier
come back. The Governor was enraged by this and much inclined to punish them. The chiefs who were their relatives implored him to order the
Indians hanged after they returned for abandoning the Christians, leaving
them behind; they had originally charged the eight with the job of accompanying Ribera's party and taking care of the Spaniards until they returned
to the chiefs' presence. The chiefs said, "They simply have not done this.
They deserve the gallows."

The Governor gave the men a reprimand instead, with a warning that
if they did it again he would punish them. As it was their first offense, he
pardoned them so as not to upset all the other Indians of their tribe.

CHAPTER SEVENTY

Captain Francisco de Ribera Gives an Account of His Exploration

T HE NEXT DAY, CAPTAIN FRANCISCO DE RIBERA APPEARED BEFORE THE GOVERNOR TO GIVE A REPORT ON HIS EXPLORATIONS. HE BROUGHT ALONG with him the six Spaniards who had gone along on his expedition. The captain said that after he left the Governor's party in the forest, he had marched along wherever the guide took him for some twenty-one days without stopping. They had traveled across a land full of thickets, with trees so dense you could not get through without dismounting and making a path for yourself. They only went a league on some days and on others, not even half a league, due to the thick brush and rock-strewn undergrowth of those woods. The only path they took was the way toward the setting sun.

The whole time they were gone they lived on deer and hogs and tapirs the Indians killed with their arrows.[1] There was so much game that they could kill everything they wanted to eat with sticks, and there was an infinite amount of honey in the hollows of the trees as well. There was wild fruit, too. All this food was certainly enough to sustain the men of the expedition.

After twenty-one days, they came to a river that flowed in a westerly direction.[2] The guide said this river went past Tapuaguazu and the settlements of the Indians. The men began to fish in it, and they pulled out a lot of fish that the Indians called *piraputanas*, which look like shad. They are excellent fish.

The men crossed the river, and going on as the guide directed they came across fresh Indian footprints. It had rained earlier, and the earth was wet. It looked as though the Indians had just gone by that day while hunting. Following the footprints, they went into some plots of corn that were starting to ripen. Not being able to hide himself, a lone Indian came out to see our men, and they could not understand his language. He had a big disc in his lower lip, made of silver, and some gold earrings. The Indian took Francisco de Ribera by the hand and by signs told the Spaniards to come along with him.

That's just what they did. They saw close by a big house made of wood and straw, and as they got nearer they noticed that the women and some other Indians were taking cotton clothes and other things out of the house and putting them into the garden plots out front. The man with the lip disc told Ribera's men to go in. The men and women inside were lifting up the straw walls of the house and throwing things outside, as they did not wish Ribera and our men to see what they were doing. There were some large earthen jars inside the house filled with corn, but Ribera saw the Indians pull a number of metal plates, small hatchets, and bracelets of silver out of the grain and throw them outside through the straw walls.

The man who seemed to be the chief in that house (from the respect the other Indians of the place showed him) took them inside and asked them by signs to sit down. The chief then told two big-eared Indians whom the others held as slaves to bring the guests something to drink out of two large vessels that were buried up to their necks right there in the ground, full of corn wine.[3] The two men ladled out the wine in some large, hollow calabashes and gave it to our men to drink.

Afterward, the two big-ears told Ribera that certain Christians might be found at three days' journey from that place, living with some Indians called the Payzunoes. After that, they showed Ribera Tapuaguazu, which is a large and very high boulder.

Just then, a lot of feathered and painted Indians began to arrive, armed to the teeth with many bows and arrows, ready for war, and the chief of the house started up a very animated conversation with them. The chief also took up his own bow and arrows, and he sent off and received Indians with a considerable number of messages. Our men suddenly understood that there had been a call to arms made to some people who had to be quite close and that these people were gathering to kill them.

Ribera said to the Christians who were with him that they should all leave the house together and retrace their steps back along the path that had brought them there before more Indians arrived. At that point more than three hundred Indians must have been mulling around the place, and Ribera let them know that he was about to call for the assistance of a lot of other Christians who were just down the way.[4] As the Spaniards prepared to leave, the Indians blocked their way. They had earlier left the longhouse out of fear of the Spaniards, and the Spaniards followed them out about a stone's throw behind the Indians, who were watching them.

With a great shout the Indians loosed a hail of arrows and chased the Spaniards until they reached the forest, where they were able to defend themselves. And the Indians, believing that more Spaniards lay in wait for them there, did not dare to go in after them. They let them escape. Everyone got away all right, but they were all wounded. They plunged down the same path that they had earlier blazed open—the one they had traveled for some twenty-one days since leaving the Governor's camp. This time it took them twelve days to arrive at Puerto Reyes.

It seemed to Captain Ribera that the distance from Puerto Reyes to the land of these hostile Indians must be about seventy leagues.

There was a lake twenty leagues from the port in which the water usually came up to your knees. It was just then rising and bursting with water, and it had expanded more than a league in the direction of the interior, from which Ribera's party had just come. Now it was more than two lance lengths deep, and Ribera's men had crossed this dangerous place on rafts only with great effort.

Anyone thinking about going to explore the interior by land would first have to wait for the water in this lake to go down.

Ribera said that these Indians were called the Tarapecocies and that they had a lot of supplies and goods of various sorts. They raised ducks and chickens much like ours in great quantity.

All this was what Francisco de Ribera and the Spaniards of his party who went out and came back with him reported. Ribera's guide chimed in along the same lines. Everyone in the party told the same tale as Ribera.

There were in Puerto Reyes just then some Indians of the Tarapecocies tribe, from the same area that Francisco de Ribera had just visited. These men had returned with Garcia the interpreter after he had visited the settlements of the interior, and they came back much the worse for wear thanks to his encounter with the Guaranis of the Río Paraguay. These Tarapecocies had escaped with the Chineses when they fled from the Guaranis' land, and both these tribes were now living together in Puerto Reyes.

The Governor wanted to find out more about these matters, so he summoned them. The Indians recognized some arrows Francisco de Ribera had in his possession; indeed, they were very glad to see them.

These had been fired at Ribera and his party during his expedition by the Tarapecocies Indians. "These came from our country," said the local Tarapecocies.

"Why in the world did your tribe want to kill the people we sent to find you and speak with you?" asked the Governor.

"Our tribe is no enemy of the Christians," they said. "We have been your friends since Garcia came to our country and contracted with us to be so."

The reason the Tarapecocies had wanted to kill the Spaniards lay with the Spaniards' bringing along the Guaranis as part of their company. "The Guaranis are our enemies," they said. In times past, the Guaranis had raided their country to sack it and kill the Tarapecocies. And then the Christians had arrived with no interpreter who could speak to and understand them. "We Tarapecocies need our visitors to tell us what their intentions may be," they said. "It's not our custom to make war on people who have done us no harm. If you will send along an interpreter, we will certainly treat him well and give him something to eat. We'll also share the gold and silver we have, which we get from the tribes in the interior."

"Which tribes might those be?" we asked. We wanted to know how they bartered for it and how it got into their hands.

"The Payzunoes," they said. These people lived three days' journey from the country of the Tarapecocies, and they traded gold and silver for bows, arrows, and slaves that the Tarapecocies had obtained from other tribes. The Payzunoes got the precious metals from the Chaneses, Chimenoes, Carcaraes, and Candirees, other tribes in the region, who have gold and silver in great quantity. Apparently the Tarapecocies barter for it, as mentioned earlier.

The Governor showed them a brass candleholder that was quite clean and polished. "Does the gold you have in your country look like this?" he asked.

"Well, the gold in your candleholder is hard and pretty vile," they said. "Our gold is soft and more yellow, and it doesn't smell bad."

The Indians then showed the Governor a gold ring, asking if it was like the rings in his country.

"Yes," said the Governor.

They showed him a tin plate, very clean and shiny, and asked if the silver in his country was like it.

The Governor replied that the silver in that plate reeked, that it was foul and soft, and that the silver of his country was lighter in color and harder and did not smell.

He produced a silver goblet, which pleased them very much, and they said that in their country there was a very great quantity of that metal in drinking vessels and other such stuff to be found in the houses of the Indians. They had plates of it, and bracelets, crowns, tomahawks, and other pieces made of it.

CHAPTER SEVENTY-ONE

The Governor Sends for Captain Gonzalo de Mendoza

THE GOVERNOR THEN SENT FOR GONZALO DE MENDOZA, ASKING HIM TO RETURN FROM THE COUNTRY OF THE ARIANICOSIES ALONG WITH HIS MEN. He wished to give Mendoza new orders and provide him with the necessities he needed to press forward with his exploration of the country, as that would best serve Your Majesty's interests. Before Mendoza came back, he was to return the Arianicosies to their houses and make peace with them.

Francisco de Ribera had already returned with the six Spaniards who had accompanied him on his own explorations of the country. All the people who were in Puerto Reyes had begun to fall ill of fever—so much so that there was no one to stand guard. And the Guaranis began to fall ill, too, and some of them were dying.

Gonzalo de Mendoza advised in a letter that all the men he had with him in the country of the Arianicosies were suffering from fever as well, and he sent them back to Puerto Reyes by brigantine, very ill and gaunt. Mendoza also said that he had been unable to conclude a peace with the Indians, although he and his men had repeated orders from the Governor to give the Indians no small number of trade goods and trinkets. The Indians showed up every day wanting to fight. It was a land of abundance, Mendoza said, as much evidenced in the countryside as in its waters. The Governor had left the men a large quantity of provisions for their sustenance, above and beyond those he had sent along in the brigantines. The cause of the illness that had befallen all Mendoza's men was the terrible water in that part of the country. As the rivers rose and crested, the water became very brackish and did them no end of harm.

In that same season, the Indians of an island that lay about a league from Puerto Reyes—Socorinos and Xaqueses by name—saw that the Christians were sick and drawn. So they began to make war on the

Spaniards. They stopped coming to the port to trade and barter as they had done previously, and they gave the Spaniards no more notice of the tribes who were speaking ill of them. This applied especially to the Guaxarapos, whom the island tribes joined and allowed into their territory in preparation for war.

The Guarani Indians who had come along in our armada liked to go out in their canoes to fish in the lake near Puerto Reyes. They and some Christians would venture on the water about a stone's throw from our camp. One morning after the sun had come up, five Christians had gone out, four of them really just boys of a tender age, with the Guaranis. As they went along in their canoes, a number of the Xaqueses and Socorinos and a lot of others from the island suddenly attacked them, capturing our five Christians. Putting them on the defensive, the island Indians killed some of the newly converted Guaranis and took many of the rest back to the island with them. There they killed them, tearing the five Christians and the Guaranis to pieces. They shared out the bits with the Guaxarapos and the Guatos, as well as with the other natives of a port town they called Old Man. They also did this with the other tribes they had gathered together to make war on the Spaniards. And after the pieces of flesh were passed out, they *ate* them, both on the island itself and in the other places where the tribes were gathered.

Not content with this, as they found their victims sick and skinny, they had the nerve to attack and try to set fire to the town where we were staying. They carried off a number of Christians, who all began to shout, "To arms! To arms! The Indians are killing the Christians!"

The whole town was armed, and we went out after them. But they got away with certain Christians nevertheless, among whom was a Pedro Mepen. The Indians also caught others who were on the lakeshore, and they killed some of our people who were out fishing. They ate up all these men just as they had eaten the first five.

Some time after the Indians had ambushed us, the sun came up. Right away we could see a very great number of canoes with many warriors fleeing across the lake, howling and threatening with their bows and arrows, holding them high to make sure we knew about their recent ambush.

And so, they ensconced themselves on the island that lies in the lake near Puerto Reyes, and they killed fifty-eight of our Christians that time.

With this fresh in his mind, the Governor spoke with the Indians of Puerto Reyes. "Ask the island Indians for the Christians and Guaranis that they've carried off," he said.

They left to do so, but when they came back they said that the island Indians had told them that the Guaxarapos had spirited all the captives away. "They don't have our people," they said.

After that, the Socorinos and Xaqueses would run the lake at night to see if they might catch some more Christians and Indians as they fished in it. They wanted to hinder anyone who might be fishing, saying the land was theirs and no Christians or outside Indians might fish there. "You must leave," they said, "and if you don't, we'll kill you."

The Governor sent word to them to quiet down and honor the peace he had already concluded with them. "Come back and bring along those Spaniards and Indians you carried off, and I'll consider you to be my friends," he said. "But if you don't want to do that, I'll proceed against you as my enemies."

Although he sent this message several times and made many entreaties, they didn't want to comply. They kept up all the mischief making and warring they could muster. The Governor finally saw that his approach gained him no advantage and gathered together his evidence against them. Having done so, he got the consent of Your Majesty's officials and the clerics to formally pronounce the island Indians enemies. This left him free to campaign against them, and he did so in order to secure the land from all the harm that they were causing every day.

CHAPTER SEVENTY-TWO

Hernando de Ribera Returns from His Exploration Along the River

O N JANUARY 30 OF THE YEAR 1543, CAPTAIN HERNANDO DE RIBERA RETURNED WITH THE SHIP AND ENTOURAGE THAT THE GOVERNOR HAD sent with him to explore upriver. And as the Governor found the captain and all his men very ill with chills and fevers when they came back, Ribera could give him no account of his discoveries.[1] In that season the river's waters had risen so much that they flooded—simply drowned—all the countryside.[2] This, of course, was the reason no one could go back and complete the exploration and discovery of those lands.

The Indians native to the place told us and swore to the fact that the high water lasted four months of the year and was so deep that it covered the land with five or six fathoms of water.[3] As I mentioned earlier, what they do is this: the locals go around in the wet season with their houses in their canoes looking for something to eat, with no chance of landing on dry ground.[4]

Throughout that country the natives follow their custom of killing and eating each other.

When the waters finally subside, they go back and rig up their houses where they were before the flooding began. The land, however, remains pestilential. The stench of the place with its great heat and all the dead fish rotting on its surface is difficult to bear.

CHAPTER SEVENTY-THREE

What Happened to the Governor and His People in Puerto Reyes

The Governor was in Puerto Reyes for three months, and all his men fell ill with fever and he with them. Everyone hoped the waters would recede and God would give them back their health, because only then could they undertake their expedition into the new territories and explore them thoroughly. But the sickness rose every day along with the waters, and it resulted in the Governor retiring his party from Puerto Reyes with enormous effort.

And after they had done us no end of harm, we took along with us mosquitoes of all kinds. They never let us sleep or rest, night or day. They were an intolerable torment to us, a worse sort of suffering than our fevers.

Considering all this, Your Majesty's officials had demanded that the Governor retire from Puerto Reyes downriver to the city of Asunción, where the men might convalesce. The Governor based his action on the opinions of our clerics and royal officials after they had looked into the problem, and he did indeed retire.

But the Governor did *not* consent to the Christians bringing along a nasty little business of some one hundred girls, whom the inhabitants of Puerto Reyes had given to our party when the Governor arrived in the place. The girls' fathers had offered them to various of our captains and other selected persons in order to butter us up. This was all done, of course, so that our men might do with the young women what they were accustomed to doing with the other young girls they already had. To avoid offending God with this sorry business, the Governor ordered their fathers to keep the girls in their houses until such time as our party returned.

The Governor did this just as our company was about to depart for Asunción so as not to offend the girls' fathers and leave the whole country in an uproar. To add a little more emphasis to the proceedings, the

Governor publicized an instruction from Your Majesty, which ordered that "no Spaniard should dare to take any Indian from his own land, on pain of grave penalties."

The Indians were quite happy with this, but the Spaniards were desperate and boiling with complaints. Some of the Governor's men wished him ill, and from that point on most of them detested him. And with this attitude and in that frame of mind, they did something I will relate in due course.

Once the people set off downriver, Christians and Indians alike, they and the Governor arrived back at the city of Asunción in twelve days. This same journey had taken the Governor two months when he had first made it in the opposite direction. Although our whole company was deathly ill, they found a little strength within their scrawny selves from the sheer desire to get home. And it was certainly no little effort to do this (to get back home, as I have noted), because they were so weak they couldn't take up arms to resist their enemies, nor take up an oar to row or guide the brigantines. And had it not been for the culverins we carried in the brigantines, our labors and the sheer danger of the place would have been all the worse.[1]

We traveled with the Indians' canoes in the middle of our ships so that we might keep them safe until the Indians could return to their own homes and lands. To make them safer yet, the Governor dispersed several Christians among these canoes, where they concealed themselves well as they guarded us from our enemies.

We passed through the territory of the Guaxarapos, who ambushed us in great numbers and with a lot of canoes. They came at us on rafts, too, which pulled right up next to us and showered us with darts. Several of these went straight through one Spaniard's chest and through the rest of him, too, and he fell down dead. His name was Miranda, and he was a native of Valladolid. The Guaxarapos also wounded some of our Indians, and if the culverins had not come to our aid our enemies would have done us much more harm.

All our people were just skin and bone because of this.

On the eighth of April of the aforementioned year, we arrived at the city of Asunción with our whole company and its ships and the Guarani Indians. And all of us, Indians, Spaniards, and Governor alike, were very drawn and sick.

The Governor met with Captain Salazar and found out that he had sent out a call for men throughout the territory. He had pulled together more than twenty thousand Indians and many canoes, and he had other people as well who were ready to go with him to search out, kill, and utterly destroy the Agaces Indians.[2]

The fact was that the Agaces had never ceased warring against the Christians who had remained behind in Asunción after the Governor had left on his expedition—and against the local natives of the place, too, robbing and killing them and making off with their women and children. The Agaces assaulted people throughout the countryside, burning towns and generally committing mayhem and other outrages everywhere.

The Governor put a stop to all this after he arrived.

We also found the caravel the Governor had ordered to be built, which was almost done. We knew that if we finished this ship, we could give Your Majesty an account of everything that had happened in this new country, from our first entry to all the later events. Accordingly, the Governor ordered the caravel to be completed.

CHAPTER SEVENTY-FOUR

The Governor and His Men Arrive in Asunción, and He Is Thrown into Chains

THE GOVERNOR HAD BEEN BACK IN ASUNCIÓN FOR A FORTNIGHT. YOUR MAJESTY'S OFFICIALS HAD HELD THE GOVERNOR IN CONTEMPT for some time due to several causes already mentioned. He never approved of their disservice—and that is certainly what it was—to God and Your Majesty or of their stripping the best port in the province of its population, with the clear aim of raising a general revolt in the country (a condition in which it currently finds itself).[1]

These men saw how he and all the Christians he had brought with him were at death's door. They met on St. Mark's Day and allied themselves with some of their other friends, and they decided that night to take the Governor prisoner.[2] To do this a little more easily, they said to a hundred men, "The Governor wants to take your estates and houses and your Indian women and give them to his dissolute followers. He wants to share all this out among the men just returned from his expedition.

"It's a gross injustice," they said to these men, "and quite contrary to the service of His Majesty. As his officials, we'll go to the Governor this very night to require, in His Majesty's name, that he not divest you of your houses or plantations or Indian women."

The officials were afraid the Governor would order them arrested, so they thought it necessary to go armed and with their friends. And so they prepared themselves accordingly and got ready to make the demands that would prove to be such a great benefit to them and, to their way of thinking, such a great service to Your Majesty.

At the hour of the Ave María, they told their men to appear with their weapons at two houses they had pointed out.[3] Here they were supposed to stay until the officials told them what they had to do. At last, ten or twelve of them entered the room where the Governor was lying gravely ill. They shouted, "Liberty, liberty—long live the king!"

These men consisted of the inspector, Alonso Cabrera; the comptroller, Felipe de Cáceres; the deputy treasurer, Garci-Vanegas; and one of the Governor's servants named Pedro de Oñate.[4] Oñate was already in the chamber, and he got the others inside, opening the door and acting as a principal in the whole business. Don Francisco de Mendoza and Jaime Rasquín were also a part of this, and Rasquín held a crossbow loaded with a poisoned dart against the Governor's chest. Diego de Acosta, the Portuguese interpreter, and one Solórzano, a native of Gran Canaria, were other members of the party. They all came in to take the Governor prisoner by force of arms, and they seized him in his nightshirt, shouting, "Liberty! Liberty!" They called him a tyrant, shoving their crossbows against his chest, and saying these and other words: "You'll pay here and now for all the abuse and damage you've caused us."

Once they were outside, they ran into the other men they had brought along, who were waiting for them. These men, seeing how the conspirators had taken the Governor prisoner in such a rough way, said to the factor, Pedro Dorantes, and the others, "Listen, blast you, you wanted us along with these traitors of yours so that we could be witnesses to what you were doing. You were going to tell the Governor not to take our estates and houses and Indian women. But you didn't ask him to stop: you just took him prisoner. Now you want to make *us* traitors against the king by seizing his Governor!"

And they reached for their swords. It was quite an uproar, and all because of those conspirators who took the Governor prisoner. They were all close to the houses of the officials, and so some of them darted inside Garci-Vanegas's houses with the Governor. A number of the others stood at the door shouting at them that they had been deceived. "Don't tell us you didn't know what you were doing!" they yelled from inside. "You should be helping us keep him prisoner." The ones inside let the others know this: "If we release him now, he'll draw and quarter the lot of us and cut off all our heads. We've all risked our lives by doing what we've done, and you need to help us carry this business forward.

"Besides," said the miscreants, "we'll split his estate and Indian women and clothes with you."

The officials went into the place where they had put the Governor (which was a pretty small room), shackled him, and set a guard. Once this was done, they went to the house of Juan Pavón, the mayor, and then to the house of Francisco de Peralta, the sheriff. In both places, the Biscayan Martín de Ure stepped out in front of the rebels and ripped the staff of office out of the hands of these lawful officers. The conspirators took them prisoner—pummeling them, shoving them, and calling them traitors. Martín de Ure and his henchmen then took the mayor and the sheriff to the public jail and put their heads in the stocks. They let all the current prisoners *out* of the stocks, and among these was a man who had been condemned to death for murdering one Morales, a nobleman from Seville.

Then they grabbed a drum and paraded down the streets, raising a ruckus and unsettling the public. They yelled, very loudly, "Liberty! Liberty! Long live the king!" And after they had made a round through the entire town, these same men went to the house of Pedro Hernández, the secretary of the province (who was quite ill at the time), and took him prisoner.[5] They also seized Bartolomé González.[6] They seized Hernández's estate and all his writings, too. Then they took Hernández along as a prisoner to the house of Domingo de Irala, where they outfitted him with *two* pairs of shackles. After they had hurled a number of insults and provocations at Hernández, they set guards to watch him.

Then they announced this: "The officials of His Majesty order that no one should dare to venture out on the street. People should stay in their homes, on pain of death and being declared traitors."

Having said that, they went back to shouting "Liberty! Liberty!" as they had done earlier. They went out proclaiming this up and down the streets, and when they bumped into people they shoved them, struck them on the back, and forced them back into their houses. They did a lot of that.

Once they were done with this, the officials went to the houses where the Governor lived and had his estate, his writings, and all the governmental dispatches sent to him by the king concerning the administration of the country. That was also where the Governor kept his writs of acceptance, which stated that the Spaniards of the province had welcomed and acknowledged him as governor and captain-general serving in the name of Your Majesty. They opened up some chests, taking all the papers that were in them. They took possession of all these documents and the chests as well. And they opened one strongbox in particular that was locked up with three keys; inside were the drafts of the proposed proceedings against the officials, detailing the crimes they had committed, which already had been sent to Your Majesty.

Then they took all the Governor's wealth—his clothes, his stocks of wine and oil, his supplies of iron and steel, and a lot of other things. Most of these items simply disappeared, everything looted. "Tyrant!" they said, walking around. "Tyrant!" That, among other names.

And what they left of the Governor's estate they put under the control of whoever was a friend of theirs, their followers, under pretext of "depositing" these items. These men were just toadies who had been helping them.

They say the Governor's estate was worth more than a hundred thousand castellanos in the prices then current in the province, and it had taken him ten brigantines to bring it all in.[7]

CHAPTER SEVENTY-FIVE

The People Gather in Front of Domingo de Irala's House

O N THE MORNING OF THE FOLLOWING DAY, THE OFFICIALS MARCHED
THROUGH THE STREETS WITH A DRUM ANNOUNCING THAT ALL CITIZENS
must meet in front of the houses of Captain Domingo de Irala. And with
Irala's friends and flunkies gathered together in that spot, all carrying their
arms, a crier backed by these people read out a scurrilous libel at the top of
his lungs. Among other things, they said the Governor had ordered that all
the citizens' estates be taken from them and that they themselves should
be taken as slaves. Irala and his men had therefore seized the Governor in
the interest of protecting everyone's liberty.

Having read out this libelous statement, they said, "Say it, gentlemen:
'Liberty, liberty!' Long live the king!"

And the crowd bellowed that out.

After doing this, people became quite angry with the Governor, and
many of them said, "Blast him, let's kill this tyrant! He certainly wanted
to destroy us. He wanted to kill us!"

But after some time, their anger and the general furor died down a little.

The officials then nominated Domingo de Irala to be lieutenant governor and captain general of the province.[1] This man was to be governor
once again instead of Francisco Ruiz, who had been lieutenant governor
of the country under don Pedro de Mendoza. The truth was that Ruiz had
been a good lieutenant and a good governor; he was deposed through spite
and malice exercised against everything that is right, and that confounded
Domingo de Irala was named as lieutenant governor in his place.

Someone then told Alonso Cabrera, the king's inspector, that he had
done Ruiz wrong, as our Francisco Ruiz had settled that country and kept
the place going with so much effort. "And now you've taken it away from
him," the man said.

Cabrera said, "Why don't you care to do what I want?"

Domingo de Irala was the most worthless of men. He would always do whatever Cabrera and the other officials told him to, and that's why they had nominated him to his position in the first place.

And so they installed Domingo de Irala in office, and one Pedro Díaz del Valle, a friend of his, was named mayor. The constables' staffs were given to one Bartolomé de la Marilla, a native of Trujillo and friend of Nunfro de Chaves, and to one Sancho de Salinas, a native of Cazalla. Then Domingo de Irala and his officials began to make public the idea that they wished to once again send an expedition into the same lands that the Governor had already explored, with the intent of searching for silver and gold. Finding it, they would send it on to Your Majesty in hope of a pardon: they believed that if they did this Your Majesty would *have* to forgive the crime they had committed. They also intended to stay in the interior and live there if they found no riches, as they didn't want to return and be punished for their misdeeds.

They believed as well that there was a chance they would find so much wealth that the king would give them a grant of land.

They went among the people with this scheme, trying to win them over. But everyone was catching on to their knavish iniquities, which were still occurring, and no one wanted to agree with the idea of the expedition.

And from that time forward the greater part of the public began to protest and clamor for the release of the Governor. The officials and the justices put in place by the officials began to harass the people who appeared, somber, at the prison, throwing them into jail, too, confiscating their estates and provisions, and wearing them out with other mistreatments.

Not wanting to be arrested, some citizens fled to the churches seeking sanctuary, and the officials placed guards around these places to keep food from getting in and made the people suffer in other ways. They shot off their guns at several people and dragged them in after putting the dogs on them and running them down. And they announced in public that they would have to destroy those who continued to show up looking grim in front of the prison.

CHAPTER SEVENTY-SIX

Turbulence and Uproar
Abound in the Land

THERE THEN BEGAN A GENERAL UPROAR AND SCANDAL AMONG THE CITIZENS, AS THOSE WHO STOOD PUBLICLY FOR YOUR MAJESTY TOLD THE OFFICIALS and their minions that they were all traitors. Day and night, these men went about with their arms in their hands, because they were frightened by the people rising up against them anew each morning. They made themselves stronger every day with the new palisades and other bulwarks they built for their defense, as if the Governor were held prisoner in Salsas.[1] They barricaded the streets and formed a defensive circle of five or six houses.

The Governor was in the tiny chamber in the Garci-Vanegas house where they had thrown him. They did this to keep him right in their midst. And every day their new mayor and constables were in the habit of nosing around the houses that surrounded the place where the Governor was held to see if they could find any freshly turned earth, which would mean tunneling in progress.

Whenever these officials saw two or three men who were partial to the Governor talking to each other, they hollered, "To arms! To arms!" And then, armed to the teeth, they would enter the place where the Governor was, put their hands on their daggers, and say, "I swear to God that if the citizens try to get in here and remove you from our grasp, we'll simply stab you, cut your head off, and throw it to them. That'll make them happy!"

To this end, the officials named four men with their four sharp daggers—those they thought were the bravest of the lot—to stand the first watch. They extracted a pledge from them that if the loyal citizens of Your Majesty came to rescue the Governor, they would rush inside the cell and cut off his head. And they honed their daggers to get ready for this eventuality and honor their oath.

Now, they did all this where the Governor could see what they were up to and hear them talking. The men who carried out these actions were Garci-Vanegas and Andrés "Flatnose" Hernández, as well as several others.[2]

In addition to all the turbulence and turmoil swirling outside the site of the Governor's incarceration, there was a lot of hotheadedness and quarreling among the cliques of the conspirators themselves. Some said the officials and their friends had been traitors and had committed a great evil when they imprisoned the Governor. They said, "We Spaniards might lose the whole country over this" (as it seemed might happen at first and each day seemed more likely). Others defended quite the opposite point of view.

Many Spaniards were maimed, wounded, and killed arguing about these matters.

Our officials and their minions said, "Those who favor the Governor and wish him his freedom are traitors and will have to be punished as such." They would not allow anyone they had arrested and held as a suspicious character to speak with anyone else detained for the same reason. If they saw two men talking to each other on the street, they would detain them and investigate. They would keep this up until they discovered what the men had been talking about. If they caught three or four men talking together, they picked up their weapons and got ready to fight.

They positioned a couple of sentinels inside two watchtowers on the roof of the house where the Governor was incarcerated. These places overlooked the entire town and the countryside beyond. What's more, they sent out some men to spy around town, watch people, and listen to what everyone was saying and doing. Thirty of their armed fellows went about at night, and they stopped all the people they bumped into, took them prisoner, and tried to find out where they were going and for what purpose.

But there was a tremendous uproar and commotion every day, and the officials and their flunkies began to get tired and worn out. So they went to see the Governor and plead with him to issue an order to the citizens telling them to calm down and not move abroad in the town. "We'll suffer a bit of embarrassment over this business, if need be," they said. They brought along the papers for this action all done up and ready, so that the Governor might sign them if he were inclined to do this for them.

But after he had done just that they didn't want to notify the citizenry, because people had earlier advised them not to do what they did. They had been pretending, walking around saying that everyone had wanted them to take the Governor prisoner. So they never sent out the Governor's notice.

CHAPTER SEVENTY-SEVEN

The Governor Is Held Prisoner in a Very Harsh Jail

A T THE TIME THESE THINGS HAPPENED, THE GOVERNOR WAS ILL IN BED AND VERY THIN. AND AS PART OF THE CURE FOR HIS HEALTH, HE HAD SOME very good shackles on his feet.

There was a lit candle on his headboard. You see, the prison was so dark that you could never view the sky and so humid that green plant life grew beneath the bed. He kept the candle close because he thought he might need it at any moment.

If you were to imagine bringing about the Governor's demise, you might search through all the people in the town for the man who most wished him ill. You would then find one Hernando de Sosa, whom the Governor had once punished for slapping an Indian chief and afterward beating him with sticks. They placed this man in the Governor's chamber as a guard who would keep a close eye on him.

The place had two doors with padlocks to keep him in. The officials and their flunkies and henchmen with all their many weapons (amounting to more than 150 of various kinds) guarded the Governor here day and night, and they were paid for their troubles out of the Governor's assets.

Even with all these guards, every night, or every third night, the Indian woman who brought him his supper handed him a letter from people on the outside. Through her, his friends let him know what was going on, and they asked the Governor to tell them what he wished them to do. Three quarters of his friends were determined to do in all the rebels with the help of the Indians, who would also assist in freeing him. They hadn't done this yet because they were afraid that if they attacked, the rebels would stab him and cut off his head. In addition, they also told him that more than seventy men who were members of the prison guard were conspiring with them to raise the main gate of the prison. These men would seize the Governor and protect him until his friends could get in.

The Governor implored them not to follow through with this plan. He thought it couldn't be done cleanly. A lot of Christians would die, and he knew that once it started, the Indians would finish off as many people as they could. The upshot would simply be the loss of the whole country and the lives of everyone in it. For all these reasons, the Governor asked his friends not to do it.

Well, I mentioned the Indian woman who took a letter to the Governor every third night. She took him yet another, passing in front of the guards. They made her strip down, checking her mouth and her ears and shearing off her hair to make sure she had nothing hidden in it. I can't even say out of propriety the sort of shameful examination they actually performed.

So, the Indian woman went along in front of everyone absolutely naked till she came to the Governor. She gave everything she carried to the guards and sat down next to the Governor on his bed. (It was a small room.)

She started to scratch her foot. Then she peeled a letter off her sole and, placing one foot in front of the other, slipped it to him. She had carried along this letter (which was half a sheet of very thin paper) subtly, very tightly rolled up and coated with a little black wax. She placed it in the little hollow just under her toes—actually, under her big toe—and tied it in place with two tiny black cotton threads. In this way, she had brought along and handed over all the letters and paper needed for her business, as well as some rock powders you find in that country that will make ink when mixed with a little saliva or water.

The officials and their flunkies either suspected or were advised that the Governor knew what was going on outside his cell and what they were up to. To find out for sure, they sought out four youngsters from among their ranks to seduce the Indian woman, which didn't call for much effort. That was because by custom the Indian women are not too shy about their bodies. They take it as a great offense to deny anyone something that is asked. They say, why were they given bodies if not for that purpose?

But the boys, intimately involved with our Indian woman and showering her with gifts, were never able to wring any secrets out of her. And all this through an intimacy and its conversations lasting some eleven months.

CHAPTER SEVENTY-EIGHT

The Insurgents Plunder the Land and Take Its Estates by Force

T HE GOVERNOR WAS NOW IN CHAINS.

AND AS SOON AS HE HAD BEEN TAKEN PRISONER, DOMINGO DE IRALA and his officials had openly allowed all their friends and toadies and servants to run amok through all the towns and homesteads of the Indians, where they took women and young girls and hammocks and everything else the people had by force and without any kind of payment. This was the sort of thing that lent very little to the service of Your Majesty and the pacification of the country.

And carrying on like this, these men went around the whole countryside beating people with sticks. Then they carried them off forcibly to work their estates and paid them nothing. So of course the Indians came to Asunción to complain to Domingo de Irala and his officials.

They said, "We've had no part in this business."

That satisfied some of the Christians, because they knew that Irala had only said this to placate the Indians. By saying such things the Indians would continue to help the Spaniards and be friendly to them.

To the Christians, Irala and his ilk also declared, "You're now at liberty to do whatever you please."

Well, the outcome of all these poor answers and mistreatments was the depopulation of the country. The natives went off to live in the mountains, where they could hide and the Christians would never be able to find them. Many of the Indians and their wives and children were themselves Christians, and going off as they did, they lost the teaching of their clerics—something the Governor had so carefully nourished.

Then, only a few days after the insurgents had taken the Governor prisoner, they destroyed the caravel he had ordered built to advise Your Majesty of the progress of the province. They thought that by doing so they might attract the men needed to continue the exploration of new lands begun earlier by the Governor; of course, they would also extract a little silver and gold from these places in the process. In addition, they believed Your Majesty would give them credit for the honor they had gained and the service they had provided on your behalf.

Well, the country was in a lawless state, and her citizens and settlers suffered an endless string of abuses. The officials and their idea of "justice" had people in their grip. They jailed Spaniards and took their haciendas.

More than fifty of these settlers, appalled by all this and very unhappy indeed, went off through the interior toward the coast of Brazil, looking for some means to leave the continent and advise Your Majesty of all the tremendous damage and disruption and wrongs they had suffered in that province.[1]

Many other settlers were forced to lose themselves in the interior, and quite often they arrested these people and took them prisoner. The insurgents took away their arms and whatever they had in the way of possessions, and they shared out all this booty among their friends and flunkies to gain their gratitude and make them happy.

CHAPTER SEVENTY-NINE

The Friars Flee Again

I N THOSE DAYS EVERYTHING WAS HARSH, REVOLTING, AND BADLY SORTED
OUT, SO OF COURSE IT SEEMED, AS FRAY BERNALDO DE ARMENTA SAID TO
his friars, that it was a good time—indeed, the perfect season—to put
into effect their standing proposal to leave (as they had earlier intended
to do). They mentioned this to the officials and to Domingo de Irala in
order to gain his favor and help as they set out for the coast of Brazil. And
these men, just to make the friars happy, and in light of the fact that they
were, after all, opposed to the Governor because he had stood in their way
before, gave the clerics license to proceed and helped them. "Let them go
to the coast of Brazil," the officials said.

To help in this effort, the friars took along with them six Spaniards
and several of the Indian girls they had been instructing in the faith.

The Governor, meanwhile, was in prison. He told the insurgents several times that they should give him the opportunity to designate a lieutenant governor who in Your Majesty's name might restore peace and justice
throughout the land, as the place was daily wracked by riots and all sorts
of ills and discontent perpetrated by the rebels. "After I've named such a
man, you may be assured that I will present myself before His Majesty to
give an account of everything that's happened, past and present," he said.

The officials responded by saying that as soon as he had been arrested
he had lost any authority he may have had. They said he might not have
any recourse to his former powers. "The man we've put in charge will
suffice," they said.

They came to see the Governor in his cell every day, threatening to
stab him with their daggers and cut off his head. He said to them, "When
you finally decide to do it, in God's name and in the name of His Majesty,
send me a friar or a priest to hear my confession."

To this they replied that if they sent in a confessor, it would be
Francisco de Andrada or another Biscayan, clerics who were the principal

religious figures of the community. "If you don't want to confess to one of these fellows, we are under no obligation to send you anyone else." They took all the rest of our clerics, you see, to be their enemies and good friends of the Governor.

And so, they had taken prisoner Antón de Escalera, Rodrigo de Herrera, and Luis de Miranda, all clerics who said that the insurgents had done a great wrong, something very contrary to the service of God and Your Majesty, and that it was a tremendous outrage to the whole country to take the Governor prisoner. Father Luis de Miranda had been locked up with the mayor more than eight months without a glimpse of the sun or moon and with the guards watching them continuously.

The insurgents never wanted, nor did they consent to, any clerics coming in to confess the Governor except for the men mentioned above.

Then, a certain Antón Bravo, a young nobleman of eighteen, said one fine day that he would produce a form stating that the Governor should be set free from prison. Domingo de Irala and the royal officials promptly seized and tortured Bravo. And seeing that they had a chance to sting and punish other people whom they hated, they told Bravo they would release him if he would only implicate all the fellows he had mentioned in the confession they'd wrenched out of him.

And so Irala and his minions arrested the men Bravo named and disarmed them. Then they gave Antón Bravo one hundred lashes publicly, in the streets, calling him a traitor, and saying that he had betrayed Your Majesty simply because he had wanted to release the Governor from his prison.

CHAPTER EIGHTY

How They Put Everyone Not of Their Opinion on the Rack

T O FURTHER THEIR CAUSE, THEY CRUELLY TORTURED MANY OTHER PERSONS TO FIND OUT IF THEY HAD BEEN GIVEN ORDERS AND THEN CONSPIRED among themselves to free the Governor from prison. Who were these people, and in what way had they been plotting? Had they been mining away under the prison?

Quite a few people were maimed or crippled in arm and leg from these sessions on the rack.

In certain sections of the town, people wrote on the walls, *By your king and your law you will die.*[1] Domingo de Irala and his officials and constables asked about to discover who had written this, swearing and threatening that if they found out who was scribbling the words they would surely punish him.

And so they did indeed take a lot of people prisoner, and put them on the rack.

CHAPTER EIGHTY-ONE

They Want to Kill an Alderman Because of the Request He Made of Them

WELL, WITH EVERYTHING IN THE STATE OF AFFAIRS I'VE DESCRIBED, ONE PEDRO DE MOLINA, A NATIVE OF GUADIX AND AN ALDERMAN OF THAT city, was observing all the destruction, rioting, and commotion going on. Out of service to Your Majesty, he determined to enter the stockade where Domingo de Irala and all the officials were staying. In the presence of these people, he doffed his cap and said to Martín de Ure, the notary who was present, that he should read to the officials Molina's demand that all the evildoing and killing and rampaging then abroad in the land due to the jailing of the Governor must cease. "Set the Governor free," he said to these people, "because by doing so all this uproar will stop. And if you don't wish to free the Governor, you must allow him to choose someone to govern the province peacefully and with justice in the name of His Majesty."

He gave this demand to the notary, who with all eyes watching him refused to accept it. De Ure finally did take it and then turned to Pedro de Molina and said, "If you want me to read it out loud, you'll have to pay me my fees."

At this Molina pulled his sword out of his buckler and gave it to de Ure. But the scribe didn't want it, saying he never took swords for security.

So Molina took off his hooded riding cape and gave it to him, saying, "Read it, as I have nothing else to offer you as security."

So this confounded Martín de Ure took the cape and the written demand and dumped them both on the ground at his feet. "I have no wish to impart anything at all to these gentlemen," he said.

At this the deputy treasurer, Garci-Vanegas, leapt up and said a lot of insulting and shameful words to Pedro de Molina, threatening to beat him to death with truncheons. "That's just what you deserve, Molina," he said, "for what you've had the nerve to say."

Well, with that Pedro de Molina left, once again taking off his cap to them (and it wasn't an easy thing to take your leave of that lot without them doing you a great deal of harm).

CHAPTER EIGHTY-TWO

The Insurgents Allow the Indians to Eat Human Flesh

To INGRATIATE THEMSELVES WITH THE NATIVE INDIANS OF THE LAND, DOMINGO DE IRALA AND THE OFFICIALS GAVE THEM LICENSE TO SLAUGHTER and eat their enemies. Many of the people who were given such liberties were recent Christian converts, and Irala told them that they need not flee the country should they do such things and that he and his friends would actually help them.

This is something contradictory to the service of God and Your Majesty and utterly appalling to anyone who might hear of it.

And of course Irala and his henchmen said more to the Indians. They said that the Governor was a bad man, and because of that he would never approve of them killing and eating their enemies. That was why Irala and his minions had made a prisoner of the Governor. Now that they were in charge, the Indians were free to do whatever they might wish.

Well, Domingo de Irala and his ilk were soon to see that despite everything they could do and had done, the rioting and public commotion continued. It just grew worse every day. The insurgents agreed among themselves to spirit the Governor from the province. Of course, these same men wished to stay in that country and not return to Spain. So they planned to content themselves with ejecting the Governor and some of his friends.

As this became known to people who favored the Governor, it turned into quite an uproar. Irala's henchmen had let it be known that they had the Governor in their hands and they would return with him to Spain in order to be there when he gave an account of himself to Your Majesty. And the people who favored the Governor said, "You've taken the Governor prisoner. Now you yourselves will indeed have to go, although you may not wish to do so, to give an account of what you've done." So they agreed that two of the officials would travel along with the Governor and two would stay in that country.

To take him away, they produced one of the brigantines the Governor had made for the exploration and conquest of the province. There was a great uproar and a number of altercations over this, as the citizens were very disturbed to see the Governor leave the country.

The officials decided to seize the perpetrators of all these disturbances —especially any figure people followed with particular interest. Everyone knew this, and so people went about their business with a sharp eye out, and no one dared detain them. Many citizens got together through the intercession of the Governor, as the officials had pled with him to restore order and command people to stop their agitations. The insurgents wanted him to get the citizens to pledge their good faith, give their word, and promise not to free him from prison. The officials and the constabulary they had put in place would not arrest anyone nor cause any aggravation, they said. "We'll release everyone we've taken prisoner," swore the officials, and they promised to do just that.

Because they had been holding the Governor prisoner and no one had seen him for quite some time, his supporters suspected and feared he had been secretly killed. So the insurgents said they would let two clerics and two gentlemen into the prison where the Governor was kept to see him and verify that he was alive and then tell everyone as much.

The officials promised to comply with this request two or three days before the brigantine was to sail, but they never did so.

CHAPTER EIGHTY-THREE

They Write to Your Majesty and Send on Their Account

WHEN ALL THIS BUSINESS CAME ABOUT, THE OFFICIALS DICTATED A NUMBER OF MINUTES AGAINST THE GOVERNOR TO BE DELIVERED TO THESE kingdoms, accusations that would condemn him in anyone's eyes.[1] And that's exactly what they wrote up. And just to give a certain flavor to their crimes, they wrote about events that had never happened and weren't true.

When the brigantine that would take the Governor back to Spain was being recaulked and outfitted, the shipwrights and their friends hollowed out a piece of wood as thick as your thigh in secret. It was three palms' wide, and inside it they placed the general case of evidence prepared by the Governor to send along to Your Majesty, as well as several other papers smuggled away by the Governor's loyal friends after he had been arrested. They were all important to him. So the shipwrights encased these papers tightly in wax and put them inside the timber, which they then secured in the stern of the brigantine with six nails top and bottom.

"We're putting this timber in to fortify the brigantine," said the carpenters, and they kept their secret so well that no one was the wiser. But the main carpenter did let a sailor in on all this, so that upon arrival in the Promised Land he would know what to do.

Irala and his men had earlier agreed that witnesses would be able to see the Governor before he was shipped off. But neither Captain Salazar nor anyone else was actually allowed to see him. One night, around midnight, they showed up at the jail with a lot of harquebuses. Each of their harquebusiers held three firing wicks or fuses between his fingers, just to make a good show, and the inspector, Alonso Cabrera, and the commissioner, Pedro Dorantes, went into the cell where the Governor was held. They grabbed him by the arms and lifted him up off his bed by his shackles, as he was in a very bad way, practically dying, and they hauled him along to the door that opened onto the street. There he saw the stars up in the sky (which he had not seen for many months) and begged them to let him give thanks to God. He went down on his knees, and when he got up, two muscular soldiers brought along by Cabrera and Dorantes carried him off forcibly (as he was gaunt and quite beaten up) toward the docks.

As they were going along, the Governor found himself among a number of people, and he said, "Gentlemen, you are my witnesses that I leave as my lieutenant Captain Juan de Salazar de Espinosa. He will serve the causes of peace and justice in this country in my name and in the name of Our Majesty until such time as Our Majesty declares what may best suit his purposes."

As soon as the Governor uttered these words, Garci-Vanegas, the deputy treasurer, attacked him with dagger in hand and said, "None of that nonsense. You won't be able to lie to the king if I cut your heart out."

Well, after this the Governor had certainly been warned not to talk, and at that point the rebels were quite determined to kill him. Everything he said made them and everyone who had conspired with them in Your Majesty's name to deliver the Governor into their hands look bad. And all the citizens were now in the streets.

Garci-Vanegas withdrew a little distance, and the Governor said the same things one more time. So Garci-Vanegas attacked him again furiously, sticking the point of his dagger against the Governor's temple and hissing, as before, "No more nonsense, if you don't want me to stick you a few good ones!" Then he nicked the Governor's temple and gave him and the men carrying him such a shove that they toppled over onto the ground. One of them lost his cap.

Seeing this happen, the soldiers carried the Governor off quickly to the brigantine, where they used some planks to shut him up in the stern. They trussed him up so tightly with a couple of padlocks that he couldn't even turn and then set off into the open water to sail downstream.

Some two days after the Governor had sailed away, Domingo de Irala, the comptroller, Felipe de Cáceres, and the commissioner, Pedro Dorantes, got together with their friends and raided the house of Captain Salazar, where they arrested him and Pedro de Estopiñán Cabeza de Vaca. They put them in chains, threw them on another brigantine, and sent them off downriver until they ran into the launch that held the Governor. And they were brought along with the Governor as prisoners to Castile.

It is certainly true that if Captain Salazar had earlier expressed his wishes, the Governor would never have been taken prisoner—not to mention been removed from the province or taken to Castile. But Salazar had been appointed lieutenant governor, and he let things go by. Catching up to the Governor's launch, he begged the officials to let him take along a couple of his servants so they could tend to him along the way and prepare his meals.

So they allowed Salazar two servants, not to serve him but to row the little ship four hundred leagues downstream. Of course, they couldn't really find anyone who wanted to come along under such conditions, so they seized a few men and took them along by force. Others fled into the interior.

The officials seized their lands and possessions, which they gave to the men who took them by force. And along the way they did another very bad thing: for some four days after they took Captain Salazar prisoner, they went around telling their own partisans and a number of their other friends a thousand terrible things about the Governor. Then they said, "Well, what do you think? Have we done a few things with your welfare in mind? Have we served His Majesty's cause? If you think so, and if you love me, would you mind signing your name at the end of our paper here?"[2]

That's how they filled up four quires of paper.[3] As they sailed downstream, they said aloud and then wrote out all these calumnies against the Governor, and the people who signed the papers remained some three hundred leagues upriver in the city of Asunción.

And that's what the evidence that they sent off against the Governor was like.

CHAPTER EIGHTY-FOUR

The Governor Is Poisoned Three Times with Arsenic While He Is on the Road

WHILE EN ROUTE DOWNRIVER, THE OFFICIALS ORDERED ONE MACHÍN, A BISCAYAN, TO COOK UP SOMETHING TO EAT FOR THE GOVERNOR. AND after cooking some food, Machín handed it over to one Lope Duarte. These men were both cronies of the officials and of Domingo de Irala and as guilty as all the others who had taken the Governor prisoner. Duarte had come along as Irala's solicitor and to carry out his business on the ship, and in front of the guards and with their blessing he slipped arsenic to the Governor three times.[1] Well, the Governor carried along with him a bottle of oil and a piece of the horn of a unicorn, and whenever he sensed he had been poisoned he used these remedies, day and night.[2] It was a very difficult business, involving tremendous vomiting, and it pleased God that he came out of it all right.

A day or so later, the Governor asked Alonso Cabrera and Garci-Vanegas, the officials who were transporting him, to allow his own servants to prepare food for him, as he would accept food from the hand of no one else. "You'll eat and drink from the hand of anyone you're given," they said to him. "Nobody's going to give us orders, and it makes no difference to us if you live or die."

And so the Governor went several days without eating anything, until necessity constrained him to comply with what they wanted. They had promised to take a number of people to Spain in the caravel that they earlier had destroyed, as these same people had approved of the Governor being clapped in irons and were not against the rebels. They had made these promises especially to one Francisco de Paredes of Burgos and to fray Juan de Salazar, a friar of the order of Our Lady of Mercy.

The insurgents were also carrying along as prisoners Luis de Miranda, Pedro Hernández, Captain Salazar de Espinosa, and Pero Vaca.[3]

And once they arrived downstream at the isles of San Gabriel, they did not want to take Francisco de Paredes or fray Juan de Salazar aboard the brigantine.[4] They were worried that these men might show some favoritism toward the Governor here and tell the truth about what had happened once they were in Spain.

The conspirators were afraid of these men, and so they put them aboard some launches that were about to sail back upriver to Asunción. The unfortunates had, of course, already sold their houses and estates before coming downriver for much less than they were worth. They complained and carried on so much that it was the saddest thing in the world to hear it all.

Here the officials also stripped the Governor of his servants, who up to that point had attended and rowed him the whole way, and it was the single thing that touched him the most, as well as the greatest anguish he had suffered in his life. And they themselves suffered no less.

They were on the island of San Gabriel for two days, and at the end of this time some of the party departed for Asunción while the rest went to Spain. After the brigantines had gone, twenty-seven people in all climbed aboard the launch that had carried the Governor, in which there were only about eleven thwarts or rowing benches. The party made its way downstream until it came to the ocean. Just as they ventured into the open sea a storm caught them, filling up the whole launch with water, and they lost all their provisions. Only a little flour, a little lard, and a bit of fish—as well as some fresh water—were left. The tempest raged, and they were on the point of drowning.

It seemed to the officials present, who had clapped the Governor in irons and wrought him many injustices and rank offenses by shackling him and taking him prisoner, that God's wrath was in the enormous storm. They decided to loosen his shackles and free him. With this in mind they did so, and it was Alonso Cabrera, the inspector, who filed them off. He and Garci-Vanegas kissed the Governor's foot, although he didn't want this, and they said in public that they knew and confessed that God had sent the four-day storm because of the groundless injustices and insults they had inflicted upon the Governor. They confessed that they had done the Governor multiple wrongs and committed many rank offenses and that everything they had said and sworn to against him was a lie and falsehood. To accomplish their ends, they had created two thousand pieces of false testimony. All this came out of the envy and malice they bore him because he had explored in three days all the byways and the countryside of the province—something they had not been able to accomplish in all the twelve years they had been in the land. They begged the Governor for the love of God to pardon them and promise not to let Your Majesty know that they had clapped him in irons.

As soon as they released him, the driving rain and the wind and the storm itself ceased. It had raged on for four days with no letup.

And so we sailed twenty-five hundred leagues back across the Atlantic in our brigantine, navigating without seeing any land—only water and the heavens above, eating just a tortilla fried up with a little fat and some sweet water to drink. We dismantled pieces of the launch at times to be able to cook up the flour tortillas that we ate. And we came in this way to the islands of the Azores, which belong to His Serene Majesty the King of Portugal, on a voyage that took us three months.

We would not have been so hungry or needy during our journey if those men who had earlier taken the Governor prisoner had only dared to touch on the coast of Brazil or go to the island of Santo Domingo, which is in the Indies. But they didn't venture to do so, as they were guilty men fleeing justice, and they were afraid that if they put in at any of these lands I've mentioned they would have been seized and tried as rebels and traitors to their king.

Fearing that, they had not wished to touch land anywhere. So when we arrived in the Azores, the officials who had taken the Governor all that distance harbored hot feelings among themselves, and they split into factions, with each taking up his own cause. They began to set sail again in different groups; but before they did so, they meant to have the judge in Angla arrest the Governor and hold him prisoner so that he might not tell Your Majesty of the crimes and acts of contempt that they had perpetrated in the province of the Río de la Plata.[5] They simply said that when the Governor had passed through the Cape Verde Islands, he had robbed that country and its port.

When they told the magistrate this, he ordered them to get out, as:

Su rey no era home que ninguen osase pensar en iso, ni tenia a tan mal recado suos portos para que ningún osase o facer. (No one should dare to think that their king was the sort of man who would believe this, nor that he governed his ports in such a sorry way that anyone would dare try this in them.)[6]

Then, seeing that their wickedness did not convince the magistrate to arrest the Governor, they all left the Azores and came home to these kingdoms of Castile. They got here eight or ten days before the Governor, who was held up by contrary weather. They arrived at the court before he did and spread it around that he had gone off to see the king of Portugal to tell him about the particulars of the La Plata province.

The Governor arrived at the Spanish court a few days later. The miscreants vanished the same night he came, heading for Madrid, where they thought the king's court might go, as indeed proved to be the case.[7] Just then, the bishop of Cuenca died; he had presided over the Council of the Indies and had possessed both the desire and the willpower to punish the great crime and contempt of authority that had been wrought against Your Majesty in the Río de la Plata.[8]

A few days afterward, everyone—including the Governor—had been arrested and then let out on bail, provided they not leave the court. Garci-Vanegas, who was one of the prisoners, died a wretched and unforeseen death when his eyes popped out of his head before he could declare the truth of what had happened. His companion Alonso Cabrera, the inspector, suddenly lost his mind and being without it, murdered his wife in Loja. And the friars who had been part of the intrigues and uprisings against the Governor also died sudden and disastrous deaths.

It all goes to show what little fault the Governor has had in this whole affair.

And after keeping the Governor under arrest and detained at the court for eight years, the authorities cleared him of all charges and set him free. But for a number of reasons that swayed the council, they took away his governorship. His opponents said that if he were to return to the Río de la Plata, there would be a lot of commotion and unrest in the land as he set out to punish the guilty.

And so they relieved him of the governorship, along with everything else, and never paid him anything in the way of recompense for the great sums he had spent in service as he went off to that distant place to lend a hand and launch his explorations.

Postscript

The Account of Hernando de Ribera Made
Before Pedro Hernández, Notary Public,
on March 3 of the Year 1545

I N THE CITY OF ASUNCIÓN (WHICH IS ON THE RÍO PARAGUAY, IN THE PROVINCE
OF THE RÍO DE LA PLATA), ON THE THIRD DAY OF THE MONTH OF MARCH, IN
the year of the birth of Our Savior Jesus Christ 1545, in the presence of
myself, a notary public, and of witnesses as noted below, all assembled in
the church and monastery of Nuestra Señora de la Merced, the redeemer
of prisoners, there appeared Captain Hernando de Ribera, a conquistador
of this province, and he said:[1]

During the time of Señor Álvar Núñez Cabeza de Vaca, Governor and
Adelantado and Captain-General of this Province of the Río de la Plata by
the grace of Your Majesty, he was in Puerto de Los Reyes, where the Governor had come to begin his exploration this past year of 1543 [sic]. He
received his orders and left to begin exploring with certain people in a brigantine, sailing up a river they called the Igatu, which is a branch of two very
large and roiling rivers. One of these is called the Yacareati and the other the
Yaiva. Following the accounts of the native Indians, they course through the
settlements of the interior.

They came to the settlements of the Xarayes, according to his report,
leaving their brigantine well secured in a river port. Ribera then went off
into the interior with forty men to explore it and see it with his own eyes.

They traveled through many of the Indians' towns, where they undertook long and copious interchanges, both with the inhabitants of these
settlements and with others from distant places who came to see the captain and speak with him. He took care with these exchanges to interrogate
them pointedly and find out the real truth about the interior, which he
could do as a man who knew the Cario language.[2] He used Cario as he

interpreted what these tribesmen told him and chatted with them, and in this way he informed himself about that country.

At this same time, Ribera had in his party Juan Valderas, one of Your Majesty's notaries, who wrote down and certified some of the events of the expedition. But the truth about the things Ribera actually found out in the way of riches or towns or the peculiarities of the people of that country was not something he wished to divulge to the aforesaid Juan Valderas for him to record in his account of the journey. He never understood matters clearly or completely. Ribera never told him anything, because it was his intention to relay his findings only to the Lord Governor. In that way, the Governor himself could mount an expedition to personally conquer that territory, as by doing so both God and Your Majesty would best be served.

Having gone on into the interior for several days, the captain returned to Puerto Reyes as ordered in a letter sent to him by the Governor. And finding the Governor and all his people to be quite ill, Ribera had not had an opportunity to make his report and give him an account of his discussions with the natives of the interior. A few days earlier, with illness constraining him, and to keep his men from dying, the Governor had returned to this city and port of Asunción. He lay ill here, and several days after his return the officials of Your Majesty had taken him prisoner (a notorious act known to everyone). So Ribera had not been able to make his report to the Governor.

Whereas, Your Majesty's officials are at the moment on their way with the Governor to the kingdoms of Spain, and as it may be that while he is gone a case of absence or murder may be the captain's fate;[3]

Whereas, the captain may have to travel to some place in which he may not be available, in which case his report and conclusions concerning his explorations might be lost;

Whereas, Your Majesty is richly deserving of his account;

And whereas, great harm and loss might come to the Governor, and for all this the captain would think himself guilty, as it would be his responsibility;

Therefore, for this reason, and to discharge his conscience and to fulfill his service to God and Your Majesty and to the Lord Governor acting in Your Majesty's name; now, before me, the notary, the captain wishes to relate the account of his exploration in order to inform Your Majesty of it.

He asked and ordered me, the said notary, to accept both his account and the tales told by the Indians, and his report is now given in the following form.

The said Captain Hernando de Ribera declared that on the twentieth day of the month of December of this past year 1543 he left Puerto Reyes in a brigantine called the *Golondrino* with fifty-two men, as ordered by the Lord Governor, and sailed up the Río Igatu, which is a branch of the aforementioned two rivers, the Yacareati and the Yaiva. This branch was quite large and turbulent, and after a journey of six days he entered into the mother of the two rivers, according to the native Indians of the country through which he was sailing. These two rivers indicated that the captain had now arrived at the interior, and the one river, which is called the Yaiva, supposedly flowed out of the Sierras de Santa Marta.[4]

The Yaiva is very big and powerful, larger than the Río Yacareati, which, according to the signs given by the Indians, comes from the sierras of Peru. And between the one river and the other lie a great stretch of land and towns full of an infinite number of people (according to what the natives say). These two rivers, the Yaiva and the Yacareati, come together in the country of some Indians who are called the Perobazaes, where they divide again. And at seventy leagues downriver, they come together once more.

Having sailed for seventeen days up this river, the captain passed through the country of the Perobazaes Indians and came to another land named after the Xarayes Indians, who are farmers of big plots and breeders of ducks and chickens and other birds.[5] It is a land of fisheries and good hunting. The people are reasonable, and they obey their chief.

Ribera and his men found themselves in the midst of this tribe of Xarayes, in a town with perhaps a thousand houses, and the chief's name was Camire. He gave them a good reception, and through him Ribera found out a great deal about the settlements of the interior. Acting on the information the Indians gave him, he left the brigantine with twelve men to guard it and set out for the interior with a guide recruited from the said Xarayes. He traveled for three days and came to the towns and lands of a tribe of Indians called the Urtueses, who are good people and farmers, much like the Xarayes.

From that point on, he traveled through a populated countryside until he came to 15 degrees south latitude minus ⅔, heading west.[6]

Now he was in the towns of the Urtueses and the Aburuñes. A large number of chiefs from neighboring towns that lay further in the interior came to talk with him, and they brought feathers that looked like those of Peru as well as plates of broken metal.[7] He asked a lot of questions of them, chatting with each one and querying them all in detail about the settlements and towns that lay ahead. And these Indians, all in conformity with each other and with no discrepancies, told him that at ten days' journey to the west-northwest, there were very large towns populated by some women who had a lot of white and yellow metal.[8] "The chairs and serving pieces of their houses are all of this metal," they said. "And their chief is a woman of the same tribe. They're warriors, and they are feared by the other tribes. And before you arrive at the country of these women, you will come to a tribe of small people."

The tribe of women fights with these small people, waging war on them and on the tribe of people who gave Captain Ribera his information. "But at a certain time of the year, the women do get together with the neighboring tribes, with whom they then have carnal communication. If those who become pregnant bear daughters, they keep them; the sons they retain until they are weaned, at which time they send them to their fathers. And around that land of women's towns there are very considerable settlements with large populations that border on the women's territory." The Indians told the captain this without his having to ask.

The Indians also told him about a certain part of a large lake they called the House of the Sun, where they said the sun was locked up.[9] The country of the women lay off to the west-northwest, between the backbone of the Sierra de Santa Marta and the lake.

Beyond the tribes that live past the women's towns, there are other enormous populations of people who are black, and—from the signs the Indians made—have sharp-pointed beards, like those of the Moors.[10]

"How do you know they're blacks?" asked the captain.

"Because our parents saw them," they answered, "and all the other neighboring tribes say the same thing about that country. They walk around clothed, and their houses and towns are of earth and stone. They are very tall people, and they have a lot of white and yellow metal, which they possess in such quantity that the serving pieces in their houses—the vessels, pots, great storage jars, and all the rest—are only this."

Captain Ribera asked the Indians in which direction lay the settlements of these black people, and they pointed him to the northwest. "If you and your men wish to go there," they said, "you will arrive at the neighboring settlements of the towns of these black people in fifteen days."

It seemed to the captain that, following what they had told him, these said towns would lie off to the northwest at about 12 degrees south latitude, between the Sierras de Santa Marta and Marañón.[11] The inhabitants are warlike people, and they fight with bows and arrows.

The Indians told Captain Ribera that, bearing from the west-northwest to the northwest, a quarter to the north, there were other populations of Indians—and very large ones at that. There were cities so big that in the course of a day you could not walk from one end to another.[12] The people of these places have a lot of white and yellow metal, and they serve food in their houses on serving pieces made of this. All the people go about clothed. "You can go there quickly," they said to the Spaniards, "and you'll travel through well-settled country."

Bearing west, there is also a lake of water, quite large, and if you stand on one side you cannot see the land on the other.[13] Along the shores of this lake, there are huge numbers of clothed people who have a great deal of metal. They also have stones that sparkle brightly embroidered into the hems of their clothes. They take these stones from the lake. These people have large towns, and all the residents of these places are farmers with very large plots of land; they raise many ducks and other fowl.

From where the captain found himself, he could travel to the said lake and its people in fifteen days (from what the Indians indicated), all through settled country, in which there was a great deal of metal and even good roads when the water went down. At that time, of course, the waters were very high. "We'll take you there," said the Indians.

But there were very few Christians, and the towns they had to pass through were large, with lots of people.

The captain also said the Indians pointed and made signs to him indicating that there were huge numbers of people lying to the west and a little to the southwest, and their houses were made of earth. These were good people, clothed and quite rich, who had a great deal of metal and flocks of very large sheep that served them in their paddocks and their farm fields, and carried burdens for them.[14]

"Are the settlements of these Indians very far away?" asked the captain.

"Well, to get to them you travel through nothing but settled country with a lot of people," they said. "You can get there pretty quickly, and among these settlements there are other people who are Christians. And there are great sandy deserts, and no water."

"How do you know there are Christians among those settlements?" asked the Spaniards.

"Well," they said, "in the old days, the people who live next to those places heard from the actual residents of those towns that they, being members of those desert tribes, had seen the arrival of a lot of people in clothes—white people with beards—who had brought along with their party some animals (which, from their signs, were horses). They were horsemen. Because there was no water, the people saw them turn back, and a number of them died."

The Indians believed that the people who had told them this came from those deserts.

At the same time, they told the captain that, lying on a line bearing west and one quarter to the southwest, there were tremendous mountains and very empty country. "People have tried to go across that," they said, "from what we know through the tribes who live over that way, but no one has been able to do it because you would die of hunger and thirst."

"How can you be so sure of this?" asked the captain.

"Because," they said, "all the people who live in and around this country talk to each other and know how things are. We've seen and talked to these other people, and they in turn saw the Christians and their horses who came across those deserts. And at the foot of those mountain ranges, off to the southwest, there are some very large settlements with rich people who have a lot of metal."

The Indians who told the captain this also said they had news that in another direction very large boats were sailing on the salt water.[15]

"Among these tribes that you mention," asked the captain, "are there chiefs who rule the people?"

"Each tribe and settlement has only one man whom everyone obeys," they said.

The captain declared that, to find out the truth of what they said, he questioned them one by one for a day and a night, posing his inquiries differently in regard to what they had told him. Having done so, he was ready to say that their story was confirmed, with no variations or discrepancies.

Captain Hernando de Ribera gave the said account with its content as indicated above, and declared it taken down and received with complete clarity and every faithfulness and accuracy, and without any deceit, fraud, or craftiness. And, as his said account can be given—and I have given it—with full faith and credibility, and no doubt may be entertained nor is entertained about all of it or any part of it, he said that he would swear, and then did swear, before God and Saint Mary and by the words of the Four Holy Gospels, as he, in person, placed his right hand on the missal book, which the Reverend Father, Francisco González de Paniagua, held in his hands and opened to the part where the Holy Gospels are written; and at the Sign of the Cross, which is like this: ✠, where the captain had put his right hand, he swore that this account, following the form and manner in which he had dictated it as it is noted above, was given, said, announced, and declared by the said chiefs of the said country and by other venerable old men, whom he questioned and examined with utmost diligence to find out and ascertain the clear truth about the nature of the interior.

Once he had obtained this account from the Indians, people from other towns came to see him—primarily from a very large town called Uretabere—and he himself went on a visit to see it. He took advice and comment from all these Indians, and they all confirmed clearly and openly his earlier accounts. The captain stated, "Neither in this account in its entirety nor in any part of it is there anything inflated or faked; there is only the truth of everything I have declared and reported without fraud or guile."

In addition, he said that the Indians of the Río Yacaraeati told him about a cataract in the river created by some high mountains and that this was actually true.[16] "God will help me if this is the case," he said, "and if not, may God deal badly and dearly with my body in this world and with my soul in the next, where I must of necessity spend an even longer time."

Upon confessing the said account, he said, "I do so swear, amen." And he asked me, and required me, the aforementioned notary, to give it as his faithful testimony to the Lord Governor, to help protect the Governor's rights.

Being present as witnesses the aforesaid Reverend Father Paniagua, Sebastián de Valdivieso, the servant of the said Lord Governor, and Gaspar de Ortigosa, and Juan de Hoces, citizens of the city of Córdoba; all of whom have signed their names here.

Francisco González Paniagua
Sebastián de Valdivieso
Juan de Hoces
Hernando de Ribera
Gaspar de Ortigosa

He came before me.

—*Pedro Hernández*, Notary.

Appendix
Original Preliminary Remarks (the Prohemio)
by Cabeza de Vaca

*T*HIS EXTRAORDINARY PREFACE IS WRITTEN AS A TRADITIONALLY FORMAL DEDICA-
TION TO THE YOUNG PRINCE, DON CARLOS. WHEN COMBINED WITH A CLOSE
study of the record of depositions from Cabeza de Vaca's lawsuits and appeals of
1545–1555, it shows the old explorer currying favor with the Spanish crown but
unmistakably a royal intimate again by 1555.

Preliminary Remarks

To his most serene, most high, and powerful lord,
the Infante Don Carlos, our Lord[4]

Álvar Núñez Cabeza de Vaca,
Adelantado and Governor of the Río de la Plata

Peace and Happiness

Having emerged in the year 1537 from that long and trying journey in Florida, where our Lord used me for so many singular ends, all of which bear testimony to His ancient mercy, exercised since the beginning of the world with men and particularly with me, Dorantes, and Castillo Maldonado, we who were all that remained of the three hundred men we were when we went into that country with Pánfilo de Narváez; and we were shielded and delivered from the many dangers facing us in that remotest of places and among those barbarous people, all of which we faced over ten long years.

And so as to serve as an example to other men so that they might be sure that the powerful hand of God (which embraces everything) will guide and assist them in any quarter of the world, I have given my brief account to His Majesty in these *Commentaries*, so that in his most mighty and unvanquished name, so wide reaching, feared, and obeyed in the greater part of the world, he may make known the memory, testimony, and example of the mercies of God to his subjects.

Afterward, as His Most High Majesty wished to continue these marvels with me, your grandfather, the emperor, was moved to send me in the year 1540 with an armada to the Río Paraná (which Solís called the Río de la Plata) to render assistance to the people there and also to continue the explorations of don Pedro de Mendoza (who they say came from Guadix). In doing this I faced many dangers and hardships, as Your Highness will pointedly see in these *Commentaries* (written out with great diligence and truthfulness by Pedro Fernández,[2] the Secretary of the Governor's Office, to whom I entrusted them), which accompany my first ventures, because the variety of occurrences in first one place and then the other as well as the many different things that happened to me may hold Your Highness's interest in this lesson with some degree of delight.[3]

Certain it is that there is nothing more delightful to readers than all the varied instruments, twists, and turns of fortune, which, at the time they are experienced, are not pleasant. But when we bring them back to mind and read about them, they become agreeable.

I have remembered how Our Lord has been served to carry forward through me His mercy and beneficence, which is indeed just and something that flows through the testimony and example that I have noted above. I have also carried forward the idea of these qualities and the wish to praise them. And just as I directed my first account to His Majesty, I should like to direct these *Commentaries* to Your Highness, to whom God has begun to reveal his dominions and the knowledge of so many lands and peoples. As the eyes of youth are opened, Your Highness may see how liberally God shares his mercy with men. And with age there will begin to grow in Your Highness the wish to recognize, with great forgiveness, love, and Christian custom—and with holy and compassionate laws—the great number of people whom God is pulling into the light through the Gospel of Jesus Christ, not permitting them to remain in the shadows and blindness and tyranny of the devil.

This has all come about for Your Highness principally from my having made my discoveries by order of the emperor, your grandfather. And that is a proper business for kings, whose resources alone are sufficient for these things. In exercising them the will of God may be followed. The proper use of these resources as well as your writings and all sorts of works is owed to the great ingenuity and ability you have shown to the world, which, most daunted and attentive, expects to receive the fruits of the most perfect king from your youth, manhood, and old age. God will grant you these things, which you will pass on to the world as its necessary king.

You should entertain no doubt that you will accomplish these ends; neither should those who may find themselves far from your house, nor those who see, serve, and deal with Your Highness every day. They cannot help being pleased with what they have begun to see. They all congratulate themselves when they view your most excellent ingeniousness well handled and disposed (which is in keeping with the nature of an accomplished young man).

You have been under the tutelage of two singular artisans: don Antonio de Rojas, your tutor and steward, and Honorato Juan, your teacher, both selected for their offices by the hands of the emperor and the prince (our lords) from amongst all the sages and gentlemen of their kingdoms with the greatest diligence, care, and timeliness.[4] These are the qualities Their Majesties must display in choosing such capable persons, to whom the royal person will be entrusted—necessary for the nurturing and teaching of the greatest successor to a throne in the world.

In regard to don Antonio de Rojas y Velasco, also of your ancient and illustrious line (what a grand addition he is to those who are close to the monarchs), with his great Christianity, prudence, and modesty, and his experience in the service of royal houses and persons, with all the other virtues and graces that are necessary in a gentleman to whom such an important business is entrusted, and considering the long experience Their Majesties have of his person and his habits from his lengthy and excellent service in such high office on behalf of the Prince, Your Highness's father: these qualities compelled His Majesty to require don Antonio to leave his personal service and undertake the rearing of his son.

With the same zeal Their Majesties selected Honorato Juan, to whom they entrusted the instruction and education of Your Highness so that you might acquire much Christianity, many virtues, and your letters from his many years of service in the royal houses—in particular, his attendance to the Prince, Our Lord, in his own studies. This same person, in addition to being a well-known gentleman from the line of the Juanes of Játiva, holds a great complement of natural talents—his science in all genres of letters is so extensive and so rare that all the learned and true doctors of our time—Italians, Germans, French, Flemish, English, and Spaniards— have testified admiringly to his most singular ingeniousness and to the wide and deep knowledge of Greek and Latin authors, natural and moral philosophy, and mathematical disciplines that he has. In all these subjects, as though he were grasping wholly the times of the ancients (when these topics flourished most), he can satisfactorily write and speak in the *style* of the ancients, with nuances only to be found in those times and authors. He does this with so much plainness and clarity that if people who hear him know the sciences, they are satisfied, and if they do not know the sciences, they understand what they are hearing as if the subject were vulgar, plain things already within their grasp.

Because of this, his conversation is of great delight and utility to all those who may hear it, full of examples and tremendous erudition, and, when speaking with him in a familiar way, he will be clear about many authors' ideas, which, when found in the works of the authors themselves, are quite difficult. And this is true not just in science but also in human affairs, in which, as he is a prudent man, he uses the substance of his knowledge of letters without appearing to do so.

All this Your Highness will experience in your studies. You will begin to see this as you progress, and so, freed of the difficulty and harshness of your beginnings, due to your being instructed by a master of such learning, prudence, and judgment, you will arrive easily and smoothly at the culmination of Christianity and sciences to which your docile and excellent ingenuity will take you, which Their Majesties desire, and which is necessary to these kingdoms.

Such persons as these and such blessings of nature as ingenuity and spirit that it pleases God to give in good time he gave to Your Highness so they might guide your person and your soul and give form to and adorn your character with clear and eternal virtues. These are, in a Christian king, namely that he be a sage; a dispenser of justice; strong, truthful, prudent, liberal, magnanimous, compassionate, humane, gentle, benign and amiable; and abhorrent of everything to the contrary.

He must be obedient to Him who, through such great kingdoms and dominions, believed in you, and to whom we must give infinite thanks, as we see so settled and firm the security of these realms and we understand clearly that His mercy and grace are in our case giving us such princes and their successors. On their behalf He has discovered so many new provinces—a great abundance of them, with all the benefits of nature and of innumerable towns and people.

And so poor is the human race and its soft laws compared to those of the Gospel that Their Majesties with so much diligence and zeal attempt to teach people, as they have been chosen by God as executors and instruments of the preaching of the Word in all the West. That is where the reign of the Gospel has increased its kingdoms and dominions, its titles, and its fame, which has become immortal for having occurred in Their Majesties' time and due to their industry and the care they have shown for the Christian religion in the world.

And we Spaniards owe a great deal for having been the ministers and participants in such a divine affair and for having been singled out for such a meritorious honor.

And though envy may attempt to impede and hinder such an obligatory and necessary work, the clear virtue and merit of these princes will defend us, giving to God the peace, calm, and tranquility that in a time of good kings may come most abundantly.

So Your Highness will succeed to the throne of calm, pacific kingdoms in order that the restitution and renovation of virtues and good letters and customs (and it seems that with your great acuity you must indeed legitimately rule) may take place. These qualities in times of discord are banished and must flee. Who might not hope for this from God's mercy, given us through such princes, and as the outcome of the virtue and holiness and magnanimity of the emperor, your grandfather?

The emperor has cleaned up in the West (as did King Josiah in Israel) the abominations and false sacrifices of the devil and has introduced and followed evangelical liberty.

And in regard to the Royal Prince, your father: the memory of him, together with that of the most Christian and fortunate queen his wife (as Ecclesiastes says of that same King Josiah), will enter into men's compositions very cordially, with their names said sweetly in men's mouths— honey poured onto the clods of the earth—for having restored the ancient Christianity of the kingdom of England to God. They will open the temples (now closed through blindness and errors) with the keys of obedience to the Pontifex Maximus.[5]

And thinking of the great obedience Your Highness shows to God, in the first instance, and to Their Majesties; and of your love and respect for your tutor and master; and of your admirable ingenuity, whose fruits we already see in your tender and not-yet-mature age—like fields in the spring, in which the genius of other men may often flourish with the sort of great perfection and ripening we are accustomed to find during fertile years, older years: of these matters you have a clear and high understanding.

Some see these things; others hear them. But everyone is happy and rejoicing with the grand expectation that Your Highness represents. We will begin to see in these kingdoms an abundance of all kinds of virtues and learning such as God imparts to those who, among all the peoples of the world, are called to Christianity—people who have been made most serene. And the Christian republic also will know all the riches and temporal wealth and peace and tranquility and growth that must indeed occur during your time.

The infidels already know great fear and dread from the news of Your Highness, and they will know it better from your works to come. This is because there is really no need to have to hope that from such great principles will come similar benefits and advantages or that the works of our Kings and Princes will tighten into narrow ends. They will, instead, extend themselves everywhere for the good and benefit of all.

This, of course, is what your tutor and teacher have counseled and taught to Your Highness (in strict conformance with the Christianity, virtue, and friendship they have always shown) when they have raised you and inculcated you with the precepts of the Christian religion, chivalry, and philosophy. Because they know that those who have administered their kingdoms with such firm, sure, and perpetual powers have left narrow holdings made very wide; suspicious holdings made more sure; very fluid holdings made quite firm; variable holdings rendered constant and permanent. And, finally, they have made mortal kings immortal.

But as to those who have wished to rule without these guidelines, though flush with the powers of riches and armies: they were not powerful enough to restrain those in their kingdoms who were against them from creating their bad effects, their ruination, their bloodletting. These rulers sometimes are changed by this sort of thing, leaving them quite infamous and hated.

Of both these types of kings Your Highness will find abundant examples in the histories you will have read. And there is no stable or perpetual thing in a kingdom that is not tied with strings of Christianity, wisdom, justice, truth, strength, and prudence. And principally for the sake of humanity and liberality, so necessary are our kings and their kindnesses that they are made in the image of God, from whom we need only await all things in abundance and perpetuity.

Frederic Remington, Coronado's March. This work depicts a Spanish exploring party in 1540 in what is now the American Southwest. Francisco Vásquez de Coronado was an exact contemporary of Cabeza de Vaca, even launching his expedition in the same year as the Governor.

Spanish caravel of the sixteenth century by De Bry.

Brigantine or launch. The brigantines constructed by Cabeza de Vaca were sturdy one- or two-mast craft used for river exploration or even ocean voyages. Sketch by Baker H. Morrow.

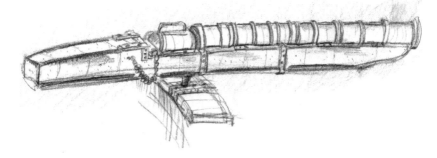

Falconet or culverin, a small cannon. Sketch by Baker H. Morrow after Hook.

Scenes from the Florentine Codex *by fray Bernardino de Sahagún. Spanish battle formations are shown in scenes 115, 116, and 117. Scene 118 depicts brigantines, much like those constructed by Cabeza de Vaca, in action.*

Indian man and woman, from Huldérico Schmidel's book (1567), The Voyage of Ulrich Schmidt [Schmidel] to the Rivers of La Plata and Paraguay, *published in Germany. Schmidel's place, personal, and tribal names are often garbled; the Scherves announced in the drawing are unidentifiable. Note the "bonnet" on the man.*

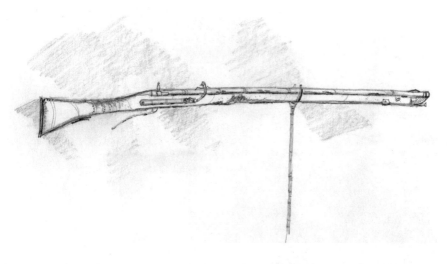

Harquebus with stand. Sketch by Baker H. Morrow after Hook.

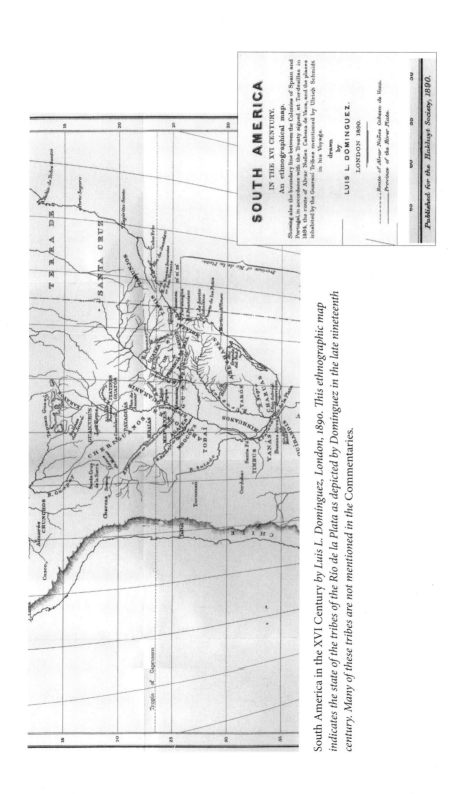

South America in the XVI Century by Luis L. Domínguez, London, 1890. This ethnographic map indicates the state of the tribes of the Río de la Plata as depicted by Domínguez in the late nineteenth century. Many of these tribes are not mentioned in the Commentaries.

Thatched-roof Indian house of the Upper Río Paraguay. Sketch by Baker H. Morrow.

Indian fisherman along the Río Paraguay. Sketch by Baker H. Morrow.

Spaniards and their Indian allies attacking a fortified Indian town in the Río de la Plata. From The Voyage of Ulrich Schmidt [Schmidel] to the Rivers La Plata and Paraguay, 1567, published in Germany.

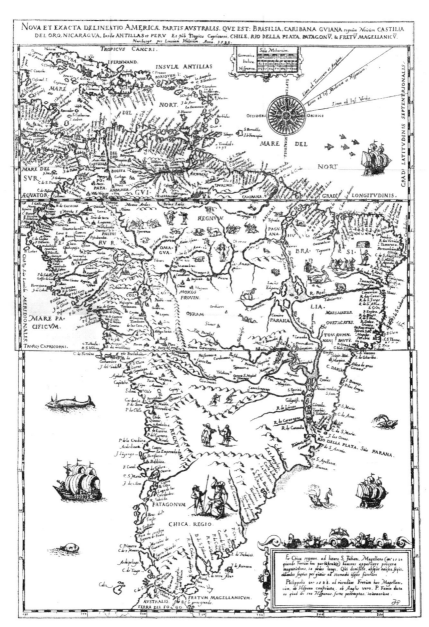

Schmidel's map of South America, taken from "Viaje de Huldérico Schmidel al Río de la Plata" (1534–1554), first published in 1567.

Reputed coat of arms of Cabeza de Vaca. This evocative insignia purporting to belong to Cabeza de Vaca is likely a fabrication concocted by the mutineers in Paraguay and used in their set of charges filed against the Governor in Spain after 1545.

Appeal of Cabeza de Vaca, in his own hand, from the legal proceedings after 1545.

Sketch of the Amazons by Hulsins.

Reception of Hernando de Ribera by the King of the Xarayes by De Bry.

Notes

Chapter One

1. Pedro de Mendoza was born in Guadix in 1487 and died in 1539 or early 1540 while returning to Spain from the Río de la Plata province. He campaigned in the Spanish army in Italy. Mendoza had been named the first adelantado, or Governor, of La Plata in 1534, where he set himself the task of finding a land route to Peru. He left Spain on August 24, 1535, with fourteen ships and 2,150 men who were, for the most part, from aristocratic families. The enterprise from its beginnings was off course, with Mendoza eventually ordering one of the party, Juan Osorio, who was a popular captain, to be knifed to death. On February 22, 1536, Mendoza founded Buenos Aires. He had to face the ferocious Indians of the place, and in the fighting against them his brother Diego lost his life. Mendoza was besieged by the Indians and only gained a respite, following great losses, by relocating the colony to another nearby site. He was resolved to accomplish his mission, and toward that end he had marched off into the interior in the same direction that his captain, Juan de Ayolas, had previously taken. He went as far north as the new settlement of Ascensión (Asunción), now capital of Paraguay. Mendoza left Ayolas and Captain Francisco Ruiz de Galán as seconds-in-command in Buenos Aires when he sailed from that settlement to Spain to give an account of the dire needs and difficulties of the province. He died aboard ship while crossing the Atlantic.

2. A ducat is a valuable, late-medieval gold or silver coin once said to be worth eleven shillings and one maravedi, or perhaps several dollars. A maravedi is worth a third of a farthing, or about one-sixth cent.

3. The nao was a sailing ship of Portuguese design in common use in the sixteenth century. Caravels, employed by both the Spaniards and the Portuguese, were first used to cross the Atlantic by Columbus. They had three or four masts and both lateen sails and a square forward sail.

4. The year is 1540.

5. La Palma is one of the westernmost of the Canary Islands, conquered by the Spaniards in 1492–1493.

6. Quintal: a hundredweight, or about 100–112 pounds.

7. This is São Tiago, the most important of these Portuguese islands located off the west coast of Africa at about 16 degrees north latitude.

8. A league is equal to about three or four miles.

9. *Doblones que reales*: i.e., more dollars than quarters. Doubloons are old Spanish gold coins, worth much more than the lesser silver reales.

Chapter Two

1. These are *botas*, with a capacity of about 125 gallons each. Cabeza de Vaca likely means that only three of his casks still held any water.

2. Cabeza de Vaca, or, more accurately, his secretary, the notary Pedro "Pero" Hernández, who is writing out this account, will refer to the author as the "Governor" for the rest of this tale.

3. Modern Cananéia is located at the far southern tip of São Paulo state in Brazil, about 125 miles southwest of the great city of the same name. It lies northwest of Santa Catarina (Santa Catalina in Spanish), an island and state of modern Brazil.

4. This is the modern Rio São Francisco in the Brazilian state of Santa Catarina.

Chapter Three

1. The enormous estuary of the Río de la Plata, some two hundred miles in width at Buenos Aires and one of the world's greatest sources of fresh water, is formed by the confluence of the Río Paraná and the Río Uruguay. It divides modern Argentina and Uruguay. In Cabeza de Vaca's day, "Río de la Plata" was vaguely defined, referring to a recently established province that included modern Argentina, Paraguay, and parts of Brazil and Uruguay.

Chapter Four

1. This sort of auditor or comptroller is a *contador* in sixteenth-century Spanish.

2. Juan de Ayolas, the founder of Asunción, was born in Briviesca, Spain, toward the end of the fifteenth century or the beginning of the sixteenth, and died in 1539. He accompanied Pedro de Mendoza, the founder of the province of the Río de la Plata, on his expedition. Ayolas explored the Río de la Plata as far upstream as the Río Paraguay. Sometime later he went up the Paraná. Following this, he remained for a while in the interior, and when he returned to his starting point, a small port called Candelaria, he found that Domingo de Irala had not waited for him as they had originally agreed. Ayolas established the city of Asunción (Ascensión), which became the center of Spanish colonization in the Río de la Plata, during his upriver explorations. Some sources refer to him cuttingly as an "assassin" and say that he died at the hands of the Agaces Indians, not the Payaguos.

3. The brigantine Cabeza de Vaca so often refers to in this narrative was a small, double-masted launch or lugger with square or lateen sails. It was relatively

simple to build, as we shall see, capacious, and ideally suited to river exploration. It was a very common Mediterranean craft of the sixteenth century. This Candelaria actually is a small river port on the south bank of the Río Paraná in what is now the province of Misiones in Argentina. The Payaguos are also sometimes referred to as the Payaguas. They were well known as fishermen and great swimmers.

4. Domingo Martínez de Irala was born in Vergara, Spain, in 1506, and died in 1577. He traveled up the Río de la Plata with Mendoza and explored the Río Paraná as thoroughly as had Ayolas. He founded the city of Candelaria in 1537 and served as lieutenant governor under both Mendoza and Álvar Núñez. Following the episodes noted in this narrative in which he was the key participant during the tenure of Cabeza de Vaca, Irala set off for the Andes. The record shows that he left virtually no stretch of land unexplored from the Upper Paraná to Peru. Notwithstanding Irala's reputation as a villain, conferred upon him not too subtly by Cabeza de Vaca, it is largely due to his relentless efforts that Spanish power was established in the South American midlands ("La Mesopotamia Sudamericana," as they are called by Dr. Julio le Riverend).

5. The original name of modern Asunción, the capital of Paraguay, was Ascensión. It was apparently founded on the site of an earlier Guarani fortress called Lambare.

6. Buenos Aires actually lies on the south side of the Río de la Plata estuary, formed by the confluence of the Río Paraná and the Río Uruguay.

7. Elsewhere, Cabeza de Vaca refers to Gonzalo as a member of the Chameses tribe. The Chanes or Chameses formed part of the larger tribal group of the Charruas, known for their warlike demeanor and their use of bows and bolas, the famous South American throwing balls tied to strings or leathers. They were nomadic and skillful hunters, living in indifferent small settlements, not much given to such domestic arts as the making of pots, and famous for their wiliness.

Chapter Five

1. A commissioner, or factor, was a commercial agent licensed by the king.

Chapter Six

1. Pedro Estopiñán was the first cousin of Álvar Núñez.

2. The Guaranis, the most famous and widespread group of the Native American peoples of southern South America, are often collectively referred to as Tupi-Guaranis. The Tupis are the coastal branch of this remarkable tribe. Guarani is one of the official languages of modern Paraguay, where it is still spoken by virtually the entire country.

3. This is *cazabi*, or cassava, a common South American food plant or plants of the genus *Manihot*, whose roots yield manioc and tapioca. It is here described for perhaps the first time in European literature.

4. Recent evidence, as well as this sort of primary, eyewitness account, indicates that chickens, probably derived from the jungle fowl of Asia, may have been

widely raised in South America before the coming of the Europeans, perhaps introduced through west coast connections with the Polynesians of the Pacific.

5. The name Vera derives from Cabeza de Vaca's father, Francisco de Vera, and from his distinguished grandfather, Pedro de Vera, the conqueror of Gran Canaria in the Canary Islands in the late fifteenth century.

6. The Iguazú is an enormous river that heads in the Serra do Mar, close to modern Curitiba, and flows directly west into the Río Paraná.

Chapter Seven

1. These slabs are a columnar, igneous rock known as "trap" and basalt, according to Domínguez.

2. This Tapapirazu may be the Tocanguanzu mentioned in chapter 6.

3. Cabeza de Vaca's recent history as an explorer and shaman among the tribes of North America made him perhaps the greatest authority in the New World at the time on good relations with local people. See Cyclone Covey's *Adventures in the Unknown Interior of America* (by Cabeza de Vaca), Adorno and Pautz's *The Narrative of Cabeza de Vaca*, or the *Chronicle of the Narvaez Expedition* for further remarkable examples of Cabeza de Vaca's efforts at diplomacy.

4. This may be the modern Rio Piquiri in western Paraná state, Brazil.

5. I.e., Guarani, or Tupi-Guarani.

6. These measurements put Cabeza de Vaca and his men roughly in southwestern Paraná state, Brazil, a little east of the Rio Paraná. Measurements of latitude in the sixteenth century are often accurate, but longitude could not yet be calculated.

Chapter Eight

1. Cabeza de Vaca likely means Tacuari, rather than Tugui, here.

2. A carack was a *carraca*, a slow-sailing cargo ship of the day.

3. *Puercos monteses* are peccaries, *Dicotyles labiatus*, distant relatives of the domestic pig.

4. The Spanish here is *gatos*. Cabeza de Vaca calls the monkeys "cats" in a passing reference, a common practice of the Spaniards in the sixteenth century.

5. Christmas was known as *la Pascua del Nascimiento* in the sixteenth century.

Chapter Nine

1. Some sources believe that the cedars Cabeza de Vaca refers to are *Araucaria* species, found in abundance in this part of the Southern Hemisphere, and here described for perhaps the first time in European literature.

2. The word in Spanish is *batatas*, which is a little problematic. Sweet potatoes or yams are West African in origin and would not likely have been distributed by the Spaniards, Portuguese, French, or other seafaring Europeans in this central part of South America by the 1540s. Cabeza de Vaca's tubers may simply be varieties of the South American native potato from the Andes, referred to here by its Portuguese name, also batata.

3. The party is probably eating the larvae of the *Calandra palmarum*, a species of weevil still fancied in South America.

4. These may be the Rio Ivahy (Ivaí) and the Rio Piquiri (Piqueri), or their tributaries, which lie north of the Rio Iguazú, in western Paraná state, Brazil.

Chapter Ten

1. These pigs are the *puercos monteses*, or javelinas, that Cabeza de Vaca mentioned earlier.

2. *Mandubies* (peanuts), here introduced by Cabeza de Vaca to Spanish literature.

Chapter Eleven

1. This is the Rio Iguaza referred to in the title of this chapter. Iguazú is its modern name.

2. Martín Alfonso de Sosa, also known as Martín Alfaro de Sosa. In Portuguese, Martim Afonso de Sousa. He was a very early governor of São Vicente in Brazil, the first official Portuguese settlement in that country, which he founded in 1532. De Sosa dispatched a small party of four under the command of Alejo Garcia to explore the Río Paraná country. Here they recruited local Guaranis and made their way west to the Andes, where they were able to amass a considerable amount of silver. They were murdered on the upper Paraná while returning to Brazil.

3. These are the famous Iguazú Falls, the greatest waterfalls of South America, on the border pocket Paraguay, Argentina, and Brazil share, here discovered and described for the first time by a European. The term *lanzas* is somewhat problematic. Cabeza de Vaca likely means *lanzamientos*, the measure of a ship from stem to stern that might yield two hundred feet or more—a reasonable estimate of the impressive mists rising from the falls.

Chapter Twelve

1. Gonçalo de Acosta was a Portuguese who had accompanied Governor Mendoza's party across the Atlantic in 1537 to report on conditions in the Río de la Plata. According to Bishop, he sailed on several round trips across the Atlantic, sometimes as a pilot. Later, he became a partisan of Domingo de Irala, lieutenant governor of the Río de la Plata and Cabeza de Vaca's great adversary.

2. The current of the Río Paraná was so strong and the river so formidable that the Spaniards had no desire and few means to go back to the other side.

3. Actually, 25 degrees 35 minutes south latitude.

4. This was an odd but consistent characteristic of Cabeza de Vaca's dealings with the Native Americans. The Governor's celebrated affability and shamanship—or perhaps showmanship—had ensured his survival and popularity among the Indians of the American Southwest and northern Mexico during his epic journey with a large native retinue across North America in the previous decade.

5. Just after Governor Mendoza had died en route to Spain in 1537, the Spanish government had sent a relief force of two or three ships loaded with provisions and men to Buenos Aires under the command of Captain Alfonso Cabrera.

Chapter Thirteen

1. Dorantes is a *factor* or commissioner, or royal commercial agent.

Chapter Fourteen

1. In this narrative the jaguar is called a *tigre*, or *tiguere*, in the Valladolid first edition of 1555.

Chapter Fifteen

1. In the sixteenth century, the flagship is the *nao capitana*.
2. The Paraná mentioned here is the modern Río de la Plata, of which the Paraná is a main tributary.
3. The year was 1542. Cabeza de Vaca is here sending two refitted launches from Asunción to Buenos Aires.

Chapter Sixteen

1. These may be war bonnets or headdresses.
2. Guarani was soon to become the lingua franca of southern South America, spoken widely by the Spaniards and Portuguese as well as the indigenous tribes. By the end of the sixteenth century it was simply called the *lengua geral*— the "general language"—of Brazil.
3. All this activity is confirmed strongly by the tale of Hans Staden, an early European visitor to the coast of Brazil (1547–1555) who also witnessed these practices among the Tupi or Tupinamba firsthand. His account was first published in 1555. The practice of cannibalism by Native American tribes remains a highly controversial subject, however, debated continuously by anthropologists and historians.

Chapter Seventeen

1. There is some evidence that the Agaces may be the same people as the Payaguas, as noted in "The Evuevi of Paraguay: Adaptive Strategies and Responses to Colonialism, 1528–1811," by Barbara Ganson in *The Americas*. I am indebted to a personal communication from Professor Ganson for this note.

Chapter Nineteen

1. These are the chiefs of the local Guaranis. The other tribe is the Guaycurues.
2. These pigs are probably puercos monteses, or javelinas.

Chapter Twenty

1. The Guaycurues, sometimes referred to as the Guaycurus, are a large collection of tribes from the Gran Chaco, a vast, hot savanna of modern northern

Argentina, western Paraguay, and eastern Bolivia that is completely inundated for much of the year. The Querandies, Tobas, and Opinones belong to the larger group of the Guaycurues. Excellent hunters, these people were much feared by the Guaranis for their ferocity.

2. Here the Spanish priests have given their new Guarani converts a number of baptismal names mostly selected from those of the local settlers, soldiers, and officials. Gonzalo Mairaru is also known as Gonzalo Mayraru (see chapter 37).

3. Modern Caaguazu, located about 110 miles east of Asunción, midway between the Paraná and Paraguay rivers.

4. Martín de Armenta was a bachelor of arts. "Bachelor" is a common Spanish honorific of the sixteenth and seventeenth centuries.

5. Tapua was sometimes transcribed as "Capua" in later Spanish editions because of the Gothic script.

6. These ostriches were *avestruces*. They are the South American rheas, *Rhea americana*, huge ratites, or flightless, three-toed birds related to ostriches, emus, and cassowarries, making their maiden appearance in European literature.

7. What Cabeza de Vaca describes here is the common American Indian practice of driving game by fire before or toward a band of concentrated hunters—hence the widespread setting of so many bushfires.

Chapter Twenty-One

1. Cabeza de Vaca may have accomplished this by lashing poles or boards over the tops of several canoes to form a kind of catamaran.

Chapter Twenty-Three

1. Ave María: i.e., at sunset. Also called the Angelus.

2. The Guatataes were also known as the Batates; see chapter 25.

3. The harquebusiers are fusiliers using the harquebus, a heavy, blunderbuss-like early firearm with a stand. It was nearly always employed in concert with crossbows as the very effective small arms of the Spanish armies of the sixteenth century.

Chapter Twenty-Four

1. This was the Spanish battle cry ever since the wars of the Middle Ages against the Moors. The Spaniards here are calling on St. James, their patron, to aid them in their fight.

Chapter Twenty-Five

1. This is the tribe referred to earlier (in chapter 23) as the Guatataes. The Guaycurues had apparently fought with them in the recent past, and the current flight of the Guaycurues across the Guarani landscape was at least partially an effort to escape their wrath.

2. Five hundred paces might be 1,250 feet or longer—an astonishing length if true.

3. The palometa, also piraña in Spanish or piranha in Portuguese, is sometimes called a pomfret. Cabeza de Vaca is here referring to its razor-sharp and fearsome teeth.

Chapter Twenty-Six

1. This is Queen Isabella of Castile, wife of King Ferdinand of Aragón, and the monarch who gave Columbus his charter to sail westward across the Atlantic in 1492.

Chapter Twenty-Seven

1. The Yapirues are also known as the Aperues; see chapter 32.

Chapter Thirty

1. The Imperues were likely the Aperues described in chapter 32, as well as the Yapirues already noted in chapter 27. The Naperues may also be the Yapirues.

Chapter Thirty-One

1. These were likely javelinas. The use here of the term *asada en barbacoa* by Cabeza de Vaca is one of the earliest mentions of this distinctive form of New World cooking.

2. These deaths apparently occurred through drowning in the currents of the Río Paraguay.

Chapter Thirty-Two

1. Aperues. These are the Yapirues Indians noted by Cabeza de Vaca in chapter 27.

2. These consist mainly of "hawk bells, looking glasses, and red cloth," according to Cunninghame Graham.

3. In many ways an anomaly, this chapter seems to be strongly based on Cabeza de Vaca's encounter with the Guaycurues in chapter 30, varying only in selected details and in the name of the tribe that serves as its subject.

Chapter Thirty-Three

1. These Indians offering obedience seem to be the Aperues of the previous chapter.

2. The alcalde mayor was the mayor, or chief official, of Asunción.

Chapter Thirty-Four

1. This is the second set of launches described in chapter 15.

2. Vergara was likely one of Irala's brigantine captains.

3. Piedras is actually at about 21 degrees south; see also Las Piedras in chapter 37.

Chapter Thirty-Six

1. This will prove to be the Río Paraguay and not the Río Pilcomayo, which leads west into the Chaco from Asunción.

Chapter Thirty-Seven

1. Las Piedras was near the modern river town of Puerto La Esperanza on the Río Paraguay north of Asunción; see chapter 34.
2. Here Cabeza de Vaca is referring not to the Río Paraná, but to the Río de la Plata near Buenos Aires.
3. By reinforcements, Cabeza de Vaca seems to mean the men in the four brigantines dispatched from Asunción.
4. Perhaps near the modern city of Campanas, some thirty miles northwest of Buenos Aires.
5. All Saints' Day is November 1.

Chapter Thirty-Eight

1. The fanega is a Spanish measure approximately equal to a bushel.
2. Fathom: A nautical measure of six feet. The heat of the flames here is likely setting fire to the thick, dry mulch on the surface of the ground over which the houses of Asunción apparently had been constructed.
3. These *tapias*, or walls, were perhaps newly constructed of adobe blocks or other durable materials.

Chapter Thirty-Nine

1. Twelfth Night, el Día de los Reyes, is the night before Epiphany, or twelve days after Christmas.
2. Also known as the Acocies Chaneses. These were probably the Xarayes.
3. The name Puerto de los Reyes is from the Spanish designation for Twelfth Night, el Día de los Reyes, as previously noted. Modern Puerto Quijarro, at 18 degrees south latitude on Lake Gaiba, in the Departamento de Santa Cruz, Bolivia, is on or near the site of Puerto Reyes.

Chapter Forty

1. This was likely on the Río Jijuy.
2. These people seem to be the Cacocies (Acocies) Chaneses that Domingo de Irala mentioned in the previous chapter, but we cannot be sure.

Chapter Forty-One

1. These ports were the river towns or villages under the guidance or control of these two chiefs.

Chapter Forty-Two

1. Cabeza de Vaca refers to the poison as simply *yerba*. It is likely curare, the notorious arrow and dart poison extracted from species of the tropical tree genus *Strychnus*.

2. Here Cabeza de Vaca refers to himself in a rare instance by one of his other titles, Captain-General of the Río de la Plata.

3. As a quintal is a hundredweight, or one hundred pounds, this amounts to more than three hundred thousand pounds (or 150 tons) of flour and meal. This is an enormous, and probably inaccurate, quantity.

Chapter Forty-Three

1. The quinto is, literally, a "fifth" or tax of one-fifth of the production, labor, or commerce of the settlers.

2. Though Cabeza de Vaca does not elaborate, Domingo seems to be a key witness against the friars and their cronies in this unhappy business.

Chapter Forty-Four

1. The factor, or commissioner, is the royal commercial agent.

2. The day of Our Lady of September is September 8.

Chapter Forty-Five

1. Tapua and the Guaviaño of the previous chapter lie some distance upriver from Asunción on the Río Paraguay.

2. Juriquizaba is also known as Yeruquihaba and Inriquizaba.

Chapter Forty-Six

1. This second Itaqui may be the name of the local Guarani people or their chief, or it may be a generic, sixteenth-century Guarani reference for a landing or small port.

2. Here, Atabare and Guacani are speaking.

3. On the Río Ipané.

Chapter Forty-Seven

1. This Guayviaño is the Guaviaño of chapter 44.

2. Almost alone among sixteenth-century conquistadors, Cabeza de Vaca always insisted that the Indians be compensated for their foodstuffs, properties, and other possessions. This approach made him many enemies among his fellow Spaniards, who were far more inclined to plunder. He continues here the pattern of generally civil behavior he established while walking across North America some ten to fifteen years before.

3. Itabitan is also known as Itapuan.

Chapter Forty-Eight

1. These puercos are possibly capybaras, also known as *capinchos*.

Chapter Forty-Nine

1. Candelaria. According to Domínguez, this port lies on Laguna Cáceres, at Corumbá in the modern Brazilian state of Mato Grosso do Sul.
2. Cabeza de Vaca's *Commentaries* were originally published in 1555.
3. The actual latitude seems to be about 19 degrees south.

Chapter Fifty

1. The cañafístola, or *Cassia fistula*, is the purging cassia tree.
2. This is the *Limon ceuti*, a lemon variety known from Ceuta on the North African coast.
3. This may be the Rio Branco or the Rio Aquidabã (Cuiaba), both of which flow into the Río Paraguay from the Serra do Bodoquena in modern Brazil.
4. According to R. B. Cunninghame Graham, Morris Bishop, and others, the Portuguese governor of São Vicente dispatched an officer named Alejo Garcia with four companions in about the year 1525 to search for gold and silver in the South American interior. Garcia seems to have traveled west through what is now the Brazilian state of Paraná until he struck the Río Paraguay north of Asunción. Here he appears to have persuaded a considerable number of Guaranis to join his party, which then made its way north and west through the Gran Chaco to Bolivia or Peru. Garcia was said to have acquired much silver in the Andes. He and his soldiers were murdered on their way back to Paraguay and the coast, and Garcia's young son was said to be the sole survivor of the expedition.
5. See chapter 45.
6. This is probably the modern Rio Napineque in Mato Grosso do Sul state, Brazil.
7. This is the modern Serra da Bodoquena in Mato Grosso do Sul, Brazil.

Chapter Fifty-One

1. The Spanish is *raizes*, perhaps manioc or sweet potatoes.

Chapter Fifty-Two

1. A league is about three miles.
2. If Cabeza de Vaca is referring to the middistance between the Tropics, then his allusion here may be to the Rio do Ouro on São Tomé, off the west African coast and directly on the equator.
3. This river fish, sometimes known as the South American salmon, is much prized for its abundance and delicious flavor.
4. An arroba is about twenty-five pounds.
5. The Río Negro flows out of the northwest into the Río Paraguay just as that river enters Paraguay from Brazil at the far northeastern tip of the country. In its upper reaches it is called the Río Tucavaca; it heads in the Bolivian

Andes and flows through the Bañados de Otuquis before discharging into the Río Paraguay. Another Rio Negro, also a tributary, flows out of the Pantanal into the Río Paraguay approximately one hundred miles to the north of the confluence described here by Cabeza de Vaca.

6. Here Cabeza de Vaca likely means that the water is relatively clear, or at least clearer than that of the Río Negro.

7. Cabeza de Vaca here arrives at the enormous wetlands of the *pantanais* (Pantanal de São Lourenco, Pantanal Matogrossense, Pantanal do Toquari, and the Pantanal do Rio Negro) in modern Mato Grosso and Mato Grosso do Sul in Brazil—the headwaters of the Río Paraguay, much like an inland sea.

8. This is likely to be the stream directly west of modern Puerto Suárez in the Departamento de Santa Cruz, Bolivia.

Chapter Fifty-Three

1. This white metal may be manganese, which is currently mined from large nearby deposits in the Bañados de Otuquis.

2. This was perhaps two hundred yards.

3. This is likely Pero Hernández, Cabeza de Vaca's secretary and the stenographer of this narrative, in a rare appearance as a participant in the story.

Chapter Fifty-Four

1. Manioc: the root of this plant, *Manihot utilissima*, is processed for its starch, which yields tapioca.

2. A very early reference—among the first in European literature—to South America's notorious vampire bats, *Desmodus rotundus* et al. The bat, of course, is a flying mammal, not a reptile, as Cabeza de Vaca also notes.

3. This span between the thumb and forefinger is a *xeme* to Cabeza de Vaca, a length of perhaps six inches.

4. Cabeza de Vaca calls the Incas "Ingas."

Chapter Fifty-Five

1. Sococies: also Sacocies; see chapter 53.

Chapter Fifty-Six

1. In the mid-sixteenth century, the tribes the Chanes chief mentions were likely residents of the modern *departamentos* of Santa Cruz, Chuquisaca, and Tarija in eastern Bolivia. Cabeza de Vaca also refers to the Paysuñoes as the Paysunoes; see chapter 70. In addition, in the same chapter he refers to the Estarapecocies as the Tarapecocies.

2. By "sheep," Cabeza de Vaca is likely referring to llamas or alpacas, common domestic animals native to the Andes.

Chapter Fifty-Seven

1. These Indians are the Guaxarapos, as will be noted in chapter 58.
2. The port is Puerto Reyes.

Chapter Fifty-Eight

1. The Todos Santos he mentions was literally, Víspera de Todos Santos, the Vespers of All Saints' Day, November 1.

Chapter Fifty-Nine

1. Some sources call this insert a *botoque*.
2. This cotton net is the famous hammock of the West Indies and South America, still a bit of a novelty forty or fifty years after Columbus.
3. These are the Andean peoples of Peru.
4. The chief is here describing the famous Mato Grosso, which is similar to the Gran Chaco west and north of Asunción. In each case the land becomes a kind of inland sea during the rainy season and even today remains largely impassable during much of the year.

Chapter Sixty

1. Barbotes are probably gold or silver jewelry in the form of light plates suspended over the forehead and nose by small chains or strings.

Chapter Sixty-One

1. The myrtle is the *arrayán*.

Chapter Sixty-Three

1. From the northerly direction of this exploration, Tapuaguazu may be a southerly outlier of the Serra das Arares near the modern town of Cáceres in the western Mato Grosso. It is more likely to be found to the west, in the modern Departamento de Santa Cruz, Bolivia. See note 2, chapter 70.
2. The Europeans are here describing with difficulty the Pantanal of Mato Grosso and its nearly impenetrable plant communities; see also Ulrich (Huldrich) Schmidel's descriptions of these thick forests.

Chapter Sixty-Four

1. This is not the same location as the Tapua mentioned in chapters 44 and 45.
2. Two arrobas weigh fifty pounds.

Chapter Sixty-Six

1. This astonishing number was likely an exaggeration.

Chapter Sixty-Eight

1. The year is 1543.
2. Rio Igatu. A good candidate for this river is the modern Rio Alegre, which lies just north of the Serra Amolar in the western part of the Brazilian Parque Nacional do Pantanal Matogrossense; see also Río Iguatu, note 8, chapter 52.

Chapter Seventy

1. These puercos are probably peccaries, or javelinas, but possibly capybaras.
2. Captain Ribera's description seems to place him and his party some-where in the middle of the modern Departamento de Santa Cruz, Bolivia. The westbound river he mentions may be the Río Quimomé, which lies near two or three freestanding monolithic mountains, the most northerly of which at 802 meters in height may be the imposing Tapuaguazu noted by Cabeza de Vaca. Alternately, the river may be another southern but west-flowing head-water tributary of the Amazon.
3. The *indios orejones* are men with distended earlobes due to their heavy earrings or earplugs. The *vino de maíz* Captain Ribera noted is one of the earli-est references in the Americas to a kind of corn liquor or whiskey.
4. Here Captain Ribera says, curiously, that the additional Christians "*vivían allí cerca*"—lived close to where he found himself.

Chapter Seventy-Two

1. See Captain Ribera's actual report of his exploration at the end of the narrative.
2. This may be the earliest European account of the remarkable floods of the Pantanal, which resemble the equally disruptive inundations of the Gran Chaco west of Asunción.
3. This would be thirty to thirty-six feet.
4. These houses were likely small huts covered with thatch, or of skin or cloth stretched over a light wooden framework, so as to fit in these vessels.

Chapter Seventy-Three

1. In Spanish, these culverins are *versos*, light cannons with long bores mounted on the decks or rails of the brigantines.
2. This immense and doubtful number (twenty thousand) suggests that the effects of the fevers had not yet worn off when Cabeza de Vaca recalled his return to Asunción.

Chapter Seventy-Four

1. The best port was Puerto Reyes.
2. El Día de Sant (San) Marcos is April 25, 1543.
3. Ave María: the ringing of church bells about half an hour after sunset, or the same bells at dawn for the morning Ave María.

4. *El veedor*. Sometimes this title is also *visitador*.

5. This, of course, is Pero Hernández, the scribe of this narrative, and Cabeza de Vaca's faithful friend and servant.

6. González seems to be at Pedro Hernández's house when this mayhem occurs.

7. The castellano was a Spanish gold coin dating from the reign of Ferdinand and Isabella, los Reyes Católicos, equal to about 10 pesetas or 490 silver maravedis.

Chapter Seventy-Five

1. Somewhat of a problematic statement. Irala already is the lieutenant governor, a post he was assigned by Cabeza de Vaca some years before. Perhaps Cabeza de Vaca means that Irala is now confirmed in this position by the officials and the street mob; certainly Irala is here assigned Cabeza de Vaca's title of captain general.

Chapter Seventy-Six

1. Salsas. This is probably Salses, a notable fortress built by King Ferdinand in the 1490s in the Pyrenees. It was designed as a bastion against the French, with massive walls in places thirty feet thick at the base.

2. This is Andrés Hernández, "el Romo."

Chapter Seventy-Eight

1. They went eastbound from Asunción into the land lying between the Río Paraguay and the Paraná.

Chapter Eighty

1. In Spanish, this is *Por tu rey y por tu ley morirás*.

Chapter Eighty-Three

1. By "these kingdoms," Cabeza de Vaca is referring to Spain—Aragón and Castile.

2. "If you love me . . ."—Here Cabeza de Vaca is apparently quoting Domingo de Irala directly.

3. A quire, or *mano*, is a medieval set of four sheets of manuscript paper, folded in half; thus, four quires would be about thirty-two sheets of paper.

Chapter Eighty-Four

1. The Spanish is *rejalgar*. Probably arsenic sulfide, a highly lethal compound sometimes also called *sandáraca* in Spanish.

2. Horn of the unicorn. Perhaps not quite as fanciful as it sounds. This may be the powdered horn of an oryx, *Oryx leucoryx* or *O. beisa*, which looks exactly like a small unicorn from the side and was found in North Africa in

Cabeza de Vaca's day. According to Bishop, this antidote to arsenic poisoning was so popular that even the Grand Inquisitor Torquemada kept some handy on his desk, perhaps with good reason.

3. The notary Pedro Hernández is also known, of course, as Pero Hernández, Cabeza de Vaca's secretary and the stenographer of this tale; Luis de Miranda is a loyal priest; Captain Salazar is the lieutenant governor; and Pero Vaca is Pedro Estopiñán Cabeza de Vaca, Cabeza de Vaca's cousin who was arrested by Irala's conspirators in the previous chapter.

4. These islands downstream are in the Río de la Plata estuary, near the confluence of the Río Paraná and the Río Uruguay.

5. This is Angra do Heroísmo, the main town of Terceira Island in the Azores.

6. Here Cabeza de Vaca transcribes the Portuguese of the magistrate phonetically.

7. The Spanish court, and therefore the capital, wandered in Cabeza de Vaca's day. The king at times held court in Valladolid, Toledo, Seville, or elsewhere. Madrid became the permanent capital of Spain in 1561 under Phillip II. Arrival in Spain versus arrival at the court is somewhat confused in this chapter.

8. The Council of the Indies was the general supervisory and administrative body of the Spanish crown for the Americas in the sixteenth century and later.

Postscript

1. Nuestra Señora de la Merced is Our Lady of Mercy.

2. Cario. The Xarayes may also be speakers of this language.

3. Here Captain Ribera seems to mean kidnapping.

4. This range may lie in the modern Departamento de Santa Cruz, Bolivia.

5. The river was the Yaiva.

6. At 14 degrees 20 minutes south latitude, this reasonably places Captain Ribera somewhere in the northern Departamento de Santa Cruz, Bolivia; he likely has not traveled as far west as the Departamento de Beni, also in modern Bolivia.

7. *Chafalonia* or *chafalonía*.

8. These are the famous Amazons, after whom the Rio Amazonas, or Amazon River, is named.

9. I.e., where the sun set.

10. *Barbas como aguileñas*, or Vandykes.

11. This places the towns of the "black people" somewhere in the Departamento de La Paz, Bolivia, or perhaps as far west as the Departamento de Puno, Peru.

12. Captain Ribera's informants seem to be speaking here of cities such as Chan-Chan, a center of the Chimu culture, on the Pacific coast. Chan-Chan held quarters of accomplished gold- and silversmiths, as well as smiths working in various metal alloys, and was indeed a vast urban complex.

13. Here the captain is speaking of Lake Titicaca, which lies high in the Andes on the modern border between Bolivia and Peru. The glistening stones may be emeralds or other gemstones.

14. Captain Ribera's Indians are describing the llamas of the Incas, which are actually camelids, not sheep.

15. Likely to the northwest, although here Captain Ribera is not specific. The boats are the Spanish caravels off the coast of Peru.

16. Río Yacareati. This river is called the Areati in the 1555 edition.

Appendix

1. Don Carlos is Prince Carlos (Charles), the son of King Philip II.

2. Pedro Fernández is Pero, or Pedro, Hernández, a notary public and Cabeza de Vaca's loyal friend.

3. Cabeza de Vaca refers here to the *Relación*, the account of his epic adventure in North America with the expedition of Pánfilo de Narváez in the 1520s. The Moor Estevanico, whom Cabeza de Vaca does not mention, was also part of his wandering band.

4. Honorato Juan, from Valencia, had been the preceptor, or instructor, of Prince Carlos since 1554.

5. The pope.

Suggestions for Further Reading

Editions in Spanish

There are numerous Spanish versions of Cabeza de Vaca's works. Among the most useful are the following: *Naufragios y Comentarios*, from the Colección Austral of the Editorial Espasa-Calpe Mexicana, 11th ed., 1992; the *Relación* and *Comentarios* in *Cartas de Relación de la Conquista de América*, vol. II, part of the Colección Atenea, published by the Editorial Nueva España, c. 1950 and edited by Dr. Julio Le Riverend; and the *Colección de Libros y Documentos Referentes a la Historia de América*, vol. 5, *Tomo Primero*, published in Madrid in 1906 by the Librería General de Victoriano Suárez and edited by Miguel Serrano y Sanz. This last edition is the best modern reprinting of the 1555 Valladolid original, and its companion volume, the *Tomo Segundo*, contains the invaluable depositions and letters of Cabeza de Vaca, Pero Hernández, Cabeza de Vaca's brother-in-law Ruy Díaz de Guzmán, Juan de Salazar, Domingo de Irala, and others in relation to the legal actions that consumed the explorer late in his life. The material by Cabeza de Vaca and Pero Hernández in the *Tomo Segundo* is considerable; in it a reader can clearly see the original outlines of the *Commentaries*.

The Crónicas de América 3 edition of the *Naufragios y Comentarios* (1984) from Historia 16, Madrid, contains useful notes by Roberto Ferrando as well as the original preface and license to print of 1555.

A very recent Spanish edition is *Naufragios/Comentarios* with an introduction by Sylvia L. Cuesy, from the Editorial Océano de México, 2001.

The original Spanish edition of the *Relación* and *Comentarios* of 1555 is one of the world's rarest books, with only three known copies still in existence. The New York Public Library holds one of these in its collections.

Editions in English

Cabeza de Vaca remains a source of great fascination in North American history. The most comprehensive contemporary study of the author and the *Naufragios* is *The Narrative of Cabeza de Vaca* and the exhaustive, three-volume *Álvar Núñez*

Cabeza de Vaca: His Account, His Life, and the Expedition of Pánfilo de Narváez (University of Nebraska Press, 1999) by Rolena Adorno and Patrick Charles Pautz. The three-volume work is a scholarly tour-de-force. Penguin's *Chronicle of the Narváez Expedition* (also known as the *Naufragios*, 2002), translated by Fanny Bandelier, is a good popular edition of Cabeza de Vaca's North American journey, with a commentary by Ilan Stavans. *Cabeza de Vaca's Adventures in the Un-known Interior of America*, a modern translation of the *Relación* by Cyclone Covey from the University of New Mexico Press (1983), has an immediacy that is very striking, augmented with a series of internal running notes in brackets from the translator.

There is only one earlier English translation of the *Comentarios*, published in London in 1891 by the Hakluyt Society as part of *The Conquest of the River Plate*. Its editor is Luis L. Domínguez, but its translator is unknown. The companion volume within this book is Ulrich Schmidel's *Voyage of Ulrich Schmidt [Schmidel] to the Rivers of La Plata and Paraguai*, written in German and first published in 1567. Its translator is also unknown, and this is the only English version of Schmidel's work. The *Voyage* is important as a distinct counterpoint to everything Cabeza de Vaca says, as Schmidel was a common soldier, a partisan of Domingo de Irala (Cabeza de Vaca's great antagonist), and the only eyewitness to write up many early Paraguayan explorations not contained in the *Commentaries*.

A Spanish version of Schmidel's narrative can be found in the Crónicas de América 15 edition of *N. Federmann / U. Schmidl: Alemanes en América* (1985) from Historia 16, Madrid, with notes by Lorenzo E. López.

Background Reading

Cabeza de Vaca is the first man in history, and the sole sixteenth-century conquistador and explorer, to produce fundamental literary works involving both North and South America. He is also the only man of the early conquistadors to hold important official positions (treasurer of the Narváez expedition in Florida; governor of the Río de la Plata province) in both continents. In a very real sense, his *Relación* or *Naufragios* (1542 and 1555) may legitimately claim to be *the* founding, original work of American literature; the *Commentaries* (1555), which form a chronicle of his South American expeditions and service as governor, may claim, perhaps along with the letters of Columbus and Cortés, an equal place in Latin American literature. But Cabeza de Vaca is sui generis; the singular achievement of his two memoirs really has no parallel in either American or European literary history.

Among the works of other sixteenth-century conquistadors, Bernal Díaz del Castillo's *The Conquest of New Spain* (*La Historia Verdadera de la Conquista de Nueva España*) is the best known. It was first published in 1632 and has appeared in many versions in both English and Spanish. Notable among these are J. M. Cohen's Penguin Classic edition (first published in 1963) and the recent translation by Davíd Carrasco (University of New Mexico Press, 2008).

The denunciation of the appalling mistreatment of the natives of the Americas during the Spanish conquest as well as its proposed mitigation became the life-work of Father Bartolomé de las Casas (1484–1576), the clerical counterpart of

Cabeza de Vaca. See his *A Short Account of the Destruction of the Indies*, translated by Nigel Griffin (Penguin, 1992), in which he singles out La Plata for a full measure of his wrath.

Hans Staden's True History, published in 2008 by Duke University Press, is a good modern edition of Staden's voyage to the coast of Brazil and his subsequent captivity by the Tupi-Guarani people from 1547 to 1554. The earlier English version of the original German work is *The Captivity of Hans Stade*, with notes by Sir Richard Burton, published by the Hakluyt Society in 1874.

Imperial Spain, 1469–1716 by J. H. Elliott (Penguin, 2002) comprehensively analyzes the social and political conditions that produced conquistadors such as Cabeza de Vaca. It deals, in particular, with the rise of Spain as modern Europe's great power of the sixteenth century. Other good contemporary accounts of Spain's ascendancy in early modern Europe are *Rivers of Gold: The Rise of the Spanish Empire, from Columbus to Magellan* (Random House, 2003) by Hugh Thomas and *Empire: How Spain Became a World Power, 1492–1763* (Harper-Collins, 2003), by Henry Kamen.

R. B. (Robert Bontine) Cunninghame Graham's *The Conquest of the River Plate* (Doubleday, Page, 1924), with its title taken directly from Luis Domínguez's Hakluyt translations of 1891, is a general history of early Spanish settlement in La Plata. Cunninghame Graham thought highly of Cabeza de Vaca, and he devotes considerable attention to the explorer's time in Paraguay. For the later history of colonial Paraguay, see his *A Vanished Arcadia* (Heinemann, 1901; reprint Century, 1988), made into a movie in the last century as *The Mission*.

A recent and more nuanced look into the history of colonial Paraguay can be found in *The Guaraní Under Spanish Rule in the Río de la Plata* by Barbara Ganson (Stanford University Press, 2003), which analyzes the controversial subject of cannibalism as well as the role of women in Guarani society. As Cabeza de Vaca notes, often with exasperation, the early Franciscans in Paraguay (as well as members of other orders) caused him many difficulties. A good study of Franciscan influence and practices in Spanish is *Presencia Franciscana en el Paraguay, 1538–1824* by Margarita Durán Estragó (Universidad Católica Nuestra Señora de la Asunción, 1987).

Biography

The three-volume *Álvar Núñez Cabeza de Vaca* by Adorno and Pautz (1999), previously noted, provides a thorough consideration of the explorer himself and his family, which is large and distinguished in southern Spain and can be traced back to the twelfth century. It also updates the outcome of Cabeza de Vaca's protracted legal battles of 1545–1555 with many recent findings. Among these is the outcome of his several appeals, which eventually led to the restoration of his good name, if not much of his fortune.

The standard biography for most of the twentieth century was Morris Bishop's *The Odyssey of Cabeza de Vaca* (Century, 1933), which deals with the explorer's journeys in both North and South America. It is now somewhat dated. Haniel

Long's dreamlike reimagining of Cabeza de Vaca's North American wanderings is *Interlinear to Cabeza de Vaca*, republished in 1992 as *The Marvelous Adventure of Cabeza de Vaca* (Dawn Horse Press).

A good recent account (Basic Books, 2007) of Cabeza de Vaca and his North American travels is *A Land So Strange: The Epic Journey of Cabeza de Vaca* by Andrés Reséndez.

The modern Spanish historian Enrique de Gandía produced his *Historia de la Conquista de la Plata y del Paraguay* in 1932 (A. García Santos, Buenos Aires), and it is still an excellent reference for Cabeza de Vaca due to its use of much original source material.

Paraguay

The narratives of Cabeza de Vaca and Ulrich Schmidel, or Schmidt, are the earliest European descriptions of the founding in the sixteenth century of the Río de la Plata, which has always vied with New Mexico as the most remote of all Spanish provinces. The isolation first outlined by Schmidel and Cabeza de Vaca has continued. Among the most evocative later descriptions of Paraguay are those found in novels such as *Yo el Supremo* (Ediciones Alfaguara, 1974; Editorial Planeta de Agostini, 1985) by Augusto Roa Bastos, concerning the reign of Dr. Francia, and Lily Tuck's *The News from Paraguay* (Harpercollins, 2004), about the dictator Francisco Solano López and Madame Lynch. Sir Richard Burton's *Letters From the Battlefields of Paraguay* (newly reissued in 2003 by University Press of the Pacific as a facsimile of the original 1870 edition) is an indispensable account of the War of the Triple Alliance by an eyewitness. The quirky and engaging *At the Tomb of the Inflatable Pig: Travels Through Paraguay* (Alfred A. Knopf, 2003) by John Gimlette concerns General Stroessner, the legacy of conquest, and the modern nation.

Index

Abacoten (chief), 39
Abangobi (chief), 15
Aburuñes people, 191
Acosta, Diego de, 163
Acosta, Gonzalo, 27, 207n1
Acuña, Héctor de, 123, 125
adelantados, xiv
Agaces people, 38; Guaycuru hostilities, 64; hostilities against Spanish, 161; Payaguas link, 208n1; peace treaty broken, 51–62; sentence against, 70; war against, 70
Alabos (chief), 39
alcohol: carob wine, 42; corn wine, 30, 126, 151, 216n3; Payagua drunken sprees, 103
Almenza, Martín de, 71
Amazons, 218n8
Andrada, Francisco de, 44, 71, 174–75
Añiriri (chief), 12
ants, 117
Aperues (Imperues) people, 64; peace arrangements, 68–69. *See also* Yapirues people
Aracare (chief), 72, 74, 77; death sentence, 77
Araoz, Juan de, 12
Arianicosies people, 143, 144, 147, 148, 155; Mendoza peace attempts, 155
Armenta, Bernardo (Bernaldo) de: desire to go to Asunción, 10; intrigues by, 90; leaving for Brazilian coast, 174; opinion about war on Guaycurures, 43–44; opinion on explorations, 71; problems for Governor, 20–21; Santa Catalina, 5–6
Armenta, Martín de, 43, 44, 209n4
Artaneses people: described, 125; facial decoration, 125; Xarayes accompanying Spaniards to, 130
Asunción: aid to colonists after fire, 81; arrival in, 30; distances, 8; fire, 80–81; founding, 204n2; friendly Carios peoples, 8; Indian reception, 29–30; letter to, 23; Miguel (Indian convert),
13–14; moving Puerto Reyes settlers to, 159–60; news of Governor's arrival, 27; officials' hostility, 41; original name, 205n5; perilous state of colonists, 28–29; poor and needy, 41; return from Guaycuru campaign, 59–60; return to, 160; trip to, 27–28; unrest among settlers, 36, 41
Atabare (chief), 85, 86, 87, 88, 89; peaceful relations, 96, 97
Atlantic voyage, 1–4
Ayolas, Juan: accounts of, 28; background, 204n2; brigantines left at Candelaria, 7–8; in Candelaria, 101; death, 29; Indians who killed, 97; Pedro de Mendoza link, xvii, 203n1, 204n2
Azores, 186

Bandelier, Fanny, 221
Barba, Diego de, 55
barbecue, 67, 210n1
battle, warnings before, 86, 87
battle cry, 52, 55, 209n1
Battle of Ravenna, xv
beheadings, 56
Big Ears, 117
biographies, Adorno and Pautz, 220–21
Bishop, Morris, 223
black people, reports of, 191–92
Bolaños, Juan de, 124
Bravo, Antón, 175
bridge construction, 17, 28
brigantines: described, 204–5n3; overloaded, 94; requested from Asunción, 27; timber, 75
Buenos Aires: abandonment, 29, 30, 34; aid to, 71; founding, 7, 203n1; location, 205n6; need to reclaim, 34; nine Christians fleeing, 7–8; population, 8; rescue of colonists, 77–79
Burton, Sir Richard, xiii